Moved by the Spirit

Moved by the Spirit

A Daily Devotional & Living Doxology

Craig M. Prather

RESOURCE *Publications* • Eugene, Oregon

MOVED BY THE SPIRIT
A Daily Devotional & Living Doxology

Copyright © 2019 Craig M. Prather. All rights reserved. Except for brief quotations in critical publications or reviews, no part of this book may be reproduced in any manner without prior written permission from the publisher. Write: Permissions, Wipf and Stock Publishers, 199 W. 8th Ave., Suite 3, Eugene, OR 97401.

Resource Publications
An Imprint of Wipf and Stock Publishers
199 W. 8th Ave., Suite 3
Eugene, OR 97401

www.wipfandstock.com

PAPERBACK ISBN: 978-1-5326-7179-1
HARDCOVER ISBN: 978-1-5326-7180-7
EBOOK ISBN: 978-1-5326-7181-4

Most scriptural references are not direct scriptural quotes, but rather paraphrased by the author to provide emphasis within the text.

Scripture quotations, unless otherwise indicated, are taken from the Holy Bible, New International Version®, NIV®. Copyright ©1973, 1978, 1984, 2011 by Biblica, Inc.™ Used by permission of Zondervan. All rights reserved worldwide. www.zondervan.com The "NIV" and "New International Version" are trademarks registered in the United States Patent and Trademark Office by Biblica, Inc.™

Scripture quotations, unless otherwise indicated, are from the ESV® Bible (The Holy Bible, English Standard Version®), copyright © 2001 by Crossway, a publishing ministry of Good News Publishers. Used by permission. All rights reserved.

Scripture quotations taken from the New American Standard Bible® (NASB), Copyright © 1960, 1962, 1963, 1968, 1971, 1972, 1973, 1975, 1977, 1995 by The Lockman Foundation. Used by permission. www.Lockman.org

All other quotations are used with permission or comply with section 107 of the U.S. Copyright Act as "Fair Use."

All poetry/musical lyrics listed in the appendixes are copyrighted by Craig M. Prather, published through BMI, and registered with the U.S. Copyright Office:

   101 Independence Ave. S.E.
   Washington, D.C. 20559-6000
   (202) 707-3000 or 1 (877) 476-0778 (toll free)
   All Rights Reserved . . .

Manufactured in the U.S.A.

To my beautiful and brilliant wife, Lisa, who loves me unconditionally, and who inspires me be a better man than I was yesterday. I also dedicate this work to my magnificent Father in heaven, from whom all blessings flow . . .

Contents

Preface | ix
Acknowledgments | xi
List of Abbreviations | xiii

1 Forgiveness (The Month of January) | 1
2 God's Dwelling Place (The Month of February) | 23
3 Our True Identity (The Month of March) | 46
4 The Passion of Christ (The Month of April) | 70
5 The Spirit of God (The Month of May) | 94
6 Obedience (The Month of June) | 119
7 The Goodness of the Lord (The Month of July) | 142
8 The Light in the Darkness (The Month of August) | 167
9 The Calm in a Time of Storm (The Month of September) | 192
10 Spiritual Battles (The Month of October) | 216
11 The Fellowship of the Saints (The Month of November) | 242
12 The Promise (The Month of December) | 266

Afterword | 291
Appendix 1: Jewish Festivals and Fasts, by Date and Month | 293
Appendix 2: "The Traveler" | 294
Appendix 3: "Crazy Life" | 295
Appendix 4: "On and On" | 296
Bibliography | 297

Preface

Devotionals are very powerful tools in which we allow ourselves to look inside our hearts and souls and admire the thoughts that dwell there. Somewhat of a juxtaposition of poetry and prose, with a touch of prophetic insight, devotions to our Lord, Jesus Christ carry with them the inner beauty of God's most precious creation. There lies the soft and benevolent voice from within whose primary longing is to praise the Savior. I've included footnotes to reference the scriptures that entered my mind as I was typing them. I hope my words, written in a stream of consciousness and co-authored by the Holy Spirit, resonate with all who read them. To God be the Glory, forever and ever, Amen . . .

—Craig Prather

Acknowledgments

I'd like to thank my dear friends and family, instructors, and colleagues for their inspiration, patience, kindness, and guidance in my spiritual, academic, and professional life. Including, but certainly not limited to:

David Quinn	Cyndi Duncan
Mike Patterson	Kati Andreano
Peter Vanderburgh	Lydia Long
Paul Gulck	Justin Jones
Professor Kathrine Berning —contributing editor	Nicole McCaskill
Professor John McKendricks	James Unruh
Professor Tony Slavin	Professor Katy Hartley
Dr. Doug Vaughan	Nathan Hartley
Dr. Timothy Allen	Bill and Breanna Ledford
Dr. Paul Louis Metzger	Nic Froese
Dr. Tom Schiave	Priscilla Rybka
Dr. Calvin Blom	Nathan Dupree
Professor Jay Hull	Professor Allen Battle
Professor Kristopher Dahir	Professor Donny Crandell
Eileen Duenas	Will Sneed
Joshua Roebuck	Dr. Brent Brooks
Professor Mike Preston	Faith Martinez
Lilly Clark	Angelo Austria
Bill Muck	Michael Williams

Carlos Orozco
Tim Lucas
Rob Caliger
Professor Bill Osgood
Brian McGhee
Danny Velasquez
The late, Joni Prather

Paul Sprauve
Brian Lucas
Professor Geneva Arnold
Professor Garrett Mcgeein
Nathan Lamaestra
Jonathan Barnard

My beautiful children

My beautiful brothers and sisters (on both sides)

My beautiful parents (on both sides)

My beautiful church family at 1st Church of God, Reno

And, all of my close friends and family …

Abbreviations

Old Testament

Gen	Genesis	Song (Cant)	Song of Songs/Solomon (Canticles)
Exod	Exodus		
Lev	Leviticus	Isa	Isaiah
Num	Numbers	Jer	Jeremiah
Deut	Deuteronomy	Lam	Lamentations
Josh	Joshua	Ezek	Ezekiel
Judg	Judges	Dan	Daniel
Ruth	Ruth	Hos	Hosea
1-2 Sam	1-2 Samuel	Joel	Joel
1-2 Kgs	1-2 Kings	Amos	Amos
1-2 Chr	1-2 Chronicles	Obad	Obadiah
Ezra	Ezra	Jonah	Jonah
Neh	Nehemiah	Mic	Micah
Esth	Esther	Nah	Nahum
Job	Job	Hab	Habakkuk
Ps/Pss	Psalm/Psalms	Zeph	Zephaniah
Prov	Proverbs	Hag	Haggai
Eccl (Qoh) (Qoheleth)	Ecclesiastes	Zech	Zechariah
		Mal	Malachi

New Testament

Matt	Matthew	1-2 Thess	1-2 Thessalonians
Mark	Mark	1-2 Tim	1-2 Timothy
Luke	Luke	Titus	Titus
John	John	Phlm	Philemon
Acts	Acts	Heb	Hebrews
Rom	Romans	Jas	James
1-2 Cor	Corinthians	1-2 Pet	1-2 Peter
Gal	Galatians	1-2-3 John	1-2-3 John
Eph	Ephesians	Jude	Jude
Phil	Philippians	Rev	Revelation
Col	Colossians		

Chapter 1

Forgiveness

The Month of January

On the First Day

A NEW YEAR IS upon us. Dark clouds and choppy waters inhabit the atmosphere as soft raindrops fall on the cold cement ground of the vacant marina in Sparks, Nevada. I cannot help but think of my Savior and the many storms that He conquered for us as I peer out into the openness of His mighty creation. He tells me to remain steadfast and to stay with the plan that has been provided for me since the foundation of the world. There were many times when I felt I couldn't persevere: that a life of serving Him was too hard. "Keep the faith my child," He says, "for I have great plans for you to flourish. Many before you and many after you will have given up on my plan. It is vital that you persevere," says the Lord Almighty. The Lord was there with me in the past, and He dwells with me now. There is no escaping the Lord's presence. There is no hiding from His almighty power.

I realize that I don't have all the answers to life's questions.

On the Second Day

God is very loving, kind, compassionate, and encouraging. I experience tremendous encouragement as doubts by the enemy begin to set in. God is wonderful. He reminds me of the various times in which He rescued me from certain dangers. He creates flashbacks in my memory to times of sorrow and despair in which His light remained shining upon me through the power of the Holy Spirit. He reassured me that He still tabernacles within me and that I need to remain on guard, bearing my spiritual armor, for Satan is constantly trying to separate me from the Holy One.[1]

---

1. Matt. 10:20 (Emphasis, mine).

I've struggled in letting my past sins and defeat resurface, which try and convince me that I cannot persevere. I've had moments of doubt, lack of faith, and questions as to my purpose in this life. Yet, through God's love and mercy, He has reminded me that my sins have been forgiven; that I live in a broken world in which He has already put a plan in motion to restore.

On the Third Day

In the silent lucidity of my home in northwest Reno, I contemplate a much simpler time in which my faith was unchallenged- even unquestioned. Peering out of my windows, I can see God move through His tapestry in the clouds. God's canvas of sunrises, sunsets, rain, and snow provide for the perfect backdrop to the glorious lake and mountains that surround Sierra Nevada.

The Father is using this time to address my issues of pride and needing acceptance from an unforgiving world. "Remain humble," I can hear Him say. "For in humility, My Son died for you." Indeed, He did. Jesus Christ remained obedient and humble His entire life up to and including His death on a cross.[2]

I need you, oh Lord, how much I need you. Your love never fails me. Time marches forward, yet you remain there, deep within me, and several steps ahead of me. You are the great and wonderful I AM. Once again, I've discovered your compassion, your quickness to forgive, and your support through this journey towards Christ' likeness.

I can feel your presence in the form of the Holy Spirit as I say a blessing for each room of my home. In the stillness of the night, I awake to discover a tugging on my heart to pray against the powers and principalities of the evil one; to dispel the darkness that inhabits this place of light.

My God is mighty to save; He provides my every need. From the time I wake up in the morning, throughout my day, and lastly when I go to bed at night, the Lord is sustaining the very life, the very breath that I take. Life itself cannot exist apart from Him. I need to continue to work on building a lasting relationship with the Father through prayer, fellowship, meditation, reading His word, and in solitude.

---

2. Phil. 2:8 (Emphasis, mine).

On the Fourth Day

Focusing on Him and His plan for me will give my life meaning and purpose. Too often, I try and set my own destiny but fail to realize that God is more than willing to guide me in the right direction. I have yet to face a hardship that God has not helped me get through. It's during the trials and tribulations of my life, that God strengthens me for the next challenge.

My wife and beautiful children are all gifts from Him. I pray that He will continue to care for and protect my children long after I've left this world. Like the mind of a child, we must be willing to put full faith and trust in the Father.[3] By infusing God's values and worldview into my children, they too will develop a loving relationship with the Holy One.

Feeling the conviction of the Spirit to focus more on my wife and children, God has spoken to me once again during this quiet time with Him. My children are only little for a little while, I must share more about my faith and principles with them before the enemy can enter their minds bringing fear, divisiveness, and separation. I must continue to pray diligently for their spiritual well-being as well as my own.

I've discovered that by having a new identity in Jesus Christ, I have already defeated Satan: now I must live like it. These times of reflection are very powerful. God has truly spoken to my heart through my solitude. I must spend alone time with God more often throughout my life. If I can be still and listen to His voice, I can accomplish all things.

I need to depend more upon God to direct my steps. Sometimes, I try to conquer my demons alone. Only through His strength can they be truly defeated. The Apostle Peter began to sink when he took his eyes off Jesus Christ. I too can fall into deep despair when I lose focus of who matters the most.

On the Fifth Day

As the rain begins to fall and absorb into the earth, the Holy Spirit speaks into my heart inviting me to allow God to transform me into the image of His Son. Christ Jesus is the one who was, who is, and who is to come.[4] No longer am I judged by the world's standards, but rather, by God's standards which He holds so high that earthly beings cannot attain them. Only through my faith and trust in Jesus Christ, can the Father see me as the finished product. Like the incense that once burned in the Holy of Holy's to

---

3. Matt. 18:3 (Emphasis, mine).
4. Rev. 1:8 (Emphasis, mine).

block God's view of the sin within the high priest standing there, I am now seen through the lens of Christ, and not of the world.

Spirit lead me to walk in the light and shield me from the darkness. Christ has paid the price for sin once and for all, so I am no longer bound by it. I am no longer held prisoner by it.[5] God has encouraged me to live as a saint who sins, not as a sinner trying to become a saint. Through faith in Him, I will always emerge victorious.

Light can never be hidden in the darkness because God's light has shined since the beginning of time; perhaps, even before the beginning of time. His love for us is immeasurable and is not bound by the physics of this earth. What a wonderful God we serve! He is in control of our every thought, our every heartbeat, our every breath.

Thank you, God, for your patience with me. Thank you for forgiving me when I fall back. Thank you for your Son for dying for me. Thank you for your Spirit for dwelling within me. I love you with all my heart, mind, soul, and strength. To you be the glory forever and ever, Amen.

On the Sixth Day

Epiphany

Blessed am I for having the power of the Holy Spirit to convict me of my wrongs. Lovingly, the Father holds me in His arms as pain and sorrow begin to dissipate over the horizon. The air radiates with His presence and the wind obeys His commands. Flowing ever so lightly, my thoughts pour into the mighty ocean of time, as I peer out at the abyss. God is love. I am love. I feel His love pour over me when I am lost or afraid.

Time seems to stand still in the evanescence of the Creator. Waiting on the moment that He returns in glory, I softly imbibe my surroundings as I journey through the desolate canyons of life. The winds of change are on the horizon now. Feeling the Spirit move in and through me, I can manifest His presence through radiant beams of light that travel from one shore to the next.

The Lord is my rock, my life, my everything. Jesus Christ paid the ultimate price for my sins, and for that I am forever indebted to Him. He took the place of my just punishment and gave His very life for my transgressions. Who, but God could have done such a thing? Demonstrating the ultimate love for His creation, the cross is both a look at the past and a hope for the future.

---

5. Heb. 10:10 (Emphasis, mine).

Eloquence and innocence taper as the fleeting envy of the enemy manifests his true colors. Don't be fooled by the lies of old. The enemy is constantly on the prowl, waiting to devour us. Resistance is key in this time of reckoning. God has already accomplished the ultimate victory. He has conquered the curse of death itself.[6] How mighty and powerful is our God.

On the Seventh Day

The Lord invites us to rest, yet we often avoid such pleasures. In the business of daily life, we tend to forget that rest is needed for both our physical state, and spiritual one. Take the time to lay in the grass of an open field, peering up at the stars above, which are too many to count.

God in all His glory took time out to rest on the seventh day. Jesus Christ invites us to rest in Him.[7] I am restless, indeed; longing and praying for that moment when Jesus releases me from my earthly burdens. Look to the Spirit of God to help you in your repose. Find in Him the power to relax and let all your worries be placed at the foot of the cross.

Jesus Christ invites us to enjoy some much-needed down time in Him. He took on the stress of the world so that we can revel in the quiet time we get to spend alone with the Creator. Taking time in solitude will not only benefit you, but benefit your Spirit as well since He enjoys connecting with the Father in this manner.

Time after time, we tend to worry about tomorrow, but, fear not, for tomorrow will worry about itself, with or without us.[8] Lost in the magnitude of the Almighty, I will spend more time in the everlasting comfort of the One who provided me with life. Before the foundation of the world, God was present. He is all-knowing, all-powerful, and all-present; giving of Himself and communing within Himself in a trifold relationship of love and omniscience.

On the Eighth Day

For three sins of my fathers, even for four, I pay the price for transgression.[9] Separation from the Father is what the enemy seeks. Don't let him take your connection to God away from you. You are a beautiful creation of the God

---

6. 1 Cor. 15:26 (Emphasis, mine).
7. Matt. 11:28 (Emphasis, mine).
8. Matt. 6:25 (Emphasis, mine).
9. Amos 2:4 (Emphasis, mine).

most high. Seek His wisdom and gain the understanding necessary to succeed in this lifetime.

Quite possibly, the end of days may be upon us. Use this time to pray fervently, meditating on His Word day and night. The hour may arrive when you least expect it and you'll want to be ready and not caught off-guard. Always rejoice in the Savior and praise His holy name. The Father, Son, and Holy Spirit are one in thought and in accord. Certainly, nothing is too powerful for them to overcome.

The Father of Abraham, Isaac, and Jacob is your Father as well. Never forget the sacrifice He made for us by sending His only begotten son to perish so that we might have eternal life. In Christ Jesus be the victory! One must put on the spiritual armor to resist the devil's temptations. Christ is always with us and in us to help with this most daunting task.

Do not be conformed to ways of this world, but be transformed by the renewing of your mind.[10] Focus on the Spirit and allow Him to wash over you, for only then can you really see what God has put before you. Spiritually, mentally, and physically, respect the body God gave to you. Teach, love, and pray for everyone around you, loving them as you love the Holy Trinity. You only get one chance on this earth to make the difference in someone's life: use it wisely.

On the Ninth Day

Dancing in the winds of change will bring upon a desire to seek the Father more than you've previously experienced. Take the time to let the Spirit resonate within and the benefits will surely be reaped. Consultation, evaluation, and exaltation are all required when meditating on the Holy One. For, even those who sow in tears will reap with joy.[11]

Illuminate yourself with the fire that burns so bright. The sacrifice of the Son gives us hope for the future. Take a brisk walk on an early autumn morning and observe the water that sparkles with translucent rays of the sunshine. The wind of the Spirit is blowing stronger as the leaves reflect His strength. I feel the encouragement of the Father as He motivates me to continue with the plan He set in motion before the foundation of the world.[12]

Footholds of the enemy may try and break your stride. Don't let him gain a stronghold. For if a foothold turns into a stronghold, the enemy no longer must try and separate you from the Holy One; he's already

---

10. Rom. 12:2 (Emphasis, mine).
11. Ps. 126:5 (Emphasis, mine).
12. Eph. 1:4 (Emphasis, mine).

accomplished his mission. Stand firm in the faith. Rebuke the enemy and Resist him![13] Your reward is already paid in full.

On the Tenth Day

As I resonate with the Decalogue, I'm amazed to realize that God's law was written to demonstrate our dependence upon Him. Written to address how we should relate to both God, and each other, the Ten Commandments were penned by God Himself and delivered to the Hebrews through Moses.[14] God's law is not to punish, but to show us how much we need a Savior to fulfill it.

Meditating on His word day and night will not only bless you but inspire you as well. Find time in your day to pray that the Spirit illumine God's word for you and enjoy the wonderful revelation that springs forth. Light a candle to help you remember that Jesus is the light of the world. His light will never fade away.

I'm reminded to speak to a brother or sister in the faith in a loving way through songs, hymns, and spiritual songs.[15] Only then, can we hear God's words whispered in divine exhilaration as the listener absorbs the fervent sounds. God will speak, but we must listen. When the Father requests our presence, be sure and answer, "Speak Lord, for your servant is listening."[16]

The vast movement of time is but a passing thought in the mind of the Creator. The Lord is beyond all space and time and therefore, does not answer to it. We are limited by our current boundaries, but take heart, for the time is drawing nearer when we will see our God face to face.

On the Eleventh Day

Sing to the Lord and praise His name forever![17] There hasn't been a time in which I felt ashamed to call upon the name of the Lord. Certainly, He is there whether I feel His presence or not. Sometimes while blessing my house, I often wondered why I didn't feel His presence tingling all over my body. His response to me was, "I'm always there, but once in a while, I like to remind you of that."

13. 1 Pet. 5:9 (Emphasis, mine).
14. Exod. 20:1-21 (Emphasis, mine).
15. Eph. 5:19 (Emphasis, mine).
16. 1 Sam. 3:10 (Emphasis, mine).
17. Ps. 96:2 (Emphasis, mine).

When I've let the enemy get me down in these cold winter months, I look to the sky to find my quickening. Something in the heavens shows me that God is magnificent. He is beyond all understanding and has unlimited power and resources. It's not that God is dependent upon me, but rather that I am fully dependent upon Him. Praying in the Spirit will ensure that our relationship remains strong.[18]

As I look back at all the blessings the Lord has given me, I realize that the curses were something I was meant to overcome. Satan is quick to convict us of wrong doing, yet the Son of the God most high is seated at the right hand of the Father in constant intersession for our salvation. Trust in Him, and He will never let you down. Don't let life's setbacks separate you from the Holy One. Satan's goal was to separate from the beginning; don't give in to him now. You've come so far, loved one, and God loves you for that.

On the Twelfth Day

He is the God of hills and valleys, and of sunsets and sunrises. There is nothing new under the sun that our God has not seen.[19] Follow Him to the deepest parts of your soul and you can rest assured that He'll cover you in His love. When life gives you set backs remember that the sun still shines even after the dark. Light will always shine in the darkness, because the darkness cannot overcome it.[20]

Take time to admire what the Father has created. A walk in the park, down the street, or in a meadow should do the trick. I often spend time early in the morning with the Father in quiet serenity watching the waves ripple towards the shore of Lake Tahoe, high in the Sierra Nevada mountains. It is there that God speaks to me: it is there that I tend to really listen.

God has provided for our every need. Don't worry about tomorrow for tomorrow will have its own worries.[21] Instead, stay focused on today. Ask yourself, "How can I better my relationship with my Savior right now in this very moment?" The relationship is key. Much like the Father relates to the Son and the Spirit, we too must relate to the Father and our fellow brothers and sisters in the faith. We are all one, with one heart and one soul.[22] Stay united with one another and enjoy God's blessings as they pour forth.

18. Jude 1:20 (Emphasis, mine).
19. Eccl. 1:9 (Emphasis, mine).
20. John 1:5 (Emphasis, mine).
21. Matt. 6:34 (Emphasis, mine).
22. Acts 4:32 (Emphasis, mine).

On the Thirteenth Day

Sometimes the road ahead can be scary. Trust in the Lord to guide you to your destination. He has everything planned out for you, so trust in the Lord and lean not on your own understanding.[23] Too often, we allow our flesh to guide our actions and decisions, yet the flesh is always at enmity with the Lord.

The Spirit of God is ripe with discernment. Allow Him to guide your path for our way is not our own; the Lord is the one who directs our steps.[24] So, be sure and allow Him to do the directing. The times I tried to go off on my own path were the times I fell or backslid. The enemy is quick to make us feel that there is no need for God to help us in this life: the enemy is wrong. We need God every day, every hour, every minute, and every second. We cannot even take another breath without God allowing it to be so.

As I walk through the valley of the shadow of death, I will fear no evil, for the Lord is with me.[25] He is quick to love and slow to anger. Let His love abound in your life by practicing obedience towards Him. The Lord knows the world is in a fallen state; therefore, don't be too hard on yourself if you fall back sometimes. Be sure and ask the Lord's forgiveness and get back into right standing with the Holy One. Be encouraged dear friends, our Savior dwells in our hearts and is always there at a moment's notice.

On the Fourteenth Day

Out of nothing, our glorious Creator created everything. Out of His very being, He spoke life into existence. When you look upon a snow-capped mountain, or gaze at a magnificent lake, remember the One who made it possible to admire. The raindrops give way to the river and oceans, and that same water gives us life.

The true road to life is not found anywhere on this earth, rather it's found within the hearts and souls of the children of God, whose source is the Son.[26] Everlasting peace is found within the Kingdom and it's there that we experience pain and sadness no longer.[27] For the Son is in the Father, and the Father in the Son.

---

23. Prov. 3:5 (Emphasis, mine).
24. Jer. 10:23 (Emphasis, mine).
25. Ps. 23:4 (Emphasis, mine).
26. 1 John 5:11 (Emphasis, mine).
27. Rev. 21:4 (Emphasis, mine).

United within each other, the Father, Son, and Holy Spirit represent the triune relationship which extends to each one of us. God was in relationship from the beginning, yet the enemy strives to break that relationship. So, it's important to stay in union with Christ by fasting, prayer, and meditating on His Word day and night.[28] Wash yourselves off through the word and enjoy the cleanliness that the Spirit accords.[29] Without spot or blemish, you will emerge victorious, if you simply keep the faith. Time, times, and a half time shall pass, yet the Word will always remain faithful and true. Trust in the Lord for He transcends all space and time and will surely lead you in the right direction.

On the Fifteenth Day

Release from the daily pressures of life is what we seek. Placing our burdens at the foot of the cross will allow us to propel our spirits into a wonderful eternal state of being.[30] God's providential will supersedes our needs in such a beautiful way. The juxtaposition of His will and ours is a mystery that remains with Him, yet we know that both take place for us right here on earth.

My Savior lives! He is alive and well and interacts with us on a daily basis. If only we would listen to Him, we would discover His never-ending love for us. God's word is active: He is the living Word.[31] God watches over us wherever we go.[32] He was there at the beginning of time, and He is there with you right now as you read these words. Like a beautiful sunset on a hot autumn day, God shines brightly from one hemisphere to the next.

Blessings and curses may befall you, but take heart that God intended you to experience them both so that you can be both thankful and determined to persevere. No one can avoid the enemy's temptations for very long before the flesh gives in. Remember, sin does not happen only in manifestation, but sin begins in the mind and then progresses into physical action. It's up to us to constantly renew our minds and hearts towards Christ. Love your enemies and pray for those who persecute you and you will experience God's forgiveness of your own sins.[33]

---

28. Josh. 1:8 (Emphasis, mine).
29. Eph. 5:26 (Emphasis, mine).
30. 1 Pet. 5:7 (Emphasis, mine).
31. 1 Pet. 1:23 (Emphasis, mine).
32. Gen. 28:15 (Emphasis, mine).
33. Matt. 5:44 (Emphasis, mine).

On the Sixteenth Day

Love abounds on this cold day in January. Many times, in the past, you may feel as if the Father's love has escaped you. Fear not, for His love never fails or fades away. God is the Lord most high and He will remain in you, and you will remain in Him for all eternity. Once you profess with your lips that Jesus Christ is the Lord and accept that God raised Him from the dead in your heart, you cannot be separated from Him, and you will have eternal life.[34]

Shadows of the enemy often cast doubt on our faith. Satan's motivation is to put fear and distrust into our minds that we may stray and question our salvation. He often prowls around like a roaring lion trying to devour us.[35] He will eventually fall like the once great cities of Sodom and Gomorrah whose very citizens allowed Satan to corrupt their hearts and minds.

Tomorrow is not guaranteed for any of us. Spend a great amount of time in worship to the Father allowing the Holy Spirit to speak through you. This way, when the Son returns, you will not be caught off guard. Be alert and ready at all times.[36] I find that in the silence of the morning, my soul and Spirit are closely connected to my Creator. Allow Him to speak and guide you like the wind guides the leaves to their final destination.

Salvation comes to us by grace through the Lord Jesus Christ.[37] If not for God's grace, we would surly perish into damnation. God is merciful and forgiving. When we fall back into the temptations of sin, remember that He selflessly sacrificed His only son for us.

On the Seventeenth Day

Enjoy time in a covenantal relationship with the Father. Like many of God's chosen before you, He has secured you as the bride of Christ long before the world was established. The Godhead dwells in constant relationship with us, much like a loving mother and father are in constant relationship with their children. There are no grandchildren in God, we are all one in the same in Jesus Christ.[38]

Raise your hands in praise to the God almighty. When the Israelites were losing the battle to the Amalekites, Moses would simply raise his hands

---

34. Rom. 10:9 (Emphasis, mine).
35. 1 Pet. 5:8 (Emphasis, mine).
36. Matt. 24:42 (Emphasis, mine).
37. Acts. 15:11 (Emphasis, mine).
38. Gal. 3:28 (Emphasis, mine).

to the Lord to secure the victory.[39] No matter what you're going through in this life, open your arms to the Father, and you will always emerge victorious.

The mountains call out His name, the birds of the air submit to His will. There is nothing on this earth that is not under the authority of our Father in heaven. For that, we should be eternally thankful, for The Lord is in control at times. If we only had the faith of a tiny mustard seed, we could command the devil to leave us, and he would.[40] He returns because of our lack of faith. Don't give in to his temptations; remove the sin from your life and experience the closeness of the Father.

On the Eighteenth Day

Who can compare to the awesomeness of the Lord? Which one of us was there when He created the heavens and the earth?[41] Who can question His decisions? As we go through this life, it's important to remember that God has a plan for us. Sometimes, in the melancholy of despair, we tend to question God's sovereignty or motives, yet that is a mistake. For God knows the plans He has for us: plans not to harm us, but to prosper us.[42]

Sometimes, I will sit in silence and look up at the stars of heaven, knowing that so many before me have admired God's skies as well. Can you count them? Abraham was shown the vastness of the heavens by God, Himself.[43] How much more should we appreciate the greatness of God?

Our God is the God of the living, not the dead.[44] You won't find Him hiding away in the endless abyss. He is right here, right now, with you at this very moment as you are reading this. God's glory is reflected in each and every one of us, whether you accept Him or not, you are still made in His image. Bear His image with pride. Accept Jesus as your personal Lord and Savior, for God and Jesus are one. Ask Jesus into your heart and start receiving the blessings He has in store for you.

---

39. Exod. 17:11 (Emphasis, mine).
40. Matt. 17:20 (Emphasis, mine).
41. Job 38:4 (Emphasis, mine).
42. Jer. 29:11 (Emphasis, mine).
43. Gen. 15:5 (Emphasis, mine).
44. Luke 20:38 (Emphasis, mine).

On the Nineteenth Day

The Messiah is the true king! He is the conqueror of death, the second member of the Trinity who has defeated Satan at the cross. Death could not hold Him, for He rose.[45] No other gods sacrifice themselves so that their followers can enter into eternity with them. When false prophets come to dissuade you from your beliefs in the one true God and His only begotten, remember that only *He* died for your sins.

We are broken, yet God is whole. There is redemption in Him if we seek it out. Always ask for His forgiveness, even in temporary moments of insanity, for God is quick to forgive and slow to anger.[46] If we fail to ask forgiveness of the Father, we further separate ourselves from Him. This allows space for the enemy to settle in. Satan is not one to give up, so how much more should we not give up on resisting him? Keep the faith, pray regularly, and allow the Spirit to pour over you.

Wonderful are the thoughts and ways of the Lord.[47] Great are His commandments and mercy. Take pride in the work you do for the Lord, for all work done is for Him. Be wise and avoid sluggish ways, for this will only lead to hardships and despair.[48] If we take pride in our work, we take pride in ourselves and the Lord will reward us greatly for it. May the Lord continue to bless you on this nineteenth day of January. Keep warm in the comfort and glow of the Holy Spirit, for He is like a burning fire that never loses its heat.

On the Twentieth Day

In the subtle stillness of the evening, I am at peace within myself. Knowing that the Lord has forgiven me of my sins puts me at ease when the enemy is on the attack. We are all susceptible and we all need the love of the Savior to forgive us our trespasses. The ambiance is refreshing as the soft wind blows against my face. I close my eyes to see a brightness that only the Holy Spirit can produce. He's always with me; He's always dwelling inside of me.

Time is moving forward whether we like it or not. The past has no place in the present, so focus on the future and how you can make it a better one for you and the ones you love. Don't let the enemy create doubt in your

---

45. Acts 2:24 (Emphasis, mine).
46. Ps. 103:8 (Emphasis, mine).
47. Ps. 92:5 (Emphasis, mine).
48. Prov. 6:6 (Emphasis, mine).

mind, for you can do all things through Christ who strengthens you.[49] The Holy Spirit is your advocate and guide while you're here on this earth. Use Him to help navigate your way in the desolation of time.

There is nothing too great for our Lord. He spoke life into existence, certainly He can speak life into you as well.[50] When you feel lonely, depressed, or saddened by the state of the world, remember that Jesus has overcome the world, so take heart, for the Lord is always with you.[51] He is sitting on the throne right now this very minute interceding for our sins, and praying for you and me. What a mighty God we serve![52] Who can compare to His greatness, power, and love? As I wake up every morning, I thank God that He allowed me to take another breath; I thank Him for not giving up on me as I live to see another day.

On the Twenty-First Day

The clouds of heaven are visible today in the cold and brooding sky. The wind blows where it chooses, much like the Spirit who gives gifts to those He deems.[53] Faith, hope, and love are just some of the gifts that the Lord bestows upon on believers, yet as Christians, we should possess all of the fruit of the Spirit as a collective whole. When you feel that a godly attribute is lacking in your life, simply pray to the Lord for Him to increase it.

Our bodies are vessels for the Holy Spirit to dwell in. Jesus is still tabernacling among us as He once did some 2000 years ago. Only now, He inhabits our body as the third member of the Trinity. He is there to help increase our faith and to guide our lives. Blessed are the poor in spirit, for they have the kingdom of heaven, and indeed they do.[54] For the spirit that Jesus is referring to, is not the Spirit of Himself, but rather the broken human spirit. Fear not if you do not possess earthly riches, even Solomon gave into temptation towards the end of his lifetime. It is much better to be rich in the Spirit than to be poor in it.

As I stare at the flames of my fireplace, I'm reminded of the fire that burns inside of me for Jesus Christ. He is the Alpha and the Omega.[55] He is in tune with the Father and Spirit at all times and works all things for

49. Phil. 4:13 (Emphasis, mine).
50. Jer. 32:17 (Emphasis, mine).
51. John 16:33 (Emphasis, mine).
52. Zeph. 3:17 (Emphasis, mine).
53. 1 Cor. 12:11 (Emphasis, mine).
54. Matt. 5:3 (Emphasis, mine).
55. Rev. 1:8 (Emphasis, mine).

good according to those who love Him.⁵⁶ He is working on you right this moment, so don't get discouraged or dismayed. The plan He has for you is still in motion. Like the waves of the sea that rise and fall day and night, then finally make their collapse on the sandy beaches of the seashore, God is in no hurry to get you to your final destination.

On the Twenty-Second Day

Like a roaring lion, Jesus will return someday when we least expect it. Be on guard, for the Lamb who dwells in the kingdom of God is the lamb that was slain, and He will come again to judge the living and the dead.⁵⁷ We are only on this earth for a moment in God's eyes. To God, a day is like a thousand years and a thousand years is like a day.⁵⁸ Time passes so slowly for us on here earth, but time is only a blink of an eye to the Lord Almighty.

Are you focusing on the earthly kingdom or the heavenly one? Which kingdom would Jesus want you to focus on? Our treasures are not stored up on earth, but rather, in heaven is where we will find our ultimate victory. God has provided for us from the beginning of time. Even after the fall, God clothed Adam and Eve as they left the comfort of the garden.⁵⁹ How much more will God provide for you, if you simply have faith in Him?

Be thankful at all times. We must expect to enter His kingdom with praise and thanksgiving.⁶⁰ The heavenly Creator has made room for you in His kingdom, so be sure and show your appreciation for this provision. Many will try and enter the kingdom through the wide road, yet it is better for us to take the road less traveled. Wide is the road but narrow the path.⁶¹

Whose ways are like the Lord's? Surely, not yours or mine. Sometimes when we question God, we are really just displaying moments of pride within ourselves. God has everything planned out, so enjoy His plan. You are an important part of it.

---

56. Rom 8:28 (Emphasis, mine).
57. 1 Tim. 4:1 (Emphasis, mine).
58. 2 Pet. 3:8 (Emphasis, mine).
59. Gen. 3:21 (Emphasis, mine).
60. Ps. 100:4 (Emphasis, mine).
61. Matt. 7:13-14 (Emphasis, mine).

On the Twenty-Third Day

Be on guard at all times, for false prophets are always in our midst. Much like the old prophet who wrongly advised the younger one, we too may find ourselves eating and drinking before the appointed time.[62] The devil is the author of all lies, and the cultivator of all deception. Wear your spiritual armor with courage and you will be able to stand up to his evil ways. A time is coming soon when his reign of terror will end.

God has love for each and every one of us. His love is limitless and unconditional. If He didn't love you, would He have sent His only begotten son to die for you and me?[63] Jesus Christ suffered and died on the cross for the sins that we should have paid for. How beautiful a thing that Jesus did for us that day at Calvary. As the dark clouds came rolling over the mountain where Christ was crucified, the earth shook, and the veil was torn.[64] No longer was God's creation separated from Him, but instead united with Him through this glorious act on the cross.

The enemy enters our minds when we least expect it. Rebuke him! Like Jesus rebuked the devil inside of Peter for trying to alter the Father's plan, we too must cast Satan out from inside of us when he tries to interrupt God's plan for us. There is power in Jesus' name. His presence is with us at all times through the power of the Holy Spirit, so remember that where you are standing at this very moment *is* Holy ground.

King David had a heart after God's, yet even he fell into temptation. No one is immune to the enemies' treachery. Prayer and reading the Scriptures will help protect us from enemy attack. Discover the didactic truths imbedded in the word of God and enjoy the freedom it gives you.

On the Twenty-Fourth Day

Hallowed be the name of the Lord. We must always remember the powerful way in which the Savior's name is proclaimed for all eternity and to the very ends of the earth. Before the end comes, the gospel of the kingdom must be preached to all the nations.[65] This reminds us of the importance to spread the good news of the life, death, and resurrection of the Lord, Jesus Christ. Without the gospel, we would surely lose hope and fall into despair.

---

62. 1 Kings 13:18 (Emphasis, mine).
63. John 3:16 (Emphasis, mine).
64. Matt. 27:51 (Emphasis, mine).
65. Matt. 24:14 (Emphasis, mine).

The horizon looks brighter now as the soft snow falls like pollen blowing in the wind from the cottonwood tree. The heavens pour out the rain that turns to snow and fills the lake high in the Sierra Nevada mountains. This same cycle has been going on since the beginning of time. God set into motion a plan to provide for our every need. Don't you trust Him? The birds ask not where their food will come from, for they know that the God of Heaven and earth will always provide for them. How much more will He provide for you? [66]

Faith, hope, and love are all required to put our trust in the One we cannot see. He dwells in the high places interacting with us at all times. God is not as distant as you might think. You merely need to call on Him, and He will make Himself known in your heart and in your mind. When you were a child, you thought like a child, but now you must put away childish things and focus on Jesus Christ who will surely help guide you through any hardship you might currently face.[67]

On the Twenty-Fifth Day

This season of life is only temporary. Other seasons will come, in which God will judge the righteous and the wicked.[68] As one of us dies, another one is born. As one of us gets sick, another gets healed. As one of us succeeds, another one fails. As one of us gets closer to God, another one gets further away. Don't despair, trust in the Lord and He will move you into a new season of life.

Children are such a blessing. God enlivens our lives with the joy and laughter of those born after us. A child's mind isn't yet cluttered by the world; therefore, to enter the kingdom of heaven we must have the mind of a child.[69] Turn and run from the sin that plagues you. If you say, "I have no sin," you only deceive yourself. We must confess our sins, and God, who is faithful and just, will forgive our sins and cleanse us from all unrighteousness.[70]

King Saul allowed the enemy to enter his heart and corrupt it. Don't let that happen to you. You have so many angels fighting for your sanctification; you would be amazed if you could see them all. Saul slayed his

---

66. Matt 6:26 (Emphasis, mine).
67. 1 Cor. 13:11 (Emphasis, mine).
68. Eccl. 3:17 (Emphasis, mine).
69. Luke 18:17 (Emphasis, mine).
70. 1 John 1:9 (Emphasis, mine).

thousands and David his tens of thousands, but the Holy Spirit slays all that come against you through the powerful name of Jesus Christ.[71]

First, there was evening, then there was morning. Despite how alone you might feel, the Father of heaven is with you. He was there at creation and He is there now. The Lord has a way of organizing all things for His good purposes. Surely, He has many good purposes for you.

On the Twenty-Sixth Day

As I stare into the clouds of heaven, I ponder what heaven might look like. The angel that spoke to the Apostle John gave him a vision of what was to come. Amazingly, the new city of Jerusalem is said to have streets of gold; pure like translucent glass.[72] This is because the dross is removed. Sin cannot occupy the new heavens and new earth; therefore, all of sins impurities are removed. And so, it should also be with us. God is working on removing our sinful impurities right this very moment. Will you help Him complete His task?

King Solomon ordered a temple to be built to glorify the Lord. Like the new heavens and new earth, Solomon's temple was also covered in gold.[73] Yet, after the temple was rebuilt, Jesus tells us that every brick will be thrown to the ground; the temple destroyed.[74] And so it was, in 70 A.D. Though physical temples can be destroyed, eternal temples last forever. The temple of God dwells inside the believer and can never be destroyed. So, rest assured that the end of the age will eventually come, and death and sin will be removed from the face of the earth.

The seas call out His name and the winds obey His commands. God's integrity cannot be compromised. The virtues of the Father are cemented into the foundation of time. His hand is mighty, and to the right of Him sits the Son, forever interceding on our behalf against the convictions of the enemy.[75] How beautiful it is to have a God that adores us so much that He redeems us without reciprocation or question.

---

71. 1 Sam. 18:7 (Emphasis, mine).
72. Rev. 21:21 (Emphasis, mine).
73. 1 Kings 6:21 (Emphasis, mine).
74. Mark 13:2 (Emphasis, mine).
75. Mark 16:19 (Emphasis, mine).

On the Twenty-Seventh day

In the days of old, the Hebrews were governed by the Judges. At first, God's chosen would obey His commandments, and God was very pleased. However, over time the Hebrews became complacent and soon forgot about the God in heaven who delivered them from their slavery in Egypt. As more time passed, they began building their own gods to worship, which angered the Lord very much. God would then send armies from nearby countries to attack the rebellious chosen ones. In a plea for mercy, the people would cry out, "Great I Am, please deliver us!"

God, being both just and merciful, would listen to their pleas and send a judge to deliver them from the enemy and help bring them back into right-standing before the Lord. The people began to worship and obey the God most high and lived in peace for quite some time; although, not much time would pass before God's chosen people would turn from the Lord again and go about life in their reckless manor, doing whatever they saw fit in their own eyes.[76]

So, it is with this generation. If we have ears, we must listen to what the Lord is saying. Like the Hebrews before us, we are God's chosen people through our faith in Jesus Christ, yet we, too, fall into the same cycle of disobedience that the Israelites did so long ago. Unlike the time of the judges, we now have an eternal king to reign over us. Only through our trust and faith in Christ Jesus, can we break this cycle. The power of the Holy Spirit dwells inside all believers for this very purpose. Jesus was genuinely tempted in all ways, yet He overcame all temptations. If He wasn't tempted in all ways that we are, how could we overcome our temptations? Break the cycle today by asking God to release you from the foothold that Satan has in your life. You won't regret it and you might just rebuild your relationship with the Father as a result.

On the Twenty-Eighth Day

Though, we often place blame upon ourselves or others for our transgressions, King Solomon once said, "there is no one who does not sin."[77] Therefore, it is impossible for us not to sin in some form. Yet, we must try to avoid falling into temptation because the enemy will often take our trials and testing and turn them into a foothold that leads to further sin. God

---

76. Judg. 17:6 (Emphasis, mine).
77. 1 Kgs. 8:46 (Emphasis, mine).

rejoices more over one lost sheep that returns to Him, than for the rest of the flock who have already repented or, still remain lost.[78]

The sunset is so beautiful tonight. I think of Adam and Eve, who surely enjoyed the same sunsets that we experience every evening. Never take life for granted. We only experience life on this earth once. Our Father in heaven has created so many wonderful things for us to admire. Some question why He would only create one planet with life on it out of the entire expanse of the universe. I think it's because He is demonstrating just how magnificent and grand He really is. Perhaps, He gives us a glimpse into His greatness by simply admiring the vastness of space and time.

Listen when the Spirit speaks to you. This world can be so distracting at times, yet the Spirit is constantly trying to communicate with us. The small voice that convicts you after you've sinned, that is the Holy Spirit, working to re-align you with the Father. How gracious was Jesus Christ for sending this gift to us? It truly was better that He left and sent us this gift.[79] The Spirit will correct and guide us, if we accept His correction. Some say, "I can fix my own issues!" Some will always remain lost.

On the Twenty-Ninth Day

The crackling of the fireplace on this early January morning sets my mind at ease as I read God's word from the comfort of my aging brown rocking chair. Regardless of the amount of times I read God's word, I always experience new and refreshing revelation. This is the power of the Holy Spirit; this is how the Holy Spirit moves us to act. For, if we simply read the Scriptures without the help of the Holy Spirit, no illumination would come.[80]

Christ is our rock, our very foundation in this sinful world. As the chief cornerstone, Christ anchors the entire temple of believers in a solid and balanced way. If we move away from Christ, we lose our balance. Remain in Him at all times and experience the joy that pours forth. The Apostle Peter was called "the rock," yet even Peter lost his balance. Stay focused on the heavenly goal and fear not, for the Lord is always with you.[81]

When we forget about all the great things that God has done for us, we tend to go the way of the world. The world is always at enmity with the Father. Mankind has repeated this disastrous cycle since the fall. Catching ourselves before we fall into temptation is not easy, yet catch ourselves, we

---

78. Luke 15:3-7 (Emphasis, mine).
79. John 16:7 (Emphasis, mine).
80. 1 Cor. 2:10-16 (Emphasis, mine).
81. Isa. 41:10 (Emphasis, mine).

must do. For, removing sin from our lives takes effort on our part. We cannot simply go through life refusing to resist sin. If we do, the great deceiver will have prevailed, knowing that you no longer have the desire to stand up to him. Continue in the way of the righteous. Trust in God and you will walk in wisdom.[82] Satan is always entering our minds, so we must rebuke him there first. Control your thoughts through the power of the Holy Spirit and then your heart will follow. Isn't it better to love than to hate?

On the Thirtieth Day

Forgiveness has been on my heart today. If God has forgiven us of our sins through the death and sacrifice of His only Son, Jesus Christ, how much more should we forgive one another? Jesus tells Peter we must not forgive merely seven times, but rather, seventy-seven times.[83] Lamech's song ends, "If Cain is avenged seven times, then Lamech seventy-seven times."[84] For the numbers seven and seventy-seven are not random. Nothing in God's word is random. Instead, those numbers speak of the reversal of the natural human tendency towards resentment and anger. No longer is forgiveness set at four hundred and ninety times per occurrence, but rather, we should forgive others in an unlimited fashion, and at all times because if we don't, we will only harbor resentment and bitterness inside of us.

Our God is a mighty fortress. Stronger than the walls of Jericho; fiercer than the roaring lion. Surely, He will return and avenge us for the wrongs of others. If He did not, would He be a just God? Therefore, forgive one another and let God judge others on the last day. Our job is to love and encourage one another. How much greater this world would be if everyone practiced those virtues. Everyone deserves to feel loved; everyone deserves to feel valued. Who have you shown love to today?

The winds of change will only blow in the direction of those who can feel them. Listen to the Spirit as He convicts us of our transgressions and encourages us in our successes. He will not lead you astray. Too often, the enemy distracts us in our mission to love and forgive one another. Forgiveness is better for the one doing the forgiving than it is for the recipient; you'll see.

---

82. Prov. 28:26 (Emphasis, mine).
83. Matt. 18:22 (Emphasis, mine).
84. Gen. 4:23-24 (Emphasis, mine).

On the Thirty-First Day

Well, we've made it to the final day in January. How are you feeling my friends? I hope you've taken the time to meditate on God's word and pray for both your friends, and your enemies. The cold month of January is only temporary. God uses the seasons to care for the earth, much like He uses the seasons of our lives to care for us. For, to everything of God, there is a purpose, even if we don't always know or understand what that purpose is.

God can harden hearts or soften them. He can cause calamity or cause peace. He causes the mighty oceans to rise and fall. He holds the world up in His mighty right hand. He overcomes His most vicious enemies, yet He humbled Himself to the point of death for you and for me.[85] We might ask ourselves, "Is it fair that God does these things that often result in our rebellion or disobedience?" "Can we really be held responsible if God predestines our movements?" Yet, we must also ask ourselves, "does the clay talk back to the potter?" For, who are we to question God?[86] Since the fall, God has orchestrated the events of mankind in such a way to accomplish His special purposes. Someday, when we see Him face to face, all of our questions will be answered.

Praise be to the One who created all things. Glory to God in the highest![87] The son of David has conquered sin! Death can no longer have a hold over us, for Jesus Christ has reversed the curse of death through His selfless sacrifice on the cross. Where, O, Death is your victory? Where, O, Death, is your sting?[88]

---

85. Phil. 2:8 (Emphasis, mine).
86. Rom. 9:18-19 (Emphasis, mine).
87. Luke 2:14 (Emphasis, mine).
88. 1 Cor. 15:55 (New International Version).

Chapter 2

God's Dwelling Place
The Month of February

On the First Day

CLEAR-BLUE ICICLES FORM ALONG the edge of the roof of my quiet little home. Their translucent glow from the reflecting sunshine reminds me of my earlier days, of time spent at a close friends' house during the cold month of February. It was a time long ago, when I was a child with no cares in the world, except to wake up and live each day like it was my last. Yet, even during those times of innocence, the temptations of the enemy were clearly present.

Long ago, the Word became flesh and dwelt among us.[1] He's still among us, tabernacling inside of those who have accepted Him into their hearts. Moses built the Holy Tabernacle in the wilderness, but it was only temporary, made of cloth and wood. Later, King Solomon built the temple made of brick, stone, precious elements, and gold, yet it was still destroyed by Nebuchadnezzar and the Babylonians in 586 B.C.E. Not long after that, the temple was rebuilt again, only to be destroyed in 70 A.D. by the Romans. However, Jesus' death on the cross marked a turning point in this destructive cycle. All those years, a tabernacle had to be built for God to dwell among His people, yet there was always separation within the tabernacle by a veil. When Jesus died on the cross, the veil was torn. His body was the veil and through Him, we enter into an everlasting dwelling place with the Lord. Subsequently, the Lord, Himself will dwell with us in the new heavens and new earth at the end of time.[2] No longer is there a separation from God Almighty and His chosen people. We are all one, dwelling with Him in an eternal jubilation.

---

1. John 1:14 (Emphasis, mine).
2. Rev. 21:2-3 (Emphasis, mine).

On the Second Day

Life is a temporary moment in the endless expanse of eternity. We often spend our lives building up earthly treasures, yet we forget that eternity is where we should place our priority. For, if we build up our treasures in heaven instead of on this earth, we will never have to worry about our treasures being destroyed by moth and vermin.[3] Is your heart in the right place?

Too often, we worry about tomorrow. God has taken care of you all along, do you think He will abandon you now? We cannot serve both God and money; therefore, we must place our trust in God to provide for us, and the money will come as a result.[4] When the Hebrews dwelt in the wilderness, God provided manna from heaven to sustain them. When they were thirsty, Moses struck the rock and water poured forth in abundance: that rock was Christ.[5]

Wealth is not the enemy of God. If it were, how could King Solomon be given vast amounts of it and still be in right-standing with the Holy One? Rather, it's the *love* of money that is the root of all evil.[6] For when we love money, we begin to worship it instead of the Lord. The money then becomes an idol that we think about day and night, and we begin to forget that God was the one who allowed us to prosper in the first place. If we have ears, we must listen to what the Spirit is saying to us.

Remain steadfast and trust in the Lord at all times and in all circumstances. Do not weary of doing good, and in the proper time you will reap the great harvest.[7] We must always love God and one another; never give up on that commandment, for the Lord never gives up on us.

On the Third Day

I can remember it like it was yesterday. Twenty years ago, at a home Bible study, I was sitting on the soft loveseat inside my friend's new home in Sparks, Nevada, and I encountered the awe and beauty of the Holy Spirit Himself. Peering out at the jubilant atmosphere, something had changed inside of me. My eyes were no longer hardened by the world and its sinful enticements. I had accepted Jesus Christ into my heart 8 years prior, yet this was different; I was now filled with the Spirit from head to toe. I could actually feel Him

---

3. Matt. 6:19-21 (Emphasis, mine).
4. Matt. 6:24 (Emphasis, mine).
5. 1 Cor. 10:4 (Emphasis, mine).
6. 1 Tim. 6:10 (Emphasis, mine).
7. Gal. 6:9 (Emphasis, mine).

tingling all over my body. Many close brothers and sisters in the faith prayed for me to receive the power of the Holy Spirit that night, and God responded in such a wonderful way, a way that has left me energized and motivated to share my faith and knowledge of God with everyone I encounter. The fire of the Holy Spirit has never left me, it's only grown stronger. Like the crackling flame atop fresh cut wood that occupies the space of a large brick fireplace, the Spirit continues to burn inside of me, attracting those whose hearts may be chilled from the emptiness of the world.

I always thank God for that day. As I got older, there were times I would venture out into the wilderness alone, yet God would always welcome me back into His loving arms. I returned to Him so that He could return to me.[8] If you find yourself out of touch with the Father, perhaps even hiding from Him as Adam once did, remember that He is slow to anger and abounding in loving-kindness, ready and willing to accept you back to Him.[9] Return to Him today, you'll be so glad that you did.

On the Fourth Day

Raindrops pour down today. The beautiful evanescent patterns are dissipating on the ground. Water has both the power to heal and to destroy. Rocks are shaped and polished by flowing rivers, yet God destroyed all creation through the heavy rains that fell for forty days and forty nights.[10] Water cleanses the earth and it cleanses us as we wash away our sins and emerge victorious as a new creation in Christ.

The Prophet Jonah was called by God to preach a message of repentance to the great city of Nineveh. Yet, Jonah feared the call, and instead traveled in a different direction through the mighty ocean.[11] During his travels, the Lord created a fierce storm, and Jonah was voted to be sacrificed to appease God and calm the storm. For three days and three nights, God preserved Jonah in the belly of a large fish who spit him out on the shore after the third day. Similarly, Jesus Christ descended into the earth for three days and three nights where He was preserved by the Lord, then having been resurrected at dawn.[12] Notice that Christ did not run from God's plan,

---

8. Zech. 1:3 (Emphasis, mine).
9. Joel 2:3 (Emphasis, mine).
10. Gen. 7:12 (Emphasis, mine).
11. Jonah 1:3 (Emphasis, mine).
12. Luke 24:1-3 (Emphasis, mine).

but rather, He embraced it for it was God's will. God chose not to remove the cup of wrath from Jesus for our sake.[13]

God often calls each one of us in different ways to accomplish His purposes. It's up to us to accept His call. Like many before us and many after us, running from God will only lead to stress and anxiety. Adam toiled the earth with sweat on his brow, not because he was physically exhausted, but because he was anxious. Like Jonah, Adam hid from God because sin had produced anxiety in him. Stress and worry are a result of the fall, yet in Christ, we should be anxious for nothing.

On the Fifth Day

This generation is always looking for a sign from God. Many people say, "If there is a God, why doesn't He reveal Himself to us?" Yet, He did over two thousand years ago, and still people didn't believe in Him. Can you not look at creation and infer that there must be a creator? For what are the chances that creation can create itself? Even the great scientists are puzzled by this. Who but the Lord Almighty, can speak life into existence?

When Jesus spoke at the Sermon on the Mount, the Apostle Matthew records the event by proclaiming, "And he *opened his mouth* and taught them, saying."[14] There is significance in the way that this verse is worded. God opened His mouth to speak creation into life (existence); Jesus opened His mouth to speak life into God's creation. Will you listen to Jesus' words today? He will speak to you if you open your heart and mind to receive what He has to say.

Jesus Christ was sent to the earth as a living sacrifice to the Lord of heaven who would forgive us of our sins once and for all. How else could mankind appease Him?[15] The blood of goats and bulls could only atone for sin once a year, and even the high priest needed to provide a sacrifice for himself and his family. Jesus is the High Priest who offered Himself as a sacrifice to atone for all of our sins once and for all.[16]

Christ was beaten, crucified, and buried, yet He rose again! This is the good news that we must proclaim to everyone around us. If Christ hadn't risen from the dead, then our faith is in vain.[17] Yet, Christ did rise from the

---

13. John 18:11 (Emphasis, mine).
14. Matt. 5:2 (English Standard Version).
15. Heb. 10:4-6 (Emphasis, mine).
16. Heb. 7:27 (Emphasis, mine).
17. 1 Cor. 15:14 (Emphasis, mine).

dead and so our faith in Him can be proclaimed in confidence to the ends of the earth.

On the Sixth Day

The sun peers out through the cold mist as I make the journey west towards the great lake. Like beams of light that shine through a cascade of water in front of the setting sun, the fire of the Holy Spirit burns brightly inside of me. In the time of Moses, the Spirit of God would rest upon God's anointed for a specific task or mission in order to accomplish His purposes.[18] Now, we experience the Holy Spirit continuously as He tabernacles inside the dwelling places of our souls.

Pentecost marked a turning point for the body of Christ. Not only was Pentecost the reverse of Babel, but it was also the starting point of the Church. For prior to Pentecost, only God's original chosen could be given the inheritance of Abraham. Now that Christ has left and He has sent the gift of the Holy Spirit to all who believe in Him, all races and people groups who are adopted by God can enjoy the eternal promised land as one unified body.[19]

We prophesy in part, yet when the perfect comes, we will do away with prophesy, because we will have all knowledge of the Holy One.[20] The time is drawing nearer to Christ's return. We must be prepared for His appearance at all times. Of the ten virgins who went to meet the bridegroom, only half of them kept their jars filled with oil. When the five foolish virgins tried to purchase the oil from those who sold it, the bridegroom had already come and gone and taken the wise virgins with Him.[21] We must always stay filled with the Holy Spirit. If you feel that His energy is dissipating, call on the name of the Lord and ask Him to fill you back up. After all, are we not empty vessels meant to house the glory of God?

On the Seventh Day

Darkness begins to settle over the horizon as the sun disappears behind the mountain tops in the west. Darkness is where the enemy dwells, for evil

---

18. Num. 11:25 (Emphasis, mine).
19. Eph. 1:5 (Emphasis, mine).
20. 1 Cor. 13:9 (Emphasis, mine).
21. Matt. 25 (Emphasis, mine).

does not like to be exposed by the light.[22] Driving through the dark streets of Reno late at night, I can feel the presence of the enemy all around me. This is the time when I need to be on guard, protecting my sanctification through the power of the Holy Spirit. Much like Jehu destroyed the evil prophets of Baal,[23] we too must fight to destroy the evil spirits around us through the sword of the Spirit, protecting our hearts with the breastplate of righteousness.

The evil one has been amongst us since the creation. Having fallen himself, Satan, in his quest to separate us from the Holy One, recruited many others that had also fallen. However, God Almighty has set a plan into motion which will redeem us back to Him and restore the earth to its original state before the fall. We are so blessed to be a part of this great plan of redemption. God cares so much for you and me that He sent His only begotten Son to die for our sins.[24] We deserved the punishment Christ experienced for us, yet the Lamb who was slain had to become a living sacrifice to atone for the sins of the whole world.[25]

The scarlet thread of redemption shines brightly throughout God's word. From Genesis to Revelation, one can see this thread interwoven in the beautiful tapestry of Scripture. We are all part of this magnificent plan, set in motion by God the Father at the creation of the world. Honor, and glory, and wisdom, and strength, be to God and the Lamb forever, Amen.

On the Eighth Day

Gentle winds blow through the air as the chill of winter begins to set in. There were many times I felt cold and alone as I traveled this earth. Yet, if I remember that my Father in heaven is always with me, then I am never really alone: He's speaking into my life and into my heart.

In the days of the Old Covenant, God spoke to us from heaven through the prophets and high priests.[26] Later, as His son walked the earth, God spoke to us directly through Him. Still later, God spoke to the Apostles through the Holy Spirit. Now, God speaks to us through the power of the Holy Spirit, whom all believers possess. Do you hear Him?

Sometimes, God will communicate with us through dreams. Both Daniel and Joseph had these experiences. I once had a dream so vivid that

---

22. John 3:20 (Emphasis, mine).
23. 2 Kgs. 10:18-28 (Emphasis, mine).
24. John 3:16 (Emphasis, mine).
25. 1 John 2:2 (Emphasis, mine).
26. Num. 12:6 (Emphasis, mine).

I reached out to the woman that was in my dream to see if she was okay. It turned out, that she had just undergone a hard breakup with her significant other of many years and had fallen into depression and despair. I wanted to meet with her and help comfort her anxiety and worry, simply by listening.

To her amazement, what I told her was completely accurate! In my dream, my old high school friend and classmate, Vanessa, was with her children at a pizza restaurant in our home town of Sparks, Nevada. After I walked into the restaurant, I found her there crying uncontrollably in the corner. As I approached her to ask if she was all right, she hugged me and wouldn't let me go. Then I woke up. I hadn't had contact with Vanessa in over twenty years. When I told her about my dream, she said, "That's crazy! Truth be told, I have been really upset over a recent break up. Thank you for reaching out to me." God can amaze even those who question their faith. By taking a step forward in our own faith, we can help increase the faith in others.

On the Ninth Day

The sunshine is peering out between the clouds on this ninth day of February. Have you ever taken notice how butterflies have a bounce in their flight patterns? It's as if they are so excited to have been set free from being bound to this earth as caterpillars, that they can't help but spread their wings and fly joyfully in the air; much like the children of God will be, once we are set free from the trials and tribulations of this earth with which *we* are also bound.

There is a freeing feeling when the bondage of sin no longer has power over us. Sin is no longer our master, because we are no longer under the law; but rather, we are now under God's grace.[27] God's grace is a wonderful thing. We are set free from condemnation[28] because of God who loves us enough to care about our eternity. I would rather be a servant of God than a slave to sin.

Sometimes we tend to punish ourselves emotionally. Break free from this condemnation, for Christ Jesus has already paid the price for your sin. Trust and follow Him, and as a result you will produce good works. The fruit of the Spirit is ripe inside of you. It's time to bring it to harvest. A good tree cannot produce bad fruit,[29] and neither can the believer in Jesus Christ. The good works produced are a means in which we share God's love with others around us. If you are not producing fruit, ask God to increase your faith and

---

27. Rom. 6:14 (Emphasis, mine).
28. Rom. 8:1 (Emphasis, mine).
29. Luke 6:43 (Emphasis, mine).

increase your passion for Him and those around you, and the good works will be sure to follow.

On the Tenth Day

Walking through the park on this cold winter morning, I feel a sense of unity amongst mankind. The various colors of leaves on the trees are all different yet they dwell together on the branches to form one unified collage of beauty. All races, genders, and socio-economic backgrounds are present today and interrelating well with each other. This is how it will be in the kingdom of heaven.[30] Sadly, this is not the case everywhere in our country, or even in our region. God created each of us in His image, and we are all beautiful in that way, regardless of skin color or physical differences. Loving God with all of our heart, soul, mind, and strength, and loving our neighbor as we love ourselves[31] does not exclude certain members of mankind, for everyone is our neighbor. I can even love brothers or sisters from other religious backgrounds because they are made in God's image, though I cannot love the gods they worship. This is why we can love our enemies and pray for those who persecute us. We are not loving their actions; but, rather, we are loving the image of God, in which they are made. Division happens when we let Satan point out our differences, instead of letting God elevate our similarities.

It's important to stay engaged with the Father at all times. He is always willing to listen, and to guide us in a better direction, but we must build our relationship with Him through reading His word, praying, and spending time in solitude, listening to the soft inner voice that speaks to us through the breath of the Holy Spirit. Pray before you read a passage of Scripture and ask the Lord to unlock His mysteries for you. The anointing you received remains in you; therefore, you can be taught by the Holy Spirit Himself, even if no one else is around to teach you.[32]

On the Eleventh Day

Each one of us has a story of where we've come from and where we are going, who our ancestors are, and what struggles they have had to endure. The Hebrew culture places its lineage in high esteem, and it goes all the way

---

30. Rev. 7:9 (Emphasis, mine).
31. Mark 12:30-31 (Emphasis, mine).
32. 1 John 2:27 (Emphasis, mine).

back to Adam. Some may read lineages in the Bible and skip right over their significance. In the Gospel according to Matthew, the genealogy of Jesus starts with Abraham, then ends with Joseph who was the husband of Mary, who was the mother of Jesus.[33] This demonstrates that even Jesus' adoptive father, Joseph, and His mother Mary, were from the line of Judah.

When we look at the genealogy as recorded in the Gospel according to Luke, we see the lineage reversed, starting with the (adopted) son of Joseph and ending with the son of Adam; the son of God.[34] We know that Jesus was called *the second Adam*. Since Jesus is God's son, He existed before Adam and is reflected within this genealogy. This magnificent truth is revealed in the first verse of the Gospel according to John, "In the beginning was the Word, and the Word was with God, and the Word was God."[35]

It's fascinating how God orchestrates things. If Ruth hadn't married Boaz, then there would be no Obed. If Obed never was, then there would never have been Jessie. If Jessie never was, there would be no David, and if David never was, there would be no earthly kings down through the line of Judah; there would be no King Jesus in the incarnate form. God has everything planned out for a reason. How blessed are we, to be part of His great plan?

On the Twelfth Day

As I awake to the sound of a crackling fire, I'm thankful for the many blessings God has given me over the years. Have I endured setbacks? Yes, quite a few; however, that has never hampered my longing to spend time with the Father in prayer and worship thanking Him for all of life's challenges and successes. It's important to thank Him at all times. If you are facing a setback or challenge, He is allowing it to take place for a reason. Rest assured, the enemy of old will be bound and everything shall be restored.[36]

Have you ever noticed that Satan starts off as a small serpent in the Book of Genesis, then grows to a large dragon in the Book of Revelation? So large, in fact, that he swept a third of the starts out of the sky.[37] This is how sin works. It starts off small, then grows to a level in which we can no longer control it. Catch the sin as it enters your heart and mind before it's acted upon. The enemy doesn't want us to be close to our creator; therefore, if you

---

33. Matt. 1:1-16 (Emphasis, mine).
34. Luke 3:23-38 (Emphasis, mine).
35. John 1:1 (ESV).
36. Rev. 20:1-2 (Emphasis, mine).
37. Rev. 12:4 (Emphasis, mine).

are struggling with a particular sin, repent constantly and run towards your loving Father in heaven. When Satan discovers that every time he tempts you, you fail to give into the temptation; and, instead, run towards the Father, he will surely give up tempting you in that area of your life. But, be on guard, for Satan always has another temptation ready to entice us.

The sun rises and falls each day. From the next beat of our heart, to the next breath that we take, there is nothing that does not happen in which the Father does not control. The glory of God is shown in every part of creation. Do you see it? Take the time to admire what God has placed before you. The stars are endless in the sky. This should reveal to us how immense our God really is. Take nothing for granted, for tomorrow is just a heartbeat away.

On the Thirteenth Day

The birds of the air glide and soar through the vastness of the atmosphere. Do they not trust in the Father to provide food for them, or that the tree branch they land on will hold them up? Surely, they have much trust, and so should we. Unlike some of our earthly friends and neighbors, the God of heaven will never let us down.

God answers the prayers of those who trust Him.[38] Trust is vital for any strong relationship. Trust is something that is hard to regain once it's lost. By building trust in our godly relationship, we can focus less on our struggles at home, and more on our earthly and heavenly goals, which should always glorify God. When we fall back, we must trust that God will catch us. Don't let the enemy break your trust in the Father. Satan is quick to turn your trial into a temptation.

God dwells in each one of us who have accepted His son as our personal Lord and Savior. The Lord has put a new Spirit in us and has replaced our hearts of stone with hearts of flesh.[39] This gives us the capacity to love Him and others, as well as to understand the words that flow from the Holy Scriptures. Take care of your body as you do your soul. Do you not realize that your body is a temple?[40] It's up to us to keep our bodies clean.

Cast your worries aside, for tomorrow will have its own worries. Your Father in heaven has taken you this far, how much further will He take you if you continue to obey His commands? Relying on the world to take care of our needs will only get us so far, yet God can take us to places unimaginable.

---

38. 1 Chr. 5:20 (Emphasis, mine).
39. Ezek. 36:26 (Emphasis, mine).
40. 1 Cor. 6:19 (Emphasis, mine).

On the Fourteenth Day

Valentine's Day

Today is Valentine's Day and many waters cannot quench love.[41] Yet, in the darkness of the evening, the spiritual realm is quite active. Often times, as I pass through the desolate streets of Reno, my senses are heightened as I observe the demons that lurk about. The chill of the winter air manifests itself as vapor that escapes my lungs and dissipates in the stillness of the night.

Though we cannot see the angelic realm, it is highly active. Angels are battling to preserve the relationship we have with the Holy One. For, did not Elisha pray to the Lord and behold, the Lord opened his eyes to see the spiritual dimension, of which angels appeared to protect him from his adversaries?[42] If one believer dwells in the household, the other non-believing members are highly favored by God, still the Christian must proclaim the good news at all times to the rest of the family so that they might believe and be saved.[43]

Perhaps, you are in a marriage covenant with an unbelieving spouse. Fear not, for the Scriptures tell us that your spouse and children are set apart in God's eyes because of your faith.[44] God has thought of your every doubt and concern and has already addressed them. This is why the Bible is so powerful. Not only is it a book about God, the creator of all things and how He relates to His creation, but it is also a book about God's son who died for our just punishment, that we might not perish, but live in eternity with the Father. God's word is both prophetic and instructional. The Bible reveals the revelation of Christ Jesus as seen through the scarlet thread of redemption.

On the Fifteenth Day

Have you ever taken the time to observe carpenter ants and how they work tirelessly day and night to provide for the queen and colony? Like one single organism, ants work in tandem with one another to achieve a single end goal. How much greater are we than the ant. Yet many believers are divided, going against the Apostle Paul who taught us to unify one another in Christ

---

41. Song. 8:7 (Emphasis, mine).
42. 2 Kgs. 6:17 (Emphasis, mine).
43. Acts 16:32 (Emphasis, mine).
44. 1 Cor. 7:14 (Emphasis, mine).

Jesus with one mind and one spirit.[45] If we have ears, we will listen to what the Spirit has to say.

How do we measure success? Quite often, we evaluate ourselves based on earthly achievements. Yet, our Father in heaven evaluates us on our spiritual achievements. David was chosen to lead Israel as a mighty king, not because of his earthly success or his appearance, but because of his heart.[46] We must keep our hearts following after God, and He will surely bless us.

Have you ever noticed that history is often written by the winners? How often do you read an autobiography or historical book that reveals the weaknesses of the author? One argument in favor of the accuracy of Scripture is that great kings and queens, prophets of God, and chosen patriarchs are exposed for their faults and sins against the Lord. Ironically, many of God's chosen had turned from God at some point in their lives. Despite his obedience and loyalty, did not the Apostle Peter deny Jesus three times?[47] God uses broken people to advance His purposes. Were most of the characters in the Bible obedient to the Lord at all times, or were many of them disobedient? If you feel as though you're not good enough to be used by God in magnificent ways, rebuke the enemy who casts that doubt in your mind. God has a purpose for you and me. Great is the Lord, and most worthy of our praise.[48]

On the Sixteenth Day

What a beautiful morning! The skies are golden yellow as the sun begins to rise in the east. All glory and majesty go to the Father in Heaven, and to Jesus of Nazareth who is of the God most high! Thank you, Lord, for blessing me today, and each and every day as I traverse this empty and desolate world. With you dwelling inside of me, I'm never alone. I feel your presence tingling all around me as the Holy Spirit manifests Himself upon my flesh.

I had the most wonderful experience at 6:00 a.m. this morning as I was blessing my home. The Spirit told me that I am anointed of God, and right at that very moment, I felt Him tingling all over my body! Amazing, indeed is the power of the Holy Spirit. He doesn't always manifest Himself in that way, but when He does, I pay attention for He is emphasizing something.

---

45. Phil. 2:2 (Emphasis, mine).
46. 1 Sam. 13:14 (Emphasis, mine).
47. John 18:15-27 (Emphasis, mine).
48. 1 Chr. 16:25 (NIV).

Jesus intercedes for our salvation,[49] but the Holy Spirit intercedes for us against our flesh. For if the Spirit wasn't in constant intersession, the flesh would tear us away from the Holy One.[50] Never think for one moment that the Lord isn't actively working on you, molding you to perfection by removing the dross of sin so that you can dwell with Him in righteousness.[51]

God's love is like a young child who runs to his father, clinging onto him and never letting go. God does not let go of us once we have accepted His son into our hearts and minds. Thomas had serious reservations about the Lord, Jesus, of whom he was witness to many miracles. Jesus told Thomas because you have seen me (*resurrected*) you believe, but more blessed are those who do not see me and yet they still believe.[52] Have you stopped doubting and believed?

On the Seventeenth Day

The pureness of the white snow that fills the ground below my feet reminds me of the white robes given to the saints in the heavenly kingdom,[53] signifying that they had suffered and died for Christ Jesus and are purified from sin. Perhaps we don't suffer physical persecution as much in the West, but all believers suffer some type of persecution for their faith. Hang in there a little while longer. Soon enough, God will deliver us from the enemy once and for all.

Our Father in heaven is full of grace and mercy. Have you not read that if you are merciful towards others, God's mercy will triumph over His judgment of you as well?[54] When the Israelites chose to worship a golden calf in the wilderness, God's anger arose against them, and He was ready to destroy them all. Yet, Moses prostrated himself before the Lord for forty days and forty nights, praying that God not do such a thing. God listened to Moses and relented.[55] Moses interceded for his people then, much like Jesus intercedes for us now. Show mercy and kindness to those who have wronged you. Our heavenly Father has shown us mercy by sending His son to die for our sins.

---

49. Heb. 7:25 (Emphasis, mine).
50. Rom. 8:26-27 (Emphasis, mine).
51. Prov. 25:4-5 (Emphasis, mine).
52. John 20:27-29 (Emphasis, mine).
53. Rev. 6:11 (Emphasis, mine).
54. Jas. 2:13 (Emphasis, mine).
55. Deut. 9:20-25 (Emphasis, mine).

Loving our neighbor involves forgiveness and mercy for their wrongdoings. For, how can you love your neighbor as yourself if you are not willing to forgive your neighbor, yet you are willing to forgive yourself? The enemy is quick to convict and slow to give up. Fight him at all costs and preserve your righteousness. God chooses to remember our sins no more.[56] How much more then, should we choose to forgive those who sin against us?

On the Eighteenth Day

The crystal-clear dew that glistens off the yellow bushels of grass reflect the brilliant light of the sun. Fine particles dance in the air as I peer out of my kitchen window at the beautiful creation of the Lord. Many people are enjoying this brisk morning as well. From people walking their dogs, to children playing in the front yard, to the neighbors shoveling snow off of their driveways, there isn't one person who's not interacting with God's intelligent design.

God has always had love for us. God has always had love for the Son, the One that He raised up from the line of David; the One that is set over God's house and kingdom forever.[57] Earthly kingdoms come and go, yet God's kingdom survives forever in Christ Jesus. God's love has been passed down through the Son since the beginning of time to all of creation. For before Abraham was, I Am.[58]

The Apostle Paul expands on many gifts of the Spirit, yet even he establishes the greatest gift of all.[59] How can we live in a world absent of all love? We have the capacity to love God and love one another because God first loved us.[60] I once used social media to reach out to someone who had hurt me many years ago. I told him that I forgave him for any pain or suffering that he caused me and that I was praying for him and his family. His response brought tears to my eyes. For he said that he too, was bullied at a young age and was so sorry for anything that he did to me. He said that he wanted to use my message to teach his own children that it's wrong to bully people, and that even people who make poor decisions deserve forgiveness. What a powerful experience for both of us. God is teaching us the importance of love and is at work doing so at all times; if we would just listen to what the Spirit has to say to us.

56. Heb. 8:12 (Emphasis, mine).
57. 1 Chr. 17:13-14 (Emphasis, mine).
58. John 8:58 (ESV).
59. 1 Cor. 13:13 (Emphasis, mine).
60. 1 John 4:19 (Emphasis, mine).

On the Nineteenth Day

Long ago, the Lord walked with our ancestors and communicated with them face to face. Yet, as sin progressed in the world, He seems to have grown more distant, or is it we who have distanced ourselves from Him? He is always willing to guide us in the direction that will glorify Him and aid us in our wishes as well. Jesus once told a story of two sons, one of which had asked to be given his father's inheritance right away, even before the father's death. After spending every last dime on personal indulgence, the son was afraid to return to the father. Seeing his son in the distance, the father ran to him and embraced him with a strong embrace. The son, being full of regret, told his father that he had sinned against both heaven and him. Instead of the father punishing him for his transgression, he forgave his son and rewarded him with the finest clothes and food.[61]

Not long after, the oldest son got word that his younger brother had returned and had been given the best provisions that his father had. Burning with anger, the older son confronted his father demanding he explain why he had rewarded someone who clearly betrayed him. "My son," the father said, "you are always with me, and everything I have is yours. But we had to celebrate and be glad, because this brother of yours was dead and is alive again; he was lost and is found."[62]

Even when we distance ourselves from our Father in heaven, it is never too late to come back to Him. Do not be afraid that He won't accept you back into His loving arms, He surely will, and He will reward you greatly for your repentance. I once was lost, but now I'm found.[63]

On the Twentieth Day

The soft white clouds begin to pour over the city as the sun rises above them. There's a chill in the air as creation wakes up and sings its songs to the Lord. God always answers me when I call.[64] It's far better to be among the righteous than to dwell with those among the unrighteous. For God blesses the righteous and covers them with His favor.[65] How many times in life do we make decisions that we later regret? Pray to the Lord at all times and He will prevent you from walking in the darkness.

---

61. Luke 15:11-30 (Emphasis, mine).
62. Luke 15:31-32 (NIV).
63. Luke 15:24 (Emphasis, mine).
64. Ps. 4:1 (Emphasis, mine).
65. Ps. 5:12 (Emphasis, mine).

The ways of the Lord are true and just. Evil tends to disguise itself as curiosity. Don't let your flesh get in the way of what the Spirit is telling you, for the three enemies of God are the world, the flesh, and the devil. We know that our bodies are temples that house the very essence of the Holy One. To give in to our temptations only helps to clutter our bodies with defilement and separate us from the Lord. We must fight the good fight, finish the course that God has laid before us, and keep the faith.[66]

Many have fallen back, yet many have repented. Does the Lord not rejoice more over one lost sheep that returns to the shepherd as opposed to the entire flock of sheep that never left?[67] Surely, the Lord is rejoicing over you at this very moment. The Christ is advocating on your behalf against the accusations of the enemy. What a beautiful Lord we serve! Submit yourselves then to God. Resist the devil and He will flee from you.[68]

On the Twenty-First Day

The mountain tops of the Sierra Nevadas don the radiant snow that fell upon them the night before. The pine trees carry the weight of the frost upon their rough branches. Below the trees, the chipmunks are searching for nuts along snow-filled hiking trails of the forest. Everything is in order by God's ultimate design; all of creation is cared for in this circle of life. How much more will God care for you, the climax of His creation?

When we set our eyes on Jesus, our healing can start to take place. Like the Israelites who were being bitten by the venomous serpents in the wilderness, gazing upon the death of sin on the cross will surely cure us from our sickness of sin.[69] Jesus paid the ultimate price for you and me. No other religion has a god of that religion who is willing to sacrifice himself so that his believers may enter into eternity with him. Moses set his people free from their bondage to the Egyptians; Christ sets us free from our slavery to sin. Only Christianity provides eternal security by God Himself, the most high, whom in Christ Jesus we are set free.[70]

The enemy was once like a guardian cherub who dwelt in the Garden of Eden and walked among the stones of fire but was full of violence and fell during his rebellion against God.[71] Sometimes it's hard to separate the

66. 2 Tim. 4:7 (Emphasis, mine).
67. Luke 15:4-6 (Emphasis, mine).
68. Jas. 4:7 (NIV).
69. Num. 21:4-9 (Emphasis, mine).
70. Gal. 5:1 (Emphasis, mine).
71. Ezek. 28:12-19 (Emphasis, mine).

wheat from the chaff. We must not judge one's heart, but rather look to the actions of the believer, which often reveal the good fruit from the bad. Paul clearly tells us not to judge those outside of the church, but we must make constructive decisions in regard to those practicing sinful behavior inside the church, lest the church increase in corruption.[72] King David surely committed sin, yet he had a heart after God, and so must we. The Lord has the power to raise us up, or to remove us from the highest places.

On the Twenty-Second Day

The birds awake this morning as the sun rises in the east. It's amazing to think that we are witnesses to the same sunrise and sunset, the same stars in heaven, and the same brilliant moon, that have all existed since the fourth day.[73] God spoke everything that exists into being; God is still speaking life into you right now. Are you listening to Him?

God's son, Jesus Christ had the power to fulfill the Law, the Prophets, and the Psalms, written over a thousand years before His earthly existence.[74] Who, other than God Himself, could be without spot or blemish? We are all broken members of the body of Christ, yet we are made whole by the blood and sacrifice of the Lamb.[75] Thanks be to God who rescued us from the devil, freed us from the ultimate consequence of sin, and brought us from death to life in Him.

The beautiful landscape of God's horizon sings praises to the Lord in majestic form. He is the light of the world and the rock in which we are anchored. Let not your troubles get the best of you, for the Lord has provided a plan to redeem you and me. Christ is the Savior of the world whose blood set us free to be people of God.

The angels sing to the Lord Almighty at all times. Holy, Holy, Holy, is the Lord God Almighty, who was, who is, and who is to come.[76] How glorious is He, who cares for our every need, who protects us from the enemy, and who brings life to the dead. Sing to the Father at all times. Rejoice in the blessings He gives you, and never forget the sacrifice He made for you and me.

---

72. 1 Cor. 5:12 (Emphasis, mine).
73. Gen. 1:14-19 (Emphasis, mine).
74. Luke 24:44 (Emphasis, mine).
75. Rev. 1:5 (Emphasis, mine).
76. Rev. 4:8 (NIV).

On the Twenty-Third Day

Walking through the park, I'm thankful to be a part of God's beautiful creation. The sound of rushing water to the right of my feet is a small reminder of the endless flow of water that pours from the great rivers. God used water to flood the earth yet provided water for the Hebrews through the Rock of Horeb. It is in water that we cleanse our sins and come out as new creations in Christ.[77] Oh, how water has the power to sustain, heal, and destroy.

At the throne sits the Father[78] with Jesus to His right, and those given the authority to judge, who sit high on the thrones.[79] In the heavenly places, all sin is removed. No longer will there be pain or suffering, for Christ is ruler over all of creation and all must submit to Him. The enemy will no longer have power over us. We will be able to resist him fully without fear of falling backwards into sin. How we should all long for that day.

Unlike the repeated sacrifices that the high priests of old had to offer year after year to atone for the sins of the Israelites, Christ entered the holy tabernacle of heaven once and for all, having placed His blood on the mercy seat to atone for our sins and obtain eternal redemption for all who believe in Him.[80] The sacrifices of goats and bulls no longer appease the Lord, for too many times, we have asked for forgiveness, only to commit a hideous sin moments later. This is why God required a sacrifice that was worthy to atone for our sins once, for all time. No one born naturally of this earth to two parents that have the imputed sin of Adam could accomplish such a task. Only Christ Jesus, who was born of God and a virgin was a worthy propitiation for the Lord Almighty.

On the Twenty-Fourth Day

Do you have a blended family? Many of us do. To love someone who was born to someone else is truly a great thing. Perhaps, you have children from different spouses? Having taught them all the ways of the Lord, you've come to discover that some of them follow your path of righteousness, and some of them do not. Do not fear, for you have still planted the seed. Other believers will water it, but God will make it grow.[81] Some of our children may never come to Christ, but that doesn't mean we must stop praying for them.

---

77. 2 Cor. 5:17 (Emphasis, mine).
78. Ps. 47:8 (Emphasis, mine).
79. Rev. 20:4 (Emphasis, mine).
80. Heb. 9:11-14 (Emphasis, mine).
81. 1 Cor. 3:6 (Emphasis, mine).

Did not David's son Absalom rebel against both David and God? Yet we know that David loved him nonetheless.[82]

Hard work gives honor to the Lord. After all, good planning and hard work lead to prosperity.[83] Adam toiled the earth long before the fall. In Adam's distress, the ground would not produce crops. Jesus Christ reverses this consequence of the fall by saying, "Therefore do not be anxious about tomorrow, for tomorrow will be anxious for itself. Sufficient for the day is its own trouble."[84]

Indeed, the Lord takes care of our every need. Worrying about the things that we cannot control only leads to more worry and anxiety. Take notice of those around you who have few worries in their lives. Do they not seem more joyful and loving than those who constantly worry about everything? Listen to what the Spirit has to say.

On the Twenty-Fifth Day

The streets are quiet in the heart of the city this early morning in February. I can almost hear a pin drop, or the faint chirping of birds as they awake to another glorious day provided by Lord above. Few roads lead to heaven; we must take the narrowest one. The world's standards are much different than godly ones. This is why we must focus our attention on the things of heaven and not of the earth.

Jesus was once asked if it was lawful that taxes be paid to Caesar.[85] Jesus asked to inspect the coin to be paid and after the Pharisees acknowledged that Caesar's image and inscription were upon it, He proclaimed, "Give back to Caesar what is Caesar's and to God what is God's." [86] The money we are in possession of is only borrowed because everything belongs to God. Yes, we individually earn money based upon our hard work, but it is God who provides us with the work. He arranged the meeting with the employer and orchestrated the events in our lives in such a way that where we are now is where He intended us to be.

As I grow older, I am less dependent upon the riches of this world, and more dependent upon God to provide for my every need. For, I would much rather do good, and be rich in good works, than be selfish and be rich in

---

82. 2 Sam. 18:33 (Emphasis, mine).
83. Prov. 21:5 (Emphasis, mine).
84. Matt. 6:34 (ESV).
85. Mark 12:14-17 (Emphasis, mine).
86. Mark 12:17 (NIV).

worldly possessions. By doing God's good works, I will already have many treasures stored up in heaven.[87]

Brothers and sisters, I encourage you to listen to the advice of the wise and godly. Do not be like Rehoboam, who listened to the unwise young men and hardened the yoke on the people of Israel.[88] The Lord places godly people in our paths for a reason; seek to understand what they are saying to you.

On the Twenty-Sixth Day

Ash Wednesday/Lent

The warmth of the sun relaxes me as I begin to write today's devotional. Certainly, God has inspired me in the most beautiful ways. Through looking at His creation, I glean a poetic sense of awe and wonder that prompts my thoughts, which are recorded from pen onto paper. In the silence of my warm home, I'm able to allow the Spirit to speak through me as I write. What a wonderful God we serve!

Today is the beginning of Lent. Lent is traditionally known as the six-week period leading up to Easter/Resurrection Sunday. Unlike the season of Advent, which is a time of anticipation and celebration of the birth of our Lord, Jesus Christ, the season of Lent involves more of a solemn observance in remembering Jesus' temptation in the wilderness, and that He ultimately sacrificed His very life for us on the cross.

Much like Jesus gave up something for us, Lent is a time in which we can give up something for Him. Thankfully, most people do not give up their lives on Lent; however, I think it is important to give up something that occupies much of our time in order to replace that time with quiet prayer and the reading of Scripture.

Many people fast on Lent but fasting from food is just one form of sacrifice. If you find it hard to refrain from your normal eating habits, I would suggest you give up time on social media, watching television, or sports and refocus your efforts on spending time with God.

The prophet Joel once heralded, "Even now,' declares the Lord, 'return to me with all your heart, with fasting and weeping and mourning.'"[89] It's never too late to sacrifice something for the Lord. After all, He sacrificed so much for us.

---

87. 1 Tim. 6:18-19 (Emphasis, mine).
88. 2 Chr. 10:8-10 (Emphasis, mine).
89. Joel 2:12 (NIV).

On the Twenty-Seventh Day

The animals of the earth often interact with one another in playful ways. Even the dog and cat can be seen embracing each other on social media. I've taken notice that the rabbit and squirrel are not afraid to be around each other in the forest. Nor are the deer and raven intimidated by one another. Animals are naturally afraid of predators, but so has it been since the fall.

Everyone has a place in God's kingdom that has accepted His Son as his personal Lord and Savior. Regardless of race, gender, or socio-economic status, we are all equally loved by the heavenly Father. The poor in spirit, the hungry, the pure in heart, and the peacemakers are all blessed by the Lord.[90] Even the meek show strength under pressure through the power of the Holy Spirit.

The Apostle Peter once had a vision in which he was told to kill and eat an unclean animal. Naturally, Peter refused to eat anything unclean, for nothing unclean had ever entered his mouth. Yet, the Lord told him not to call anything impure what God has made clean. This happened three times.[91]

Thanks to the death and resurrection of Jesus Christ, we are no longer separated from the Father for not being part of God's original chosen people. The Holy Spirit falls upon anyone who believes in the Son, regardless of ethnicity. This is why God gave Peter the vision. No longer do we adhere to civil and ceremonial laws to be considered righteous before God. For, now both Jews and gentiles are made righteous through our faith in Christ Jesus.[92]

On the Twenty-Eighth Day

The morning is upon me once again on this last day of February. Beautiful shades of yellow and crimson fill the skies as the sun peers out from under the clouds. How are things going my friends? How is your relationship with Jesus Christ? Are you finding yourself closer to Him or farther away from Him? I'm praying that your relationship will strengthen mightily.

The Father dwells inside each one of us. His image is reflected in our very being. For those of us who have chosen to follow Jesus Christ, His essence is manifested in us in the form of the Holy Spirit. The Spirit is always there to guide, correct, and convict. Have you had temporary moments of

---

90. Matt. 5:1-10 (Emphasis, mine).
91. Acts 10:9-16 (Emphasis, mine).
92. Phil. 3:9 (Emphasis, mine).

insanity in your past, of which you would give anything to turn back the clock and relive the situation in a more godly way? We all have. Yet, under the New Covenant, once we ask the Father for forgiveness, He blots out our transgressions like a cloud.[93]

God is merciful and just; He is loving and kind. There is nothing that happens in our lives that God has not foreseen and directed. You are here for a reason; I am writing these words down this morning for a reason. You are reading these words right now for a reason. Don't let the enemy get the best of you. You have so much to offer to this world. God loves you and would never lead you astray. Trust in Him at all times and enjoy the blessings that pour forth. You have so much light inside of you that others need to see. Let your light shine before all of mankind that they may see your deeds and glorify your Father in Heaven. Does a lamp do any good hiding under a basket?[94]

On the Twenty-Ninth Day

Leap Year

"An Ode to the Father" by Craig Prather

God is relational.
He was there when I was afraid for my life;
He was there when I wanted to take my own life.

He was there when I was struggling to make it;
He was there when I succeeded.
He was there when I felt ashamed;
He was there when I felt victorious.

He was there then,
And He is there now.
With me at all times,
Guiding my thoughts and dreams;
Helping to curb my fleshly desires.

---

93. Isa. 44:22 (Emphasis, mine).
94. Matt. 5:15-16 (Emphasis, mine).

Like a loving earthly father,
He is both caring and disciplinary.
He lets me tread lightly in unknown waters,
But only for so long,
Before He brings me back,
Under His protective grace.

Chapter 3

Our True Identity

The Month of March

On the First Day

THE MORNING RADIATES IN God's brilliance as the snow begins to melt from the warmth of the sun. The mountains of the Sierra Nevadas are beautifully adorned with snow as the skiers get their last bit of fun on the ski runs before the season comes to a close.

Jesus is the Lamb of God! He is the Alpha and Omega, the beginning and the end, the perfect sacrifice, who gave His own life for our sins on the cross. How wonderful it is to have someone care for us as much as God does.

The passion of our Savior, Jesus Christ is unparalleled. Completely free of sin, He became sin for us so that we might become righteous.[1] No other sacrifice was worthy to atone for, not only our sins, but for the sins of the whole world.[2] The Son of the God most high has defeated death at the cross! Worthy is He who has conquered death and sits at the right hand of the Father.

To have a soul that thirsts for God is like an arid desert that has never seen the rain. If you feel that you are not thirsty enough, pray that the Lord increases your desire for Him, and enjoy the pleasures of His sustenance. For, we are not alone in this life. Even when those closest to us have abandoned us, the Father remains. God is always with the broken-hearted; He is always with us when we are in need. Sometimes in the quietness of the morning, I can feel His presence all around me. You have strength in Jesus Christ. Trust in Him and you will persevere.

---

1. 2 Cor. 5:21 (Emphasis, mine).
2. John 2:2 (Emphasis, mine).

On the Second Day

The evening skies are full of whispers from the gentle breeze blowing in the dark. A streetlamp lights up my path as I walk through the empty streets alone. With only my thoughts to occupy my mind, I use this time to meditate on my Lord and Savior and the price that He paid for my sins.

Have you given to the church lately? Many churches go by the Old Testament standard tithe of ten percent, yet under the New Covenant, God actually expects one hundred percent from us because everything belongs to the Lord.[3] Not only should we give of our money, but we should give of our time, talents, and resources as well. Abraham gave a tenth of everything he had to the priestly king, Melchizedek.[4]

I once attended a large church in Sparks, Nevada, and served there as a volunteer in the youth ministry. Due to the recession, my wife had recently been laid off from her full-time employment and my hours were being cut as well. I remember praying that God would help us in some way since we just had our second child, Michelle and rent was due within a few days. I had about thirty or forty dollars in tips from the night before, so in faith I put it in the offering box. Amazingly, the next day, we had a deposit for $2,300.00 in our bank! Not knowing exactly where it came from, we were finally able to trace the money back to a grant that my wife never received from her community college due to a computer error six months prior.

God's timing is not the same as our timing, yet He is able to provide for our every need, sometimes when we need Him the most. So, don't be afraid to give in faith, the Lord will surely pass the test and open the floodgates of heaven to you.[5]

On the Third Day

Walking down the windy path next to the great Truckee River, I run into all types of people of all races, genders, and financial backgrounds. There are wealthy people, homeless people, happy people, sad people, confident people, depressed people, large people, small people- men and women of all colors and ethnicities. I can picture all of these people in heaven. All tribes and tongues gathered together in unity worshiping and glorifying the Father. How boring this world would be if we were all the same. God has made

---

3. Ps. 24:1 (Emphasis, mine).
4. Heb. 7:1-2 (Emphasis, mine).
5. Mal. 3:10 (Emphasis, mine).

each one of us different for a reason; therefore, be proud of your diversity, God certainly is.

How do you identify yourself? Most of us are asked by someone we meet, where we are from and what our occupation is. We might reply, "I work in sales," or "I work in construction." Yet, almost nobody says, "I am a Christian." Our true identity is not found in what we do, but in who we are. We are new creations in Christ Jesus and no longer have to identify with labels that the world places upon us. God sees you through the lens of Jesus Christ, as the finished product, perfect and blameless in every way.[6] Just think of how much better the world would be if we all concentrated on our true identity in Jesus Christ, as opposed to the mask we wear which shields us from the judgement of others.

We are beautiful in God's eyes. If you are insecure or upset with your appearance, fear not, for the Lord sees only your heart. The world can never judge us because the world does not truly know us. Work on your heart before you work on your appearance. God cares about the heart so much more.

On the Fourth Day

The air is cold this morning as I wake up to the sound of birds singing in the distance. All of creation are ambassadors of the Father, demonstrating how glorious He is simply by being alive. We are a testimony to the awesome splendor of the Lord's presence in everything, and through everything that we do.

Jesus once told a parable of the kingdom of heaven being like wheat and tares.[7] The wheat grows alongside the chaff and no one can tell the difference. Do you find that to be the case at your church? Sometimes, God will allow events to take place so that the chaff can be easily exposed, but many times, He does not. This is why we must never judge the heart of a fellow believer; however, it is biblical to stay away from our brothers or sisters who lead undisciplined lives.[8] Often times, we can tell if a brother or sister is going astray by the lack of spiritual fruit they produce. Though, at other times, they may seem godly and upright. Can you tell the difference?

I've discovered that one of the gifts of the Spirit that I have been given is the gift of discernment. The Holy Spirit inside of me will usually connect quite rapidly with a fellow believer yet will be very hesitant to bond with a

---

6. Col. 1:22 (Emphasis, mine).
7. Matt. 13:24-30 (Emphasis, mine).
8. 2 Thess. 3:6 (Emphasis, mine).

non-believer. At times, I'll be driving clients around at my secular job, and will suddenly be inspired to talk about Jesus with them. I'll often mention that I'm in college full-time. When they ask what I'm studying, I tell them, "theology." If they are believers, they will chime in and ask all kinds of questions, but if they are not believers, they will often simply say, "ok," or not respond at all. It's funny, my accuracy rate is almost one hundred percent. Those, with whom I don't feel the Spirit's prompting to talk to, often end up mocking Christianity in their conversations with other passengers.

On the Fifth Day

The sunsets are so beautiful in Northern Nevada. Tonight, the skies are full of red, blue, and purple as the sun sets in the west. Sometimes, I wonder why God is so good to us, even when so many don't acknowledge that He even exists. It makes me sad to think of all the great things that *could* take place if we would simply turn from our sins and believe in His Son. Have you accepted Jesus into your life yet?

Obedience is often not pleasant, or easy for that matter. Perhaps, you can remember back to your childhood when your parents set curfews and expected you to abide by them. I not only came home late, but more often than not, I would even sneak out sometimes after everyone fell asleep. Not all of my escapes resulted in sinful behaviors, but most of them certainly did.

In this way, our loving Father in heaven expects, and deserves our obedience to Him. The Lord allows for a lot of freedoms in this life, yet sin takes place when we know the right thing to do yet consciously rebel against God, causing further separation from Him.[9] When Adam and Eve ate the forbidden fruit, their disobedience instantly resulted in separation. Separation was and is Satan's goal. If you feel separated from the Father, reflect upon your sins. Remember, sin starts in the mind before it's ever brought to fruition.

Be encouraged, loved ones! You are not alone in your battle. We all have battles of the flesh. God's angels are helping to battle the spiritual enemies you face, as we speak.[10] God is with us, advocating for us at all times; therefore, we can rest in the assurance that He will never let us down.

---

9. Jas. 4:17 (Emphasis, mine).
10. Ps. 91:11 (Emphasis, mine).

On the Sixth Day

The trees sway as the winds of Lake Tahoe blow through the mountains. Life continues to move forward despite the challenges and setbacks that we all face. Imagine the early settlers who traversed the great mountains by horse and carriage with only the stars and dirt trails to guide their way. They persevered, will you?

I was pleasantly surprised at Church last week when one of our former congregants moved back into the area and joined us for service. She said that she missed the family feel of our church and that her twenty-two-year-old son was moving back to Reno soon and said he would not attend any other church but ours. I asked her why he enjoyed our small church so much. She said it was because I inspired him to be a better person. It was such an honor to hear that I had affected someone's life in such a dramatic way. I take no credit: The Holy Spirit does all the work. I simply follow His directions.

The Holy Spirit directed the Apostle Paul's path as well. In fact, He prevented Paul from preaching in certain areas of the Middle East until the appropriate time.[11] Quite often, I find myself asking scriptural questions as I lay in bed at night. After adamantly praying for the answers, the Holy Spirit often speaks into my mind and leads me to the passage that directly relates to my question!

Who do you get your inspiration from? Personally, I draw my inspiration from Jesus Christ, yet there are others around me who inspire me to do better; to be a better servant of the Lord. I suppose that if I listed them all, there would not be enough paper to contain all of my words. But, if you're reading this right now and know me personally, please realize that you have inspired me to be a better man than I was yesterday; for that, I am forever grateful.

On the Seventh Day

There is so much beauty in creation! I took my family on a road trip to visit my parents in Denver, Colorado, for Christmas a few years ago. Though it took more than sixteen hours to get there, looking at what God created along the way was definitely worth the time. From the flat lands of eastern Nevada to the red rock canyons at the border of Utah, from the flat parries of Wyoming to the Majestic mountains of Colorado, the world is a giant canvas, and the Lord is a brilliant artist.

---

11. Acts 16:16 (Emphasis, mine).

The Lord had gifted me with the ability to sing and play the piano at a young age. Music was a great escape for me during my adolescence. It gave me the ability to leave my teenage worries behind and immerse myself in the glorious sounds that the Holy Spirit provided. Yes, you read that correctly. The Holy Spirit was even involved in the creative process of songwriting, which would later lead from hosting a small open mic show in Reno, Nevada, to headlining my own album release party. Would you believe that my Christian music video, "Crazy Life" garnered over 750,000 views on YouTube? And, guess how long my music ministry lasted? It was successful for three years. To God be all the glory! God is so amazing, why must we give Him less credit than He deserves?

I assure you, if you simply make an effort to walk in obedience to the Lord, He will reward you greatly. This is how I choose to live my life. Do I make mistakes? Do I sin? Of course, I do! I still have flesh, but I continue to strive for excellence in my walk of faith; I continue to look to the cross for forgiveness; I continue to bask in the everlasting glow of God's Spirit, and I continue to allow the Lord to shape me into the best representative of His Son that I can be. Don't give up! With man, this is impossible, but with God, all things are possible.[12]

On the Eighth Day

International Women's Day

The warm spring is a pleasant change from the cold of last winter. Record snow fall, car accidents, and higher heating bills were just some of the challenges Renoites faced last winter. March is one of my favorite months of the year to enjoy time in the sunshine again.

Today is known around the world as, "International Women's Day." In honor of women everywhere, I'd like to share a little bit about them from the Bible. The first woman we see in Scripture is Adam's wife, Eve. There's a well-known quotation by the late Matthew Henry that goes, "Women were created from the rib of man to be beside him, not from his head to top him, nor from his feet to be trampled by him, but from under his arm to be protected by him, near to his heart to be loved by him." I think this is true in the sense that there was equality between men and women in God's original design. It's only because of the brokenness of a fallen world that men try and force women into submission.

---

12. Luke 18:27 (Emphasis, mine).

Another prominent woman in Scripture is Ruth. Having been an outcast of Moabite descent, Ruth defied the odds by winning over the heart of a kinsman redeemer named, Boaz. Through their son, they continued the tribal line. Obed's grandson, David would become the great king of Israel, accepting the covenant of eternal reign through the tribe of Judah.

And, of course there's Mary, the mother of Christ. Facing criticism for being pregnant out of wedlock, Mary persevered, knowing that God had intended for her to give birth to His only son, Jesus Christ. Trusting God, Mary and Joseph made the journey from Bethlehem to Egypt, and stayed there until Herod's death.[13]

I hope you have a wonderful Woman's Day. Your companionship and loving hearts are so very needed. Thank you for bringing all of us into this world.

On the Ninth Day

Purim

The emerging sunrise casts beautiful colors of bright blue and golden yellow between the hovering clouds that seem to stand still in time as the earth continues to rotate, day after day. The rabbits can be seen relaxing in the meadow as the world hurries around them.

I try and wake up earlier than my wife and children so that I can enjoy time with the Lord in unhurried solitude. Sometimes I prevail, sometimes my kids prevail, but at all times, God is telling me to slow down and just enjoy His presence.

In the West, we tend be in such a rush for everything. Many other countries do not function in this way; yet, ingrained in our culture is this idea of needing everything immediately. I'm no exception, but the Lord truly prefers that we slow down, be still, and enjoy life in Him.[14]

We should always listen to godly wisdom. God's wisdom existed in the pre-incarnate Christ, even before the world was formed.[15] Therefore, it is of the upmost importance that we fear the Lord, for the fear of the Lord is the beginning of wisdom.[16] As we go through life, we experience blessings and curses, but the one who perseveres gains the eternal blessings of God. If I recounted all of my trials and setbacks, the list would surely be quite end-

---

13. Matt. 2:13-14 (Emphasis, mine).
14. Ps. 46:10 (Emphasis, mine).
15. Prov. 8:14-31 (Emphasis, mine).
16. Prov. 9:10 (Emphasis, mine).

less. This is why I focus on the future and not the past; to God, my past sins are remembered no more.[17]

Be encouraged loved ones! We all face similar struggles and challenges in this life. Though each of us is unique and face our own unique experiences, we can surely relate to others in the sense that all of us have had to deal with the enemy who haunts us at one point or another. Cast him out and place your worries at the foot of the cross. This is why Jesus died for you.

On the Tenth Day

The streets are empty this morning as the cool air blows in from the west. The menacing clouds make their way over the mountaintops towards the valley below. The smell of rain is in the air as the creatures of the land find shelter between the rocks. The ants make the treacherous journey back into the earth where they are protected from nature's elements.

Have you ever taken the time to observe the rock badger? Rock badgers were around in King Solomon's time, for he mentions them in the book of Proverbs.[18] They can see over half a mile away and blend in nicely with their environment. When a predator is nearby, the rock badger finds its security and its protection in the rock. If we had the brains of a rock badger, we would know where our security lies.

If biblical history has taught us anything, it's that God will only allow for disobedience towards Him to take place for so long before He intervenes. Look at all of the times His chosen people were placed under the control of their enemies. Don't think that society is immune to God's wrath just because certain people choose not to believe in Him.

With everything going on in the world around us, we need to stay focused on Jesus Christ. Jesus will never lie to you, never cheat on you, never hurt you, and never let you down. We make up the Holy Temple; God's house is built on the foundation of the apostles and prophets, and Jesus Christ is the chief cornerstone.[19] Therefore, find your security in Him. After all, He laid down His very life for you and me so that in following Him, we can enjoy the presence of the Father during this age, and in the age to come.[20]

---

17. Isa. 43:25 (Emphasis, mine).
18. Prov. 30:26 (Emphasis, mine).
19. Eph. 2:20 (Emphasis, mine).
20. Mark 10:29-30 (Emphasis, mine).

On the Eleventh Day

Personal testimonies are such powerful tools of evangelism. All of us have a story that we can share with someone else. The Lord will use your story to spark interest in someone who has yet to come to faith. This is the power of the gospel message. Jesus' story, along with our own can make a huge impact on someone who is curious about Christianity.

There was a time many years ago when I did not know Jesus Christ, at least not intimately, yet He already knew me. I grew up in Sparks, Nevada, after having moved from Northern California with my parents around the age of six. Life at home was a struggle for me emotionally. I felt very little love or appreciation from my stepfather, and rarely felt close to my mother. This led to a constant feeling of rejection early on in my childhood. I can't say that I participated in many sins prior to my salvation because I was saved at the age of twelve; however, I did feel an overwhelming sense of love and peace in my life, only *after* I accepted Jesus Christ into it.

One morning in the fall of 1986, I encountered, who would later become my best friend. The first person I met in this new town of Sparks, Nevada, was Paul. Paul was a year older than I was and heavily involved at Lord of Mercy Lutheran Church. The church was only a few blocks from our house, so we would enjoy riding our bikes or walking there on Sunday mornings together. Despite the fact that both of my parents were non-believers, they didn't mind letting me out of the house to indulge in a formal religion that would help keep me out of trouble. After several church services and Sunday school classes, I made the conscious decision to accept Jesus Christ into my heart, and subsequently underwent a water baptism ceremony at the Lutheran Church in 1988. I still have the Good News Bible that was given to me that day, with the inscription of my very first Sunday school teacher, Mary, on the inside cover.

On the Twelfth Day

I ran into a dear friend and colleague the other day at Multnomah University. After catching up a bit, Priscilla said to me, "A lot of people before they are saved deal with fear." I thought about it a while and concluded that she was most certainly right. There are many people who are saved later in life who probably did experience fear of the unknown prior to their salvation.

Joseph was once cast into the pit by his brothers. Lacking food and water, Joseph surely anticipated his death in those fearful moments, yet the

Lord was still with him.[21] The great prophet, Daniel was thrown into a lion's den by King Darius. Yet, God rescued him.[22] If the Lord was with these men at their greatest time of need, how much more will He be with you during your personal hardships and times of need?

All of us have something that we fear in this life. Perhaps, it's financial security, or fear for our health, or fear of the unknown? Whatever distress you might have, let it go and take Jesus' yoke upon you, for His yoke is easy and His burden is light.[23] I have full confidence that the Lord has placed you exactly where He wants you to be. I have only become stronger because I've persevered through the difficult times, and you can too.

If you are not at a place in your life where you want to be, don't give up, letting Satan get the best of you. Persevere through it and enjoy the rewards the Lord has waiting for you. Don't worry about the unknown, the Lord knows exactly what is happening, and what will happen to you in the future. It is all part of His plan, so be strong and courageous, for the Lord will never leave you.[24]

On the Thirteenth Day

I love getting together with family and friends over dinner. It's so nice to catch up on life, celebrate a loved one's achievements, or simply enjoy the company of those around us. Jesus enjoyed eating with His disciples as well, both before and after His resurrection.[25] Yet, too much indulgence of food or wine can be sinful.

Gluttony is one of those sins that we often overlook or consider as of little importance. In fact, I was debating even including gluttony in this devotional, but then I thought, it's not what is important or is not important to me that matters, it is what is important to God that matters, and gluttony is apparently important to Him.

There are actually several Bible verses that address gluttony, but I find the one from Paul's letter to the Philippians quite telling: "For, as I have often told you before and now tell you again even with tears, many live as enemies of the cross of Christ. Their destiny is destruction, their god is their stomach, and their glory is in their shame. Their mind is set on earthly things."[26]

21. Gen. 37:23-24 (Emphasis, mine).
22. Dan. 6:16-23 (Emphasis, mine).
23. Matt. 11:28-30 (Emphasis, mine).
24. Deut. 31:6 (Emphasis, mine).
25. John 21:12 (Emphasis, mine).
26. Phil. 3:18-19 (NIV).

Like many other sins, overeating can lead to destruction of, not only our bodies, but our relationship with the Holy One as well. By constantly setting our thoughts on the earthly food that we live to enjoy, we forget about the spiritual food that we need to sustain life. Christ once provided bread and fish to feed the multitudes; Christ still provides food for our souls through His body and blood, which we remember during Holy Communion.[27]

So, enjoy eating meals with others, but try not to overindulge; unless it's overindulgence in the Word of God.

On the Fourteenth Day

Not too long ago, one of my friends, and well-known pastor in the community was caught by law enforcement soliciting a prostitute and providing alcohol to a woman under the age of twenty-one. Sadly, his poor choices led to his removal from a successful ministry, expelled from school, and separated from his beautiful wife and children.

This is where the enemy deceives and devours. It's not hard to participate in sinful behavior. If it wasn't enjoyable, we wouldn't do it, but what about the consequences? There's always a consequence for our actions, whether it's earthly, heavenly, or both. We must be diligent in our fight against the enemy. We often hear the words of God, and they are sown in us, yet Satan can easily take those words away.[28] Don't give up the fight! The enemy is certainly not giving up, so we must remain strong.

I used to believe that the sins I struggled with would never go away; that the past would always come back to haunt me, but I was wrong. With persistent prayer and washing by the Holy Spirit, I was able to conquer my demons and live a healthy Christian life.[29] Like everyone, there are still sins that I struggle with, but that is why sanctification is a life-long process. We must constantly work towards it. It's never too late to stop committing sin. If you have sins that are constantly plaguing you and wish to remove them from your life, pray to the Lord this very moment for deliverance. After all, if you do what you do not want to do, then it's no longer you that is doing it, but rather, it's the sin that lives within you,[30] so cast it out and live a productive life.

---

27. Luke 22:19-20 (Emphasis, mine).
28. Mark 4:15 (Emphasis, mine).
29. 1 Cor. 6:11 (Emphasis, mine).
30. Rom. 7:16-20 (Emphasis, mine).

On the Fifteenth Day

The morning awakens to the sound of creation as it echoes beautiful praises to the Father. Day and night the heavenly hosts bow down and praise the Lord.[31] How fortunate we are to live in a time and place where we can worship our God openly without fear of retaliation. Our brothers and sisters of the faith were not so lucky during the time of the early church. The Saints often gave up their very lives for Jesus' name.

When observing leaders in the church, be sure to pay attention to a few things. Do they practice what they preach, or do they preach gospel truths that they, themselves do not adhere to? Does the relationship they have with Christ and other believers reflect a heart after God's own heart? Do they live humbly, or do they act as if they are entitled to prosperity? And, finally, do they appear to have a servant's heart, or do they prefer to be served?

Jesus came, not to be served, but to serve others and lay down His life for them.[32] In college, we used to call this an upside-down pyramid / servant-leader model. Most businesses are structured in such a way that the people at the bottom of the company pyramid serve everyone above them, finally culminating in the wealth and success of the person at the top, usually the owner. However, if you follow Jesus' life as recorded in the Gospels, you might notice a different type of leadership model. Christ, who is God, Himself incarnate, teaches, preaches, heals, and delivers with little concern for His own well-being. In fact, when Peter refuses to have his feet washed, Jesus tells him that unless he allows Him to do this, he will have no part of Him.[33] This is because Jesus was washing him clean of his iniquity and cleansing him from his sin.[34]

On the Sixteenth Day

The calm of the lake helps to relax me as I stare out at it this cold sixteenth day of March. The reflection of the morning sky transforms the water into glass; the tiniest ripples can barely be seen from the marine life travelling carelessly towards the other side.

About a year before my grandparents on my stepfather's side passed, I made the four-hour road trip from Reno to Vacaville to visit them. They seemed active and in good spirits, though their battle with cancer had taken

---

31. Neh. 9:6 (Emphasis, mine).
32. Mark 10:45 (Emphasis, mine).
33. John 13:8 (Emphasis, mine).
34. Ps. 51:2 (Emphasis, mine).

its toll on their health. I always loved spending time playing chess with my grandfather or talking about life and politics with my grandmother. As I grew older, I always seemed to have an excuse not to get away and visit family more; occupying my time with work, church, commitments, and my own family. I wish I could have been there for them during their final days on this earth.

Make the time to enjoy life. It's so important to find balance in our hectic lives. I know too many people, including myself, who look back on their lives and only remember working. My beloved grandmother, Ursula once said, "Family is important, Craig." Not long after that, she passed away. Much like a scale that is not balanced properly, life can tend to get heavy in certain areas. Therefore, give a just amount of weight to everything in your life and delight in the Lord.[35] For, how many times have we said to ourselves, "I wish I could have been there?" So, go there. Quit making excuses for yourself and make the time for those who care about you. This life is much too short not to enjoy what the Lord has given us. There is a time and a season for everything under the heavens.[36]

On the Seventeenth Day

How are you at loving someone made in God's image? We can show our love for others in many ways. Helping someone in need does not always mean that we have to help them financially. Sometimes, people just need someone to talk to. I find that the time I spend with others is much more valuable to them than money.

I have a friend and brother in Christ, who is part of a deliverance ministry that provides prayer, deliverance, healing, and resources for those in need in our community. My friend, Paul and the other volunteers spend hours on Sunday afternoons inside of prayer tents praying and preaching to the lost and downtrodden in some of the roughest neighborhoods of the city. Love in action involves: caring for others, honoring others, serving the Lord, rejoicing in hope, being patient in tribulation, showing hospitality, blessing those who persecute you, rejoicing with those who rejoice, weeping with those who weep, being consistent in prayer, and living in harmony with one another.[37]

Several years ago, after writing a sermon on loving one another, I decided I buy a t-shirt with a big red heart on it, go to the local Walmart, and

---

35. Prov. 11:1 (Emphasis, mine).
36. Eccl. 3:1 (Emphasis, mine).
37. Rom. 12:10-16 (Emphasis, mine).

stand out front telling people that they are loved, and that they are valued- a social experiment of sorts. I didn't tell anyone that I was a pastor, or even that I was a Christian. I simply wanted to show complete strangers that there is a God who can use people to love them. Out of hundreds of people that I spoke to, very few of them ignored me, or were upset that I, a stranger, spoke to them. Ninety-nine percent of them gave me a hug, smiled, and said it back to me. There is no lack of people hurting in this world. This is why we must preach the gospel of hope to the ends of the earth. Someone always needs to hear it.

On the Eighteenth Day

Do you ever feel as though the good deeds you do for others go unnoticed? Or, that if you help others financially, you won't see any benefit from it? Yet, surely someone, at some point, has helped you during a challenging time of your life; did anyone notice? The hypocrites will often do good deeds for others yet expect something in return. You might notice that they are fasting because they walk around with their cheeks sunken in, hoping that someone will notice and acknowledge how great they are. Yet, Jesus says that their reward is already paid in full.[38]

I enjoy doing yardwork. Well, I should say, I enjoy mowing and edging the lawn. So, last summer, I took notice that my elderly next-door neighbor was letting the edges of his lawn and grass between the cracks of his driveway grow wildly out of control. Not wanting to let him know who it was, I waited until he left with his wife for the day, then ran over to his house with my lawn edger, edged the entire lawn and swept up all the debris. I spent about an hour working on his lawn and finished just in time for his wife and him to return. I have to be honest, part of me was hoping that he'd take notice, come over to my house, and thank me for my efforts, but he never did. Perhaps, it was for the better, lest I end up just like the hypocrites I'm describing in this devotional.

The Bible says that we should be doing things for others in secret, not letting the left hand know what the right hand is doing.[39] In this way, we are simply paying forward our reward in heaven. So, take some time out of your day to do something anonymously for someone else in need. The Lord will truly thank you for it.

---

38. Matt. 6:16 (Emphasis, mine).
39. Matt. 6:3-4 (Emphasis, mine).

On the Nineteenth Day

I used to fear that I would make the wrong choices regarding the direction of my life. Should I join this church, or that church? Should I go to college, or not go to college? Should I work for such and such employer, or work for myself? I suppose we all worry about these things from time to time, yet for some, it can really bother them, not knowing what their future is *supposed* to hold.

I've worked several types of jobs throughout my life. I started out delivering papers for a local newspaper around the age of twelve. At fifteen, I passed a lifeguard training exam and worked for the Cities of Sparks and Reno as a lifeguard. I was later promoted and worked as an aquatic's manager. Not long after that, during a more stressful time in my life, I lost my family, home, employment, and will to live. Shortly after that, I regained my focus, drive, and desire. I found new employment, I started a business, I met my wife, I had children, I received *The Call* to the ministry, I started college, I pastored a church, I graduated college, and I built a stronger relationship with Jesus Christ than ever before.

All of these events (and many more that are not listed) happened exactly according to God's plan. If we fear where life will lead us next, we simply need to ask God to direct our steps. We mature in our Christian walk through our experiences, regardless if they are good, or bad. If you feel the Lord leading you in a certain direction, follow your passion. If it doesn't work out, then the Lord has something better planned for you, more plans than can be numbered.[40] If it does work out, great! Either way, you can find comfort in the fact that you had the faith to trust in God. I no longer worry about where tomorrow will lead. Instead, I put my faith and trust in the Lord and let Him plan my life out for me. It's much less stressful that way.

On the Twentieth Day

We are often our own worst critics. I remember the first time I ever preached a sermon. I filled in for a friend of mine from college at a small Baptist church. He was headed out of town and asked if I could preach for him. Excitedly, I said, "Sure, I'd be happy to." I spent a few days preparing my message on the heart of King David. Dressed in my Sunday best, I proceeded to wow the audience with my wonderful words and biblical knowledge. Unfortunately, only every other word came out because I was so nervous that I constantly

---

40. Ps. 40:5 (Emphasis, mine).

said, "um" in between practically every single word! Fortunately, I got better, but only after several years of practice.

My wife, Lisa had a hard time taking clear x-ray photographs when she first began radiology school. She used to get frustrated and say that she would never be as good as the school expected her to be. I told her to just stick with it, everything gets better with practice. Sure enough, after taking hundreds of practice photos, her images began to improve drastically, and her instructors began complimenting her on how good they were. God is great, indeed!

Much like bettering ourselves through practice in public speaking, or manual tasks, building our relationship with God requires practice as well. The enemy is quick to deceive us and make us doubt ourselves and our position within the kingdom of heaven. We must rebuke him and know that even if our hearts condemn us, God is greater than our hearts.[41]

If you are not at the place of sanctification in your life that you would like to be, keep practicing! Stay persistent and faithful that you will ultimately prevail. Pray for success and know that God is with you.

On the Twenty-First Day

The Bible has many stories of redeemers. The Old Testament lists kinsmen redeemers who had the rights to an inheritance that had been sold to strangers, or another Jew. Patriarchs such as Boaz, Jeremiah, and God, Himself often redeemed people, land, or property throughout the Old Testament. Job once called upon God to redeem him from his affliction.[42]

The biblical term *redemption* can be defined as: "Paying a price in order to secure the release of something or someone."[43] Indeed, those who are in sin are in need of a redeemer, someone who is considered a worthy sacrifice to God that can redeem mankind from their bondage to sin by dying in their place and paying their ransom.[44] That someone is Jesus Christ: Who is, who was, and who is to come.[45]

Christ paid the price for you and me to be redeemed back to the Father, since we were once eternally separated from Him as a result of our transgressions. Jesus gave His own life for complete strangers who could care less about Him. Sometimes, the thought of it makes me cry. Who else

---

41. 1 John 3:20 (Emphasis, mine).
42. Job 19:25-26 (Emphasis, mine).
43. *Holman Illustrated Bible Dictionary*, s.v. "Redemption."
44. Matt. 20:28 (Emphasis, mine).
45. Rev. 1:8 (Emphasis, mine).

would do such a selfless act for a people who refuse to worship, act like, or even respect Him?

We must show our appreciation for the Son at all times through prayer, worship, and studying the word. So many believers only show up on Sundays to worship God, or worse yet, they only attend church on Christmas and Easter. Yet, what about the rest of the week? How are you worshiping the Lord the other six days? I suggest you keep your Bible underneath your bed, so that when you wake up each morning to read it, you are already on your knees, ready to pray to the Father.

On the Twenty-Second Day

The day breaks, and the sound of the birds singing in unpredictable harmonies can be heard in the distance as the sonorous pine trees sway in the wind that blows gently from the west. The warmth of the sun melts away the fallen snow that blankets the valley. In the distance, one can see the footprints of a deer embedded in the wintry wonderland. Time seems to stand still like the waters of Lake Tahoe before they are disturbed by the wind and seafaring sailors.

Like many things among God's creation that have ceased to function properly after the fall, we too are in need of restoration. When Satan spoke to God, he was in the presence of the Holy One.[46] Yet, how can this be? Satan can be found, even in the heavenly realms? I'm afraid so, loved ones. The heavenly battles of good and evil are fought daily, just like the earthly battles of good and evil are fought daily.[47] Do not be saddened by this, for God has already set in motion His plan of restoration. God's plan is often revealed to us in stages. Some of the stages have already been fulfilled according to the prophets; some have yet to be fulfilled. Satan and his angels will lose their fight against the sons of man; some have already been kept in darkness, bound with everlasting chains for judgment on the great Day.[48] Satan was *already* defeated at the cross. The new heavens and new earth will be truly glorious, for the presence of evil will no longer be a factor because evil will be eternally confined to the fiery lake of sulfur in the second death.[49]

Pray that Jesus will return swiftly to end our pain and suffering. We are living in turbulent times, so we must remain strong during our battles.

---

46. Job 1:6 (Emphasis, mine).
47. Eph. 6:12 (Emphasis, mine).
48. Rev. 12: 7-9/Jude 1:6 (Emphasis, mine).
49. Rev. 21:1-8 (Emphasis, mine).

With faith, hope, and love, we will emerge victorious through the power of the Holy Spirit.

On the Twenty-Third Day

It's always a reality check for me when I hear of a well-known brother or sister in faith fall from their elevated position of leadership. My Spiritual Formation professor used to remind us that our sins will eventually find us out.[50]

Too many of our brothers and sisters in Christ have fallen in ways that could have been prevented. We all know of popular evangelists who have fallen away from God due to sexual immorality, or other prominent sins that were allowed to take strongholds in their lives. Sadly, the suicide rate of pastors and ministry leaders is quite high. There are several factors for this, but the main ones are: loss of trust, loss of church leadership, loss of a spouse, if applicable, and loss of religious employment; essentially, loss of everything that one spends their entire life working towards. So, I have to ask, if you are currently involved in sinful behavior, are the consequences worth it? The Bible says, "If we say we have no sin, we deceive ourselves, and the truth is not in us. If we confess our sins, He is faithful and just to forgive us our sins and to cleanse us from all unrighteousness."[51] This is why God sent His only Son to die for us. For if it were possible to cleanse ourselves, become righteous, and remain sinless through the Law, then Jesus died for nothing.[52] Even though we continue to sin, it is possible to refuse the practice of sinning because God's seed is inside of us. This is what distinguishes us from the children of the devil.[53]

If you are struggling with a sin that dominates your life, seek help from both God, and your brothers and sisters in faith. Do not be afraid to seek the help of other believers who will restore you gently.[54] Believers should be involved in restoration, not condemnation.

On the Twenty-Fourth Day

My ten-year-old son, Brett is very curious. He has always had an inquisitive mind. I remember when he was only four or five years old and would ask me

50. Num. 32:23 (Emphasis, mine).
51. 1 John 8:1-9 (ESV).
52. Gal. 2:21 (Emphasis, mine).
53. 1 John 3:9-10 (Emphasis, mine).
54. Gal. 6:1 (Emphasis, mine).

questions about everything from how a car engine works to how our bodies fight off viruses. Before he could even read, he was on YouTube watching complex videos on the immune system and mechanical engineering. His school took notice of this and had a psychologist test his I.Q, which the results came back as "highly gifted" with a score of 136! Lisa and I are so blessed to have such a beautiful and brilliant boy.

Now that my son is a little older, his questions have slowed down a bit, perhaps because he already knows most of the answers. He did ask me about debts and loans the other day. Most likely, he picked up on some of the conversations that his mom and I have had about our own personal finances. In North America, most families have some type of debt, whether it be from student loans, credit cards, home mortgages, or personal loans. But, paying back our debts is not only responsible, it's quite biblical. Paul writes that we must pay taxes to authorities and give to everyone what we owe them.[55]

In time, our debts will be paid, and we can enjoy life without financial burden. In Moses' era, God declared that at the end of seven years the Hebrews were to cancel all debts.[56] This would eliminate financial debt, but only Jesus Christ can cancel our eternal debt to the Father. God, Himself canceled the debt of our sins, which stood against us and condemned us; He took it away by nailing it to the cross.[57]

On the Twenty-Fifth Day

In college, I was affectionately known as the "overachiever." I worked hard to get my assignments done early, and spent many hours studying to earn the A. In fact, I worked so hard during my undergraduate program, that I graduated top of my class with high honors. Yet, despite this outward success, inside I was still dealing with the insecurities of my youth, which involved feeling as though I had some inferior intelligence.

The enemy wants nothing more than for us to feel as though we do not amount to anything. He revels at the thought of our insecurities, because that is when we're most vulnerable to his attacks. We may feel as though we are the only one facing temptations and insecurity, yet the Bible tells us that no temptation has overtaken us except what is common to mankind.[58] Even though we struggle with temptation, God will always provide a way out for us.

---

55. Rom. 13:5-7 (Emphasis, mine).
56. Deut. 15:1 (Emphasis, mine).
57. Col. 2:14 (Emphasis, mine).
58. 1 Cor. 10:13 (Emphasis, mine).

If we're honest with ourselves, we will admit that we sometimes wear a mask to hide what is going on inside of us from the rest of the world. It's not always easy to be yourself among people that hold you up on a pedestal. Yet, time and time again, we've seen God remove people from places of authority who have abused their God-given position. Did not Jesus tell the disciples, "whoever wants to become great among you must be your servant?"[59]

Therefore, rely upon the Holy Spirit to help you overcome your insecurities; take off your mask and breathe fresh air. Be the best representation of the kingdom of God that you can be. There is no need to place yourself on a pedestal to please mankind. On the great day of Judgment, God might just ask you, "What did you do with all of the gifts I had given you?" Will you answer him, "I got straight A's?" God is more pleased with what you have done, and what you continue to do to advance His kingdom. In the end, that's all that will matter.

On the Twenty-Sixth Day

The beauty of the sunrise is something I truly look forward to seeing. It reminds me that there is always light after the dark. I will often wake up before dawn to write this devotional, since there are fewer distractions to hinder my thoughts. Although, my kids seem to instinctively know when I'm awake, and will often come out of their bedrooms earlier than usual to greet me.

I used to attend a small Lutheran church in Sparks, Nevada. There were only a handful of members, but all socio-economic status', ethnicities, and ages were represented on Sundays. I've always enjoyed singing, so I looked forward to the contemporary Christian songs that the guitarist or pianist would play during the worship portion of the service. I couldn't help but notice that many church members stood in silence while the rest of us sang. Since I had so much wisdom at the age of ten or eleven, I was convinced they were offending the pastor, or perhaps they were offending God, Himself!

Worship comes in many forms. Most of us worship the Lord by singing to Him on Sunday mornings or during a mid-week service. Yet, other forms of worship can also be meaningful. Silent prayer during worship, lifting our hands up, or simply meditating on the lyrics can all be ways in which introverted believers display their love for Jesus Christ. During ancient times, sacrificial offerings were considered a form of worship that were pleasing to the Lord.[60]

---

59. Mark 10:43 (NIV).
60. Exod. 10:24 (Emphasis, mine).

Whichever way you choose to worship, be sure and take the time to thank and praise the Lord for everything He has done in your life. After all, we must enter His gates with thanksgiving and His courts with praise.[61]

On the Twenty-Seventh Day

Walking along the Truckee River is very relaxing. Watching the currents ripple over the rocks reminds me of a much simpler time. The birds of the air float gleefully by as they sing their morning songs. Passersby greet me with a friendly "hello" as I walk down the same bright cement path that so many have walked down before me.

Vengeance is one of those concepts that we feel guilty for thinking yet hope that it takes place for someone who has wronged us. Certainly, there are people from our past who may have mistreated us in such a way that we are eager to seek revenge upon them, but this is not what Scripture teaches us. The Apostle Paul tells us, "Beloved, never avenge yourselves, but leave it to the wrath of God, for it is written, 'Vengeance is mine, I will repay, says the Lord.'"[62]

There are people from my past who have hurt me or caused me emotional pain; but after time, I realized that my job is to forgive them and allow God to deal with their transgressions. One person, in particular, was a boy named Matt who used to yell and threaten me every day in P.E. class when we were in middle school. I dreaded going to P.E. and eventually started skipping class to avoid him. The following year, I ended up training in martial arts and boxing to physically improve myself so that I was ready to face him in high school. Ironically, he ended up being zoned for a different high school than me and I never had to deal with him again.

You may remember reading that I later found Matt on Facebook, so I thought I'd write to him and tell him that I forgave him for our past and that I was praying for him and his family. You would be amazed at how powerfully that message came across. Not only did he thank me and apologize profusely for what he did, he also said he would use my message to teach his children the importance of forgiveness and treating others in a loving way. God is great, indeed.

---

61. Ps. 100:4 (Emphasis, mine).
62. Rom. 12:19 (ESV).

On the Twenty-Eighth Day

The study of language has always been something of interest to me. How we communicate with each other has changed greatly over time. The Bible tells us that at one time, we all spoke a single language.[63] After the languages were confused, people dispersed. As a result, the pronunciation and dialect of words began to morph and change.

When I took Greek in graduate school, I had a slight advantage over my classmates because I already had a minor in English. Most students jokingly confessed that they learned the rules of English grammar from their Greek class. Greek has certainly helped me brush up on the mechanics of the English language. My wonderful Greek professor used to tell us, "You won't get better at translation by simply memorizing the paradigms and mechanics of the language. You'll only get better by spending time in translation." And, he was right. Though I dreaded spending three to four hours a chapter doing workbook translations, I eventually got better, and cut my translation time in half.

Much like practicing Greek translations can allow for us to better understand the original intent and message of the author, we too must practice communicating with each other to better understand who we are in God's image. We must strive to communicate with each other more effectively, and we must desire to improve our communication with the Father.

If you have the gift of a prayer language, be responsible with it. For does not the Apostle Paul tell us, "When you are praising God in the Spirit, how can someone else, who is now put in the position of an inquirer, say 'Amen' to your thanksgiving, since they do not know what you are saying?"[64]

On the Twenty-Ninth Day

High in the Sierra Nevada mountains, the crystal blue waters of Lake Tahoe can be found. Various shades of blue and emerald are transcended by the white sands below them. On the mountains of Incline Village, one might see a black bear with her cubs seeking shelter from the wind and rain. The majestic deer come down to graze at the edge of the road as passersby approach them ever so cautiously.

I've been very blessed to have so many spiritual mentors in my walk with Christ. My early mentor and Lutheran Sunday school and confirmation teacher, Rev. Mike Patterson, ended up becoming a very close friend of

---

63. Gen. 11:1 (Emphasis, mine).
64. 1 Cor. 14:16 (NIV).

mine over the years. He furthered his own walk with Christ and eventually became an ordained Episcopal priest. Another good friend and mentor of mine, David Quinn is so gifted in teaching God's word. He knows the Bible inside and out. Though, if you were to ask him, he might humbly admit that he's really only scratched the surface.

As I began my college career, writing mentors have helped me to progress both in writing and in godly wisdom. My wonderful, knowledgeable, and compassionate theology professors were, and still are, very instrumental in my spiritual development.

It is so important to have positive mentors and role models in our lives. We can all learn from someone who has been through the fire and lived to tell about it. The Bible tells us that it's like iron sharpening iron.[65] So, allow your iron to be sharpened by another brother or sister in Christ. You'll truly be the better for it.

On the Thirtieth Day

Sometimes, we feel powerless to defeat the enemy when he encroaches upon our lives. How many times have you given into temptation, asked for forgiveness, then gave into the same temptation all over again? I know I certainly have. Yet, through it all, I stayed focused on Jesus Christ. Praying, and requesting that He deliver me from whatever mental or physical temptations I might be struggling with. After time, those temptations were no longer in my life, because I stayed fervent in prayer and rebuked the enemy before me in Jesus' name.

You have the power to witness, overcome temptation, and communicate with Jesus Christ, for with the Holy Spirit comes great power. Being first baptized in the Holy Spirit, then led into the wilderness, Jesus later came out of the wilderness in the power of the Holy Spirit to begin His public ministry.[66] Jesus has the same Holy Spirit that we do. In fact, Jesus and the Holy Spirit are one in the same. Had Jesus not been genuinely tempted in all things, we would have an excuse to give in to our sins, but since Jesus was genuinely tempted in all things, as we are, we can overcome our temptations just as Jesus overcame His.[67]

Nothing is impossible with the Lord. I've accomplished things I never thought I would be able to, since I've been obedient to God's call. I have a great marriage and beautiful kids, I've went to college, graduated, and am

---

65. Prov. 27:17 (Emphasis, mine).
66. Luke 4:1-14 (Emphasis, mine).
67. Heb. 2:18 (Emphasis, mine).

currently half-way through my master's degree. I've been blessed with a lead pastor position at a very Christ-centered church. I've been able to live in a nice home in a great neighborhood. I've been honored with the opportunity to publish this book, and so much more. You see, none of these things are of my own accord; but rather, I'm blessed because I put God first and foremost in my life. Remain obedient to God's call in your life and enjoy the blessings He has in store for you.

On the Thirty-First Day

The morning is quiet as the children lay soundly asleep. I have the privilege of sharing with you, thoughts that are inspired by the Holy Spirit each and every morning. What an honor it is to be able to do something that I love and use what God has given me to inspire someone else. I hope I've served you well in that sense.

We have made it to the end of March. How did you do this month? Were there days in which you struggled? Were there days in which you had much joy? I hope so. I've found that everything in this life has a balance. Too many care-free days can lead to us taking what we have for granted or leave us ill prepared when the enemy attacks. Too many challenging days can lead to us giving up or feeling like there's little hope. A few of each is just fine.

How have you identified yourself lately? When someone asks you what your interests are, or where you work, do you immediately tell them a hobby or your earthly vocation? Or, do you add in that you are a Christian and your identity is found in Jesus Christ? I feel as though too many of us are afraid to admit that we love Jesus and love others. If we lived in the Middle-East, admitting our faith could be quite costly to us, but living in the West, we have little fear of physical retaliation. Other religions have many members who do not seem to fear proclaiming their faith, so be proud of who you are and what you believe in. Christ died for you and me so that we no longer fear eternal judgment but can enjoy everlasting life.[68]

Our Lord is so great! If we only took the time out each day to thank Him for what He's done in our lives, we would be so much more blessed than we already are. I try and thank Him at least once a day, if not more. If you are in a place in which you feel the Lord far from you, invite Him back into your life. You might just find, that He never left in the first place.

---

68. John 5:24 (Emphasis, mine).

Chapter 4

The Passion of Christ

The Month of April

On the First Day

April is upon us! Glorious are the Father, Son, and Holy Spirit from whom all things are given. I am truly blessed to be able to write these words to you today, and I thank you for taking time out of your day to read them. I hope that you find today, and every day, edifying to your soul.

This first day of April is known to us in the West as, "April Fool's Day." Yet, Jesus is very prohibitive when it comes to referring to someone as a "fool."[1] We do not use the word *fool* in the same way that those of biblical times used it. When they called someone a fool, they were basically saying that someone was damned to hell for not being saved.[2] This is why Jesus can instruct *us* not to call someone a fool, yet still do it Himself. We simply refer to anyone without commonsense as foolish in our attempt to judge them; whereas, Jesus did have the ability to judge their salvation.

Never take any precious moment for granted. Every opportunity to interact with another brother or sister made in God's image is a beautiful one. I love being around people, getting to know them, and finding out what makes them tick. I also enjoy encouraging others to better themselves. If I can do it, anyone can do it; you simply need to step out of your boat of comfort into the sea of faith. Sometimes, there are intimidating storms over the sea, but Jesus will surely be there to lift you up, should you fall.

On the Second Day

Warmth begins to prevail as the winter season draws to an end. The glow of the sunshine upon my face makes me smile inside as I think of creation

1. Matt. 5:22 (Emphasis, mine).
2. 1 Cor. 1:18 (Emphasis, mine).

waking up to enjoy a new day under heaven. No longer are the frigid qualms of winter manifesting in menacing ways; but rather, the confidence in the coziness of the Father's love has taken a prominent position during this stage of life.

Be on guard at all times, dear friends. The spiritual realm is very much alive and active. Satan and his demonic followers are fierce and, on the attack, aggressively entering our minds to try and convince us that we are not worthy to be in the presence of the Holy One. Yet, doesn't Scripture tell us that Christ's sacrifice was sufficient enough for God's creation to now be made holy and dwell in His presence?[3]

The Lord has taken our punishment upon Himself. Generation after generation have rebelled against the Lord. How hard is it to practice obedience to the creator of all life? I promise if you do, you will reap the rewards ten-fold. When I strayed from the Lord's presence at an earlier season of my life, I was very much in a depressed state of mind, having allowed the devil to enter into it and manipulate my thoughts. Yet, God Himself initiated my return by allowing my mind to be affected by my Spirit. You see, once the Holy Spirit is inside of you, He doesn't go away. He dwells there permanently, allowing you to journey only so far, before bringing you back into right standing before the Father.

Time on this earth will pass away, seasons will pass away, yet eternity never passes away because God is eternal. So, it is the eternal Holy Spirit that dwells inside each believer. The Father, the Word, and the Spirit are everlasting, fixed firmly in the heavens.[4]

On the Third Day

Have you ever experienced the beauty of Napa Valley, California? The grape vineyards spread out as far as the eye can see. The wheat colored rolling hills give way to their agricultural valleys below. In the distance, there is an old rustic barn that houses some of the finest black stallions and brown quarter horses around. Think about God's creation around you. Surely, your surroundings will inspire you to glorify Him, if you simply observe what He has created. There's so much beauty in this world right in our own backyards. Don't allow the enemy to take away your sense of awe at what the Creator has made for us to enjoy. The vastness of space exists to glorify

---

3. Heb. 10:14 (Emphasis, mine).
4. Ps. 119:89 (Emphasis, mine).

God. God created everything we see in nature simply by speaking it into existence. God said that it was very good.[5]

YHWH plants us from the very best seed, like the choice vine of the vineyard. How then can we turn against Him into a corrupted and wild vine?[6] The Lord only has the best intentions for us. Does not Jesus represent the true vine and we are His branches?[7] For, if the fruitful branches are not pruned, they too will end up wild and be cut off. Listen to what the Spirit has to say.

We must remain devoted to the Father; constantly working towards bearing good fruit. If you find yourself allowing wild vines to uproot in your life, cut them off and throw them into the fire. For, it's better that one part of your conscience be cut off, then your entire soul be burned up in the eternal fire. You can do it. I will be praying for your success. God is in your corner, always willing to lift you back up after you have fallen.

On the Fourth Day

My children are sleeping comfortably in their beds this morning. As the birds wake up to sing a new song, they too have little cares in this world because God provides for their every need. Humbling themselves before their parents and trusting in them, children must have great faith that their needs will be met. This is why Jesus tells us, "Truly I tell you, unless you change and become like little children, you will never enter the kingdom of heaven."[8] For, whoever is least on earth, is truly great in heaven.

How many times have we turned from the Lord and He has accepted us back? Past seasons of life have taken me to places where I felt distant from God, yet God never gave up on me. He orchestrated events in my life to allow for me to return to Him. He accepted me back into His loving arms like a long-lost child who is reunited with his father. This too, can be the case in your life. If you feel distanced from the Father, simply pray for forgiveness, turn and run from the sins that have strongholds in your life, and enjoy the freedom from the eternal consequences of sin that Jesus has provided for you.

Jesus suffered a horrible death for you and me to not have to worry about being separated from God because of our sinful nature. The least we can do is try and honor His death by repenting our sins, and then allowing

---

5. Gen. 1:31 (Emphasis, mine).
6. Jer. 2:21 (Emphasis, mine).
7. John 15:5 (Emphasis, mine).
8. Matt. 18:3 (NIV).

the Lord to refresh us.[9] God is slow to anger and quick to forgive. What great patience He must have for us. For, how many times did Ezra the priest tell the Israelites that God had punished them less than they deserved?[10]

On the Fifth Day

Holy Week Begins

Palm Sunday/Passover Preparation—10th of Nisan

A glorious occasion is upon us this beautiful fifth day of April. The vegetation is beginning to grow again, and spring time takes over from the cold winter months. The animals come out of hiding now as the sun warms the earth. I thank God for the opportunity to serve Him again.

Today we remember the beginning of the Jewish Passover festival. Jesus Christ, the Savior of the world entered into Jerusalem riding on a colt on Palm Sunday as the crowds before Him shouted, "Blessed is the one who comes in the name of the Lord, Hosanna in the highest!"[11] Jesus then went to the temple and was there on display.[12] Nothing in the Holy Scriptures is there by chance. Indeed, everything in the Old Covenant is fulfilled by Jesus Christ in the New Covenant. Did not Moses instruct the Israelites to select a lamb without blemish and keep it for four days between the tenth of Nisan and the fourteenth of Nisan, before its slaughter at twilight?[13] And, is not Jesus the Lamb of God?[14] Therefore, listen to what the Spirit is teaching you.

Many will come in Jesus' name claiming to be Christians yet will not possess the fruit of the Spirit. God has an order for everything; First Christ, the first fruits, and after that, all who belong to Christ at His coming.[15] Surely, one should expect to possess the fruit of the Spirit if we are to call ourselves followers of Christ. If you are lacking fruit in a certain area of your life, pray that the Lord will increase your zeal for Him and watch the fruit pour out.

---

9. Acts 3:19 (Emphasis, mine).
10. Ezra 9:13 (Emphasis, mine).
11. Matt. 21:1-9 (Emphasis, mine).
12. Matt. 21:12-17 (Emphasis, mine).
13. Ex. 12:3-6 (Emphasis, mine).
14. John 1:29 (Emphasis, mine).
15. 1 Cor. 15:23 (Emphasis, mine).

On the Sixth Day

Passover Preparation—11th of Nisan

Mist rises off of the great lake as the sun rises over the mountains. God is very much active in this process; He deserves praise, for the sun rises and sets because of Him.[16] The wind softly blows as the majestic pine trees sway ever so slightly in the breeze. Another glorious day is upon us. Have you thanked God lately for the ability to wake up and enjoy it?

Rebellion has always existed, even before the fall. Satan brought rebellion into this world and as a result, we are naturally opposed to the Father before our conversion. Jesus Christ died on the cross so that we can be reconciled back to our loving Father and experience a beautiful relationship with Him once again.

Jesus dwelt in the temple for four days and four nights. Upon His arrival, He discovered money changers in the temple; turning a place of worship into a den of thieves.[17] Driving them out, Jesus purged the sin from within God's Holy Temple. Similarly, Jesus purges the sin from our Holy Temples through the power of the Holy Spirit, for is it not written that our bodies are temples of the Lord?[18] Therefore, allow the Holy Spirit to cleanse your body by resisting temptation, praying on God's word day and night, and repenting of your sins. Active repentance is very important because the enemy is not willing to give up easily, and neither should you.

The Spirit of the Lord is inside of you for a reason. Allow Him to point you in the right direction. Sometimes, we can give into our temptations and allow Satan to convict us of our sins; yet, it is written that there is now no condemnation for those who are in Christ Jesus.[19] So rejoice in the love of the Father. Surely, He loves you. Do you love Him?

On the Seventh Day

Passover Preparation—12th of Nisan

Have you witnessed any miracles lately? I certainly have. I've witnessed people being healed of various diseases and ailments. I've seen people with severe addictions come to Christ and be cleansed of their dependencies. I've

---

16. Ps. 113:3 (Emphasis, mine).
17. Matt. 21:12-13 (Emphasis, mine).
18. 1 Cor. 6:19 (Emphasis, mine).
19. Rom. 8:1 (NIV).

seen people prayed over, prophesied over, and evil spirits cast out of them in the name of Jesus Christ.

I was once at a high school party in which a college-aged man was encouraging us to drink. As we drank to excess throughout the night, many of us became unable to move or function. This person attempted to molest me in the bathroom that evening. Realizing that someone else might take notice, he told me he would be downstairs and come back a few minutes later. I was terrified because after drinking so much, I was not in a physical state to defend myself. I clearly remember praying to God asking Him to help get me out of the situation. Immediately, I was completely sober! My intoxication was replaced with adrenaline and I was able to make my way downstairs without notice, run over three miles in the dark (in what seemed to be less than ten minutes to where my car was parked), and drive safely home. I will never forget how God rescued me that evening in my time of need. If you find yourself still skeptical of the power of God, I promise you, Jesus can heal you.

The blind and lame visited Jesus in the temple and He cured them.[20] Is not God restorative? When a blind man came to Jesus to restore his sight, the Lord took some of the earth and rubbed it on his eyes, and after his faith in washing, he was suddenly able to see.[21] Man was formed from the earth by God, Himself; sinless and blameless, and without deformity. This is how God will restore mankind at the end of the age. Listen to what the Spirit has to say.

On the Eighth Day

Passover Preparation—13th of Nisan

The hummingbirds are gathering around the bird feeder this morning as the sun rises over the hilltops. The earth is warming up as spring flowers begin to blossom all around me. God reminds us that in life, there are different seasons. What season are you in right now?

Human nature is a curious thing. We tend to be happy when others fail and upset when others succeed. Unless, of course, it is us doing the failing or succeeding, then our emotions are in their proper order. One may ask, "Isn't the Lord, Himself a jealous God?" It is true that the Lord mentions jealousy in Scripture, yet as with all things of God, His is righteous and

---

20. Matt. 21:14 (Emphasis, mine).
21. John 9:1-6 (Emphasis, mine).

ours is not. For God's jealousy is spurned because of mankind's' worship of idols;[22] whereas, our jealousy is spurned because we worship ourselves.

While Jesus was visiting the temple during the Passover festival, He performed many miracles and cured many people that came to Him. The chief priests and teachers of the Law became jealous and angry at Jesus' fame and glory.[23] Even Jesus, doing all things for the glory of God, was viewed by the Pharisees in a jealous and angry manor.

Perhaps, someone is more successful than you, has more material possessions that you do, or has something of value that you do not; making you feel as though you have failed. Yet, if you have a strong relationship with Jesus Christ, you have already succeeded. Do not let the world value your success. You have more in Christ Jesus than all of the world's material possessions combined. You cannot take your possessions with you; have you ever seen a moving truck at a funeral?

On the Ninth Day

Passover Feast and Seder

Jesus Tried, Beaten, Crucified, and Buried—14th of Nisan

Jesus Christ was a true friend to sinners. If Christ were here today, I imagine we would not be able to find Him in the luxurious shopping malls of the city or living in the suburbs. I imagine that, just like when He walked the earth, He would be walking among the lost and downtrodden, giving them hope and encouragement, teaching them, and healing them; delivering them from all kinds of evil.

It may be hard to believe, but even Jesus had some among Him that He could not trust. Judas Iscariot betrayed Jesus for 30 pieces of silver, the exact price that was used to purchase a slave in ancient times.[24] During the Last Supper, Jesus proclaimed that someone would betray Him, and that it would be better if that person was never born.[25] Yet, Jesus also said, "Father, forgive them, for they know not what they do."[26] Judas realized what he had done, but by then it was too late.

---

22. Ps. 78:58 (Emphasis, mine).
23. Matt. 21:14-16 (Emphasis, mine).
24. Ex. 21:32/Zechariah 11:12 (Emphasis, mine).
25. Mark 14:21 (Emphasis, mine).
26. Luke 23:34 (ESV).

Our Lord was beaten, crucified, and buried, more than two-thousand years ago. Having become the Lamb that was slain, His blood set us free from our bondage to sin.[27] Jesus changed the lives of so many people, even while He was hanging on the cross. Did not one of the criminals hanging next to Jesus acknowledge that He had done nothing wrong, and ask to be remembered once He came into His kingdom?[28]

We must always think about our actions and how they will affect others around us. For, we are commanded to love our neighbors as ourselves.

On the Tenth Day

The Feast of Unleavened Bread

High Sabbath—Jesus is Buried in the Tomb—15th of Nisan

The fifteenth of Nisan was the beginning of a seven-day feast in which Israel was to eat bread without leaven in remembrance of their escape from Egypt. We often miss the significance of bread as it relates to Scripture. In the Bible, leaven is almost always associated with sin. Jesus Christ is the bread of life;[29] Having been born in Bethlehem (*house of bread*), Jesus later suffered the affliction for our sins, which is why the bread that the Hebrews *could* eat during The Feast of Unleavened Bread was known as *the bread of affliction*.[30] It was Christ's body which God provided as manna in the wilderness. Jesus would later feed the five-thousand with only five loaves of bread and two fish.[31]

After Jesus died, His body was lowered, wrapped in linen, covered in spices, and placed in a garden tomb by Joseph of Arimathea and Nicodemus.[32] One may question whether or not Jesus could have been entombed for a full three days and three nights based on the dates given in the Scriptures. Jesus said more than once that His time in the tomb would be three days and three nights, just as the prophet Jonah had spent three days and nights in the fish's belly.[33] The Apostle John reveals that the bodies would

---

27. 1 Pet. 1:18-19 (Emphasis, mine).
28. Luke 23:41-42 (Emphasis, mine).
29. John 6:35 (Emphasis, mine).
30. Deut. 16:3 (Emphasis, mine).
31. Matt. 14:13-21 (Emphasis, mine).
32. John 19:38-42 (Emphasis, mine).
33. Matt. 12:40 (Emphasis, mine).

not remain on the cross on the Sabbath, for it was a "high day."[34] Therefore, the week of Jesus' death was a "High, or double Sabbath" week; which was celebrated only during certain seasons of the year. The Hebrew day starts at sunset, not at midnight, this is how Jesus was able to eat the Passover meal and still become the Passover sacrifice on the same day.

On the Eleventh Day

Feast of Unleavened Bread

Jesus is Buried in the Tomb—16th of Nisan

God wrote nothing through His prophets and scribes by accident. Everything has its rightful place and purpose. Interestingly enough, there is a children's game that is played during the Passover Seder in which three pieces of unleavened bread are placed in a bag. The middle piece is removed, broken, wrapped in linen, then buried somewhere in the home. Towards the end of the Seder, the *afikomen* or wrapped bread, is searched for by the children. The one who finds it is given a gift. This gift is known as the promise of the Father. Similarly, after God raised Christ from the dead, then through our faith, we too receive a gift from the Father; the gift of eternal life.[35]

Haman represents a type of false Messiah in the book of Esther. A decree was sent out on the thirteenth of Nisan that all Jews would be killed.[36] After hearing the news, Esther proclaimed a three-day fast (*14-16 of Nisan*).[37] On the sixteenth day of Nisan, Esther risked her life before King Ahasuerus by asking the king to invite Haman to the banquet.[38] The King then asked Esther what she wanted, and she asked that the king come to another banquet the next day, which would have been on the 17th of Nisan. Haman was hanged on this day. Likewise, Christ's resurrection on the seventeenth of Nisan marks the death and defeat of Satan, for from that point on, Satan could no longer separate us from the Holy One.

Blessed are those who find hope and comfort in Christ Jesus. Faith in Him is the path to eternal life. Jesus rightfully proclaims that "No one comes to the Father except through me."[39]

---

34. John 19:31 (Emphasis, mine).
35. Chumney, *The Seven Festivals of the Messiah*, 61-62.
36. Esth. 3:12 (Emphasis, mine).
37. Esth. 4:16 (Emphasis, mine).
38. Esth. 5:4 (Emphasis, mine).
39. John 14:6 (NIV).

On the Twelfth Day

Regular Sabbath—The Festival of First Fruits

Resurrection Sunday—17th of Nisan

Spring time tends to bring the joy out in people. The harvest is soon to be reaped and the blessings will be plentiful. Our remembrance of this spring day, which took place over two thousand years ago, is no different. In fact, you could say that the best of the harvest was presented to God in the form of the Son. The festival of First Fruits had begun. Christ was the first fruits of those who had fallen asleep.[40] Though, God had raised some from the dead in the past, they were sure to face death again. Yet, Jesus Christ, who died once for our sins, now lives forever in the kingdom of heaven.

Death was defeated at the cross! Have you not heard that you were buried with Christ at baptism?[41] Therefore, we may also walk in the newness of life, thanks to His resurrection. What a glorious event the resurrection was, which took place specifically for you and me. Through our faith and trust in Christ Jesus, we no longer need to fear eternal death, for though this body will go back to the ground, our soul and Spirit will go back to our Father.[42]

Mary entered the tomb of Jesus Christ, only to discover that His body was not there. Not long after, Peter and John rushed to the tomb, looked inside, and believed.[43] Jesus then called out to Mary, who was weeping next to the tomb, and she went to embrace Him, yet Jesus told her, "Do not hold on to me, for I have not yet ascended to the Father. Go instead to my brothers and tell them, 'I am ascending to my Father and your Father, to my God and your God.'"[44] Sin can no longer cling to us, and death no longer has control over us.

On the Thirteenth Day

The beauty of the morning is upon me once again as I sit down at my desk to write today's encouraging words from the Father. The coffee maker has just

---

40. 1 Cor. 15:20 (Emphasis, mine).
41. Rom. 6:4 (Emphasis, mine).
42. Eccl. 12:7 (Emphasis, mine).
43. John 20:1-8 (Emphasis, mine).
44. John 20:17 (NIV).

finished brewing, creating a wonderful aroma of French roast in the air. I am moved by the Spirit to complete the task that the Lord has set before me.

Setting goals is so important. God wants you to achieve your dreams, yet He does not want to do everything for you. You must persevere in your goals and dreams together with God's help. Have you not read that the heart of a man plans his way, but the Lord establishes his steps?[45] God orchestrates all the events in our lives to achieve His good purposes. We must listen to the Spirit who guides us in the direction of His glory. Whatever we do, we must do it in the name of the Lord.[46]

Do you sometimes doubt your faith? Perhaps, you have doubts of Jesus' resurrection? Lack of faith is nothing new. Even the Apostle Thomas had doubts of Jesus' resurrection, and he had walked with Him for three years prior, witnessing the ushering in of the kingdom of heaven on earth.[47] It's vital to ask the Lord regularly to increase your faith. Once the enemy places doubt in your mind, he gets a foothold in that area. If not put in check, footholds can become strongholds that are nearly impossible to remove. You have all the strength you need through the power of the Holy Spirit. Put your hope in the Lord and trust in His holy name.[48] Do not fear the enemy, for he has no power over you. Resist Satan's temptations and turn towards the Lord. You'll be so glad that you did.

On the Fourteenth Day

The leaves are starting to form on the trees now as the spring season is upon us. The cold of the winter gives way to the warmth of the sunshine. I pass by many cheerful people as I walk along the river's edge in downtown Reno. How wonderful it is to be alive to enjoy God's creation.

It's important to show love and support for one another. The Lord is very encouraging and supportive. Scripture tells us, "Therefore encourage one another and build one another up, just as you are doing."[49] Everyone deserves to feel loved and everyone deserves to feel valued. Have you encouraged someone around you lately?

The tongue has much power. It can heal or destroy, it can bless or curse, it can accept or reject.[50] Therefore, use your words wisely. Show respect

---

45. Prov. 16:9 (ESV).
46. Col. 3:17 (Emphasis, mine).
47. John 20:27 (Emphasis, mine).
48. Ps. 33:20-21 (Emphasis, mine).
49. 1 Thess. 5:11 (ESV).
50. Jas. 3:9-10 (Emphasis, mine).

for one another. We are all made in God's image. Someday, you may need to hear kind words as well. The Apostle Paul tells us that love is patient.[51] Sometimes in the business of life, we tend to lose patience for those we love most. This is where the enemy begins to settle in the minds of those who believe in the Holy One. A minor frustration can turn into a major argument if we are not careful.

When we feel bitterness or contempt building up inside of us, we must reject and rebuke the evil spirit that is causing it. Love does not manifest itself in hatred. Even God's anger is loving because it's not based in hate; but rather, it is based in correction for the betterment of His creation. When Jesus entered the temple of His Father, He was angry at the moneychangers that dwelt there.[52] His anger was loving because He was zealous for His Father, who *is* love.

On the Fifteenth Day

Life has woken up on this glorious fifteenth day of April. Birds sing in the morning air as the sound of a train passes by in the distance. The fresh steam from the ground rises as the sun peers out between the clouds. The lights of the city go out as the sun illuminates the buildings of the valley.

The passion of Christ is so prevalent in our lives. How wonderful it is that important historical events can be celebrated and remembered each year. Christ was perfect in all ways. He was genuinely tempted but overcame temptation in order to remain pure for God.[53] In this way, we have hope to overcome our own temptations. Was not Jesus tempted in the wilderness for forty days and forty nights?[54] Despite hunger and thirst, pain and suffering, Jesus did not give in to Satan's seduction. Indeed, this is a great example for us as believers. We have the power of the Holy Spirit within to overcome any obstacle the enemy places before us.

Some may boast that the Lord has gifted them in better ways than others. Surely, the body of Christ is made up of many parts. Does not the Apostle Paul say that we all have one baptism in one Spirit?[55] We have one Spirit that gives different gifts to different people. Therefore, do not be dismayed if you do not have the same gifting as a different brother or sister in Christ. Surely, God has gifted you in ways that you cannot imagine. For, if

---

51. 1 Cor. 13:4 (Emphasis, mine).
52. John 2:13-16 (Emphasis, mine).
53. Heb. 4:15 (Emphasis, mine).
54. Matt. 4:1-11 (Emphasis, mine).
55. 1 Cor. 12:12-13 (Emphasis, mine).

we all had the same gifts, how could we be made up of different parts? We must all work in harmony together for the betterment of the church. Division takes place when we allow the enemy to convince us that we are better than someone else. Listen to what the Spirit has to say.

On the Sixteenth Day

The warm evenings often give way to frigid mornings, as they reveal their mist within the atmosphere. The edges of the lake are frozen, revealing the reflection of God's beautiful cloud formations like a mirror. The city is quiet as I walk along the desolate streets alone. Sometimes solitude is a good thing because it allows us to really listen to what the Spirit has to say; sometimes solitude is a bad thing because it can allow the enemy to cause us to doubt. Which spirit will you listen to today?

Trust is an important thing. Perhaps someone has betrayed you, hurt you, or broken your trust. Have you forgiven them? Have they asked for your forgiveness? If you cannot forgive them, is it because you feel that you cannot trust them again? Trust takes so long to earn yet can disappear so quickly. If you are in a relationship where the trust has been shattered, ask God for the ability to forgive, and for the courage to build the trust back again. If you are the one who has broken the trust of someone you care for, ask God for forgiveness and repent of the sin that is separating you from the one you love. When we break someone's trust through our sinful actions, we not only betray the one we love, but more importantly, we are betraying the One who loves us. Does Scripture not tell us to, "Trust in the LORD and do good; dwell in the land and enjoy safe pasture?"[56] Therefore, build your trust with your heavenly Father and you will be able to build the trust in your earthly relationship as well.

Be cautious of the *friends* that advise you in this life. Are they really looking out for your best interests, or are they simply advising you to make themselves look better? Did Zophar not tell Job that God should speak and open His lips against him?[57] Godly friends are hard to find, but if you have some, cherish them with all of your fervor.

---

56. Ps. 37:3 (NIV).
57. Job 11:5 (Emphasis, mine).

On the Seventeenth Day

The bright sunshine peers out from the east as the morning wakes up from its evening slumber. The dawn is approaching rapidly as creation is quickened to glorify the Father. My home is quiet this morning as I pen these words through the power of the Holy Spirit. The Spirit dwells and empowers, not just me, but all who have accepted Christ into their hearts. For, was not the prophet Micah filled with power by the Spirit of the Lord?[58] Are you listening to what the Spirit has to say?

God is in the business of restoration. Perhaps, you have fallen away from God and are looking to reconnect with Him? Fear not, for God is also eager to reconnect with you. Jesus not only preached the good news and taught those around Him the true interpretation of the Law, but He also healed and delivered those suffering from demonic afflictions. The same is true today. Jesus is the name above all names, which is why there is so much power in name of Jesus Christ.[59] You may have noticed that non-Christians often have no issue with using the name "God" in conversation. Yet, as soon as one proclaims the name of Jesus Christ, anxiety, fear, and apprehension begin to build up in the unbeliever. This is because their flesh is at enmity with the Holy One until such time that they accept His only begotten son into their hearts and minds.

I encourage you, loved ones, to look inside yourselves and ask where you want to spend your time long after this lifetime has passed. Do you want to spend eternity in a place of glory, next to the radiance of the Father, Son, and Holy Spirit; absent of tears and suffering? Or, would you rather spend your eternity in the place of weeping and gnashing of teeth?[60] Aren't you growing tired of what the enemy is doing to you here on earth?

On the Eighteenth Day

The beautiful flowers begin to blossom as they enjoy the warmth of the sun on this eighteenth day of April. Feral cats scurry along the empty roads in search of their next meal and human interaction.

Long ago, God spoke through His prophets, but in these last days, He has spoken to us through His Son and Holy Spirit.[61] For, did Moses not say that God will raise up a prophet even greater than he that we must listen

---

58. Mic. 3:8-10 (Emphasis, mine).
59. Phil. 2:9 (Emphasis, mine).
60. Luke 13:28 (Emphasis, mine).
61. Heb. 1:1 (Emphasis, mine).

to?[62] The Bible itself is the living Word for a reason. It's not only a book of the history of God's chosen people, but also a book of relationship between God and mankind. It reveals who God is and how His Son is a necessary part of our salvation. It has recorded many of the prophecies that spoke of Jesus Christ long before His incarnation. The Scriptures also reveal to us the messages that the Holy Spirit intends for us to receive.

When you read the Bible, you are not just reading words on paper. The Bible is the only book in all of history that has had a one hundred percent prophetic accuracy rate. Even the most well-known seers of the past predicted several future events that never took place. Everything written in the Old Testament has been fulfilled in the New Testament, with the exception of Christ's return. Surely, we can trust that will be fulfilled as well.

Almost without fail, I open the Bible on a daily basis and read the many narratives and poetry that are written on its pages. The sacredness of the Holy Scriptures must be respected at all times. The authors were all inspired by God to record His most precious thoughts and revelations. We are so lucky that we have a loving Father in heaven who longs to communicate with us through Spirit and Word. Have you read about Him lately?

On the Nineteenth Day

As the morning begins, the bright and seductive lights go out on the casinos and resorts of Northern Nevada. As you enter the casino, you might take notice of the fact that there are no clocks inside. Gamblers sometimes spend all night trying to win money back that they have lost or trying to win the next big jackpot; some do, but many do not.

One may ask, is it a sin to gamble or play the lottery? It was certainly customary for people in biblical times to cast lots to decide upon certain matters. However, casting lots rarely resulted in direct financial gain for the one who was chosen. In many cases, the lot that was cast only reflected upon the anger of the members that did the casting.[63]

Not everything that we have available for entertainment today existed in biblical times. This is why God always looks to the heart to reveal our true intentions. For, does not Paul tell us that all things are lawful, but not all things are helpful or build us up?[64] Satan certainly knows that money is one of our weaknesses. We depend upon it to survive and depend upon more of it to live a prosperous life, yet does not the Bible tell us that the *love* of

---

62. Deut. 18:15 (Emphasis, mine).
63. Jonah 1:7 (Emphasis, mine).
64. 1 Cor. 10:23 (Emphasis, mine).

money is the root of all kinds of evils?⁶⁵ This is why we must depend upon God to provide for our every need. Through our faith in Him, we will always be prosperous; if not financially, we will at least prosper spiritually, and that is worth more than all of the diamonds in the world.

We must curb our desires of indulging in the pleasures of the world. Does Paul not tell us to let our reasonableness be known to everyone?⁶⁶ The acts of the flesh will become obvious to you once you give in to them. Pray that the Holy Spirit will protect you from the enemy's desires.

On the Twentieth Day

In the early spring mornings, I often walk along the cement path by the river near downtown. I like to smile and say, "good morning" to passersby. Most of them smile and say, "good morning" back to me. However, some are upset and angry, and even reply with unpleasant words.

Have you taken notice that lately, people seem to be more comfortable using foul language in public? Certainly, foul language has been around for quite some time, yet in recent years, it appears to have taken aggressive inclusion in normal conversation. Many Christians like to argue that only using the Lord's name in vain is considered sinful; however, the Apostle Paul once wrote, "Do not let any unwholesome talk come out of your mouths, but only what is helpful for building others up according to their needs, that it may benefit those who listen."⁶⁷ Jesus also tells us, "What goes into someone's mouth does not defile them, but what comes out of their mouth, that is what defiles them."⁶⁸ Therefore, always use your words to glorify God and build others up. It's too easy to slip into language that dishonors God and others. After all, the tongue can both heal and destroy, so choose your words wisely.⁶⁹

Jesus Christ was yelled at, spit on, abused, and tortured. Yet, instead of seeking revenge, He asked the Lord to forgive His abusers because they knew not what they were doing.⁷⁰ Indeed, many of the actions taken by others that hurt or harm us are done under Satan's influence. This is why we must pray for those who persecute us. Pray fervently that God will deliver them from the evil one; everyone deserves prayer.

65. 1 Tim. 6:10 (ESV).
66. Phil. 4:5 (Emphasis, mine).
67. Eph. 4:29 (NIV).
68. Matt. 15:11 (NIV).
69. Prov. 12:18 (Emphasis, mine).
70. Luke 23:34 (Emphasis, mine).

On the Twenty-First Day

This morning, I'm enjoying a hot cup of coffee at one of my favorite coffee shops near the beautiful Truckee River in Reno, Nevada. I patiently wait for a young man who reached out to me through his mother who is a friend, of a friend, of a friend, of mine on social media. He believes in God yet is suffering from depression. I pray that the Holy Spirit will give me the right words to say to him.

I've discovered that God sends those to us that He knows need caring for. When I first began in formal ministry, I was worried that I would have no one to share my love of God with. I soon discovered that I didn't have to search them out at all! Complete strangers were sent regularly by God to me for godly advice and healing. When someone reaches out to you, ask the Spirit if He was the one who sent that person; He probably was.

Spending time with others can be very powerful, and costs us nothing, except our time. So many people in the world are hurting. There is no shortage of those who need God in their lives. We must always proclaim the good news to others around us, and maybe throw in a loving embrace or kiss for good measure.[71] Satan does battle in our minds; and, therefore, we must be mentally strong; praying in the Spirit at all times with every kind of prayer and supplication.[72]

In the same way, we must reach out to another brother or sister of the faith when we are feeling lost, upset, or in need of help. After all, two are better than one.[73] Who are you planning on sharing God's love with today? You don't have to have all of the answers. You don't even have to talk that much. Simply being willing to spend time listening to someone who's made in God's image will speak volumes.

On the Twenty-Second Day

The quiet streets of downtown Reno reflect the dissipation of life that normally inhabits the landscape as I walk the silent streets alone, in search of my innermost thoughts and emotions. These are the times that I feel closest to God, for I have little distraction keeping me from communicating with Him.

I stopped in at the local convenience store this morning for some coffee, cream, and pastries. Since it was four in the morning, I was one of very

---

71. Rom. 16:16 (Emphasis, mine).
72. Eph. 6:18 (Emphasis, mine).
73. Eccl. 4:9-10 (Emphasis, mine).

few people in the store at that time. As the cashier was ringing up my items, he began to tell me all about his life. How he had worked a second job at another convenience store, just got out of a relationship, and how he was very good at saving up money for the slow winter season. I was very tempted to tell him all about myself as well; how I work full-time as a chauffeur, substitute teach, write music, run a small church, write books, attend graduate school full-time, take care of my wife and three children, etc. Yet, something inside told me to let him have his moment, so I did.

Self-control is not always an easy practice to adhere to. Lack of self-control is like opening a wall of your home to the outside world and allowing others to pillage it.[74] We must set boundaries for ourselves. Satan makes it so easy to give in to our temptations, which is why we must control our urges and prevent him from interrupting our right standing before God.

Pray with diligence and faith. Prayer is our direct line of communication with the Holy One, and the Lord always listens to us. Sometimes the answer to our prayers is yes, sometimes it's no, and sometimes it's, not yet. Quite often, I will pray before bed and fall asleep praying. This does not offend God, for it's better to fall asleep to the sounds of prayer than to suddenly awake in His silence.

On the Twenty-Third Day

Technology can be a double-edged sword. On the one hand, it helps with instant communication, locating lost relatives, and making our lives more convenient. On the other hand, technology limits our physical interactions, leaves little room for privacy, and distracts us from many other things.

Once, not long ago, I forced myself to take a break from social media. With divisiveness and hatred at an all-time high, I figured it was best not to expose myself to the temptations of the flesh. I was able to resist social media for about 3 weeks, then I found myself reconnecting with the virtual world much sooner than I expected.

The Bible teaches us of the importance of fasting. Many people equate fasting to the removal of food, yet fasting is really anything that you indulge in that could be replaced with prayer. For me, fasting from social media allowed me to spend more time reading and praying over God's word. For others, it may involve skipping a meal or taking a break from television. Jesus Christ instructs us to fast with humility. He says, *when* we fast, not *if* we will fast.[75] Therefore, the Lord Himself expects us to participate in fasting on

---

74. Prov. 25:28 (Emphasis, mine).
75. Matt. 6:16-18 (Emphasis, mine).

a regular basis. This rhythm of fasting will allow you to grow in discipline, as well as allow your relationship with the Father to develop even stronger.

If we are honest with ourselves, we will admit that we live a more comfortable life than most people around the world. Even the homeless in the United States have shelters, donations, governmental assistance, and opportunities to improve their lives, if they so choose. Third-world countries have little to offer people who are in poverty. This is why Jesus tells us that the poor will always be with us.[76] Therefore, never take God's blessings for granted.

On the Twenty-Fourth Day

Springtime is a time of love. Indeed, love is in the air as many lovers choose to marry each other in the spring or fall. I married my beautiful wife on March 2, 2008. Even though all relationships have challenges and disagreements, it feels so wonderful to be loved by someone else. I would argue that the joy surely outweighs the heartache.

Jesus Christ loves us in the best way. Much like a bridegroom who loves his bride unconditionally, we have truly captivated the Lord's heart.[77] From His example, we should be loving those closest to us in an unrestricted way. When we constantly put down those whom we love, or place unrealistic expectations on others, we are displaying the exact opposite of God's love. For, God does not love us with conditions.

If you are in an unloving relationship with someone else, look inside yourself and question whether or not you have loved that person unconditionally. If you have, then ask them to do the same. Even if you are not in a relationship with someone else, realize that neither height nor depth, nor anything else in all creation, will be able to separate us from the love of God that is in Christ Jesus our Lord.[78]

I personally try to show love for everyone that I encounter, because everyone that I encounter deserves to feel loved. It's not hard to smile at someone as they walk by you, or to engage in conversation with someone you've just met. Christ's love is living and active inside each one of us who believe in Him. There are very few things that I'd like to be remembered for long after I leave this earth; but, in the end, what matters to me most in this life is that I was able to love, and to be loved.

---

76. Mark 14:7 (Emphasis, mine).
77. Song. 4:9 (Emphasis, mine).
78. Rom. 8:39 (NIV).

On the Twenty-Fifth Day

A healthy marriage takes work. Having officiated several weddings, and having been married for many years myself, I can attest that it is not always easy. Marriages, or long-term relationships tend to go through stages. The first year is much like a honeymoon phase, in which everything is great and small annoyances are often overlooked. After some time, children may enter into the picture and the bond grows stronger as you raise them together. But, be careful of the next stage of marriage. This is where the enemy enters into the relationship trying to, once again, separate us from, not only God, but each other as well. We may feel less loved or cared for by our spouse. The little things we once overlooked may start to really bother us. Instead of dwelling in intimacy with our partner, we are simply co-existing. Satan can turn emotional sickness into physical and spiritual sickness, if we don't make the effort to remove him from our lives. This is where most marriages fall apart.

The good news is that we have a way to overcome this stage and persevere in our marriage through repentance and forgiveness. We can overcome Satan's divisive attacks through our faith in Jesus Christ. Jesus tells us, "What God has joined together, let no one separate."[79] My wife, Lisa and I went through the "stage of destruction" just like everyone else. Don't think that just because I'm a pastor, it can't happen to me; Satan tends to attack us even more severely. Yet, instead of blaming each other for how we were acting, we started investigating *why* we act the way we do. Some of it is environmental, some of it is genetic, yet that is who we are, so we can either accept each other for who we are, or we can give up on each other like so many failed marriages do. We chose the former. I'm praying that your relationship is a healthy and lasting one. In faith, God will help you get through any relationship stage that may challenge you.

On the Twenty-Sixth Day

The ominous clouds are making their way over the valley as rain begins to fall. The symposium of citizens meets to discuss ways of bettering our city for the area's homeless population. Blissful teenagers frolic in the shallow ponds that rapidly form on the cold cement ground.

We all face struggles in life. Sometimes those struggles are minor: sometimes the struggles are major ones. Like being trapped in a raging storm, we may find ourselves defenseless against life's bitter attacks. Yet, did

---

79. Mark 10:9 (NIV).

not Jesus calm the storm on the Sea of Galilee after His faith allowed Him to sleep through it?[80]

Too often, we lack faith in the One who has cared for and loved us all along. I used to worry about making the wrong choice as to where to serve in ministry, or where to serve secularly, or what city to live in, etc. Yet, all through my life, the hand of God has been guiding my steps. I have never had to worry about finding work, caring for my wife and kids, or having a roof over my head, because I constantly walk in faith and obedience to Him.

I once had a great conversation with a young Russian man who works in the transportation industry with me. During our conversation, he said that the financial world and religious world are two separate entities that have nothing to do with each other. I thought about it for a moment and replied, "You are right, yet everything we have and do falls under the care of Jesus Christ." In other words, if we place our focus on God first and foremost, then He will provide us with the financial security we need. If we place our focus on our love of money, we may or may not have endless wealth, but we will certainly forsake God in the process. He later told me that he was very inspired by that conversation, and that he never forgot those words.

On the Twenty-Seventh Day

The warmth of the morning sunshine radiates as the vegetation grows abundantly in response. Another beautiful day is before us as the Lord anticipates our interaction with Him. Like a loving parent, God is always interested in what we are doing and what we desire. When we pray, we should pray with this idea in mind. We can communicate with Him through our prayers and deeds; we can talk to Him just like might talk to a spouse or a parent.

We are never alone, for God is always with us. It was foretold long ago that God would dwell with us;[81] He is dwelling among us right now in the form of the Holy Spirit. When we feel lost or afraid, we can always pray to the Father, for He is listening to us at all times.

I have been in several situations in which I felt like there was no way out of them. Perhaps you have as well? Yet, through fervent prayer and trust in Jesus Christ, I have been rescued from things you couldn't imagine. Sometimes it's hard to put our trust in something that we cannot see, yet surely, we trust that the winds will blow the clouds from the oceans to the valleys and provide water for the inhabitants below. We cannot see the wind, but we can see the results of the wind through leaves that are blown

---

80. Mark 4:35-41 (Emphasis, mine).
81. Ezek. 37:27 (Emphasis, mine).

or whitecaps that form on the great lakes. Jesus said, "The wind blows wherever it pleases. You hear its sound, but you cannot tell where it comes from or where it is going. So, it is with everyone born of the Spirit."[82]

We are the winds of change, and we manifest that change through the power of the Holy Spirit who dwells inside of us. If you are unhappy with your life, you can change it. Jesus is there to help you every step of the way. Put your faith and trust in Him and enjoy the relaxing breeze of the Holy Spirit.

On the Twenty-Eighth Day

Unabashedly, my little five-year-old daughter will approach anyone and say hello to them. Whether we are walking down the street, in the grocery store, or playing in the front yard as someone walks by, my daughter, Makayla is always happy to see other people and interact with them. I feel as if most of us were that way at five years old.

So, what happened to us over the years that resulted in our reluctance to love someone else? Was it something you went through? Someone who hurt you emotionally or physically? How can we get back to the place of loving others for being made in God's image? The answer is not as complex as social science may want you to believe that it is. We must first forgive those who have wronged us, and then turn to Jesus Christ to build us back into the innocent child that we once were.

Jesus Christ loved children when He walked this earth, and loves being with them even more in heaven. I have a few friends who have lost their children. The grief they must experience is unimaginable, yet to their children, the kingdom of heaven belongs.[83] This can bring some comfort amongst the sorrow. Earth has lost a precious child, but heaven has gained a beautiful saint. David lost his first child with Bathsheba, but David knew that someday he would go to him in heaven.[84]

We should try to love and comfort those around us. No one knows what they are really going through except the Father. Therefore, pray to the Lord and ask Him how you can comfort them in their time of need. Surely, He will have the answer.

---

82. John 3:8 (NIV).
83. Mark 10:13-16 (Emphasis, mine).
84. 2 Sam. 12:22 (Emphasis, mine).

On the Twenty-Ninth Day

The grass is starting to come alive again as the spring rains provide life-giving water to the earthly vegetation. God created all that has life and all that is needed to sustain life. Like the lifeless planets in outer space, or the endless sands of the desert, some things in creation are simply there for us to admire.

It's amazing to see where God is going to take us in our lives. Looking back on my life, I felt as if it was full of both challenges and triumphs. Though parts of my life were certainly not pleasant, it was all orchestrated that way to strengthen my faith. The Apostle Paul once said, "Three times I was beaten with rods, once I was pelted with stones, three times I was shipwrecked, I spent a night and a day in the open sea."[85] And, that was just a fraction of what he experienced during his missionary journeys. Yet, Paul, who was once a persecutor of Christians, was later happy to be persecuted in the name of Jesus Christ. As a result, martyrdom would be considered honorable to Jesus Christ for many centuries.

Sometimes, we can't see any light when we peer into a dark tunnel. We must start walking through the darkness to see the light at the other side. The light shines in the darkness, and the darkness has not overcome it.[86] Therefore, let the light of Jesus Christ shine brightly inside of you by casting out all of the darkness that tries to make its way in.

It is important to rely upon other believers to help in the sanctification process. This is why church is so important. We must encourage one another in these tumultuous times.[87] It's very difficult to work on our relationship with Christ alone; although, some time spent in solitude with the Lord is always a good thing.

On the Thirtieth Day

The mountains in the west reflect God's majesty as the dew forms on the sagebrush that inhabits them. The sun is just rising over the horizon as the sky turns shades of light blue and golden yellow. The majestic pine trees tower over the animals of the forest as they scurry to find their daily provisions.

My friends, beware of deceptive spirits. For not every spirit that tries to communicate with us is from God. Indeed, the enemy has been a deceiver from the very beginning, leading Adam and Eve astray by convincing them

---

85. 2 Cor. 11:25 (NIV).
86. John 1:5 (NIV).
87. Heb. 10:25 (Emphasis, mine).

that he had their best interests in mind. We must test the spirits by asking them if Jesus Christ has come in the flesh. If they deny this, then they are not of God. However, if they confess this truth, then they are from God.[88]

Beware of the spirit of the antichrist, for he is in the world already.[89] You can see him manifested as one who deceives, perverts, harms, and corrupts those closest to God. But fear not, for He who is in you is greater than he who is in the world.[90] Christ has already overcome the world through His sacrifice on the cross. He has resurrected; therefore, death no longer has control over Him.[91] The enemy will attempt to draw us away from the Holy One. Yet, if we stand firm in our faith and rebuke him, then we will surely break free from our allurement to sin, and instead, build our relationship with the Father. Everyone backslides sometimes. Do not let the enemy convince you that you cannot persevere in faith. You are a saint who sins in God's eyes because Christ has already paid the price for your transgressions.

---

88. 1 John 4:1-2 (Emphasis, mine).
89. 1 John 4:3 (Emphasis, mine).
90. 1 John 4:4 (Emphasis, mine).
91. Rom. 6:9 (Emphasis, mine).

Chapter 5

The Spirit of God
The Month of May

On the First Day

THE BRISK WINTER GIVES way to the warmth of the spring as I make my way through a nearby field which is alive with vegetation. The latter rains have brought beautiful flowers, roses, tulips, orchids, and lilies. The atmosphere feels brighter as I watch my neighbors wash their cars and mow their lawns. I usually start mowing my lawn around the middle of May.

We have great power in the Holy Spirit! The Apostle Paul tells us that we all are baptized by one Spirit to form one body.[1] Therefore, one brother or sister in faith does not have a different Spirit dwelling within them than another brother or sister in faith has. In fact, the same Spirit that descended upon Jesus Christ at His baptism over two-thousand years ago, descends upon us now when we accept Jesus Christ into our hearts. This is why all Christians should possess every fruit of the Spirit, which are: love, joy, peace, forbearance, kindness, goodness, faithfulness, gentleness and self-control. Against such things there is no law.[2]

Perhaps, you are full of love, yet lack self-control. Or, maybe you are kind, but are not faithful. We must pray that the Lord increase our fruit in these areas. Some Christians claim that they have some of the fruits, but not others. They do this by saying, *fruits* of the Spirit. Yet, is the Holy Spirit divided amongst itself? Certainly not, for the fruit of the Spirit is listed as one comprehensive and complete unit in the New Testament. Therefore, no believer should be lacking in any area of fruit, for does not a good tree bear much good fruit?[3]

---

1. 1 Cor. 12:13 (Emphasis, mine).
2. Gal. 5:22-23 (NIV).
3. Matt. 7:17 (Emphasis, mine).

On the Second Day

How is your prayer life? To be honest, there are times when I'm too preoccupied to think about prayer, or too tired, or too busy, or too . . . you get the idea. Yet, that doesn't give me an excuse not to pray. When my son, Brett was around six or seven years old, he used to remind me every night to pray for him and the rest of our family. Regardless of how tired I was from working a long day, or attending classes all day, his request for prayer always made me get out of bed and honor it.

Prayer is important to God because it opens up the lines of communication. Jesus would often pray for hours to the Lord before making decisions about something. Once, Jesus prayed to God all night before choosing His disciples.[4] Many people like to treat God like Santa Clause, but when we pray, we shouldn't ask for a wish-list of items. I will always open up in prayer thanking God for what I have and what He has planned for me. If I've sinned in some way, I ask for God's forgiveness. Then, I like to switch the focus to someone that I personally care about, or someone that has sent me a prayer request. Lastly, I pray for my friends and family, and if it dawns on me, I might ask that God's will be done in my life as well. You'd be surprised at how many blessings pour out when we take the focus off of ourselves and place it upon God and His creation instead.

If you struggle with prayer, look no further than the Scriptures themselves. God has provided many great prayers in the book of Psalms and other wisdom literature books that will help to get you started. When Job's friends sinned against him, God instructed them to have Job pray on their behalf so that His anger might turn from them.[5] God is ready to listen; we must be ready to speak.

On the Third Day

Spring rain begins to fall on the thick grass and cement porch in my front yard as the neighborhood gets cleansed from the dusty streets and sidewalks that inhabit it. I love the sound of rain coming down like pellets of sand that bounce off the sides of rustic buildings in the midst of a windstorm.

It's common to hear people to say, "Surely, I'm going to heaven, for I am a good person." Yet, Scripture tells us that the fool says in his heart, "there is no God," and that no one is good, not one.[6] This is why we must

---

4. Luke 6:12-13 (Emphasis, mine).
5. Job 42:7-9 (Emphasis, mine).
6. Ps. 14:1/Romans 3:10 (Emphasis, mine).

share with people the good news of Jesus' life, death, and resurrection. If we could be saved simply by being good people in the eyes of society, then Jesus was persecuted, beaten and killed for nothing. God has much higher standards than we do. To him, even our best earthly deeds are but filthy rags.[7]

I'm afraid, our best deeds will not be sufficient for us to dwell in eternity with the Holy One. Only our faith in Christ Jesus will guarantee us the arrival of our heavenly destination. We must confess with our hearts that Christ is Lord, and in return, He will confess us to our Father in heaven.[8] James tells us that faith without works is dead.[9] Therefore, you will surely produce good works if you first have faith, for once you are baptized into Jesus Christ, the good works will naturally pour forth.

Let your words be used to encourage and build up your brothers and sisters in Christ. Be sure to use your words carefully, for every man will give an account on the day of judgment for every careless word that was spoken.[10]

On the Fourth Day

One of the beauties of spring is that the warmth of the sunshine lasts all day into the evening. Going for a walk at dusk helps me relax from a hectic day of work and school. Breathing in the fresh air that God provides for us every day is a blessing in itself, for as soon as we start taking life for granted, someone is lost unexpectedly.

Never be afraid to witness the Gospel of Jesus Christ. The Apostles were beaten and threatened never to speak a word about Jesus Christ, yet they could not stop proclaiming what they had seen and heard.[11] One of the reasons the Scriptures have much power is that they reflect accurate historical accounts of miraculous events that took place in front of thousands of eye witnesses.

When Peter and the other Apostles were facing certain death from the high priest and council of the Sanhedrin, the honored teacher of the Law, Gamaliel proclaimed, "In the present case I advise you: Leave these men alone! Let them go! For if their purpose or activity is of human origin, it will fail. But if it is from God, you will not be able to stop these men; you will

---

7. Isa. 64:6 (Emphasis, mine).
8. Matt. 10:32 (Emphasis, mine).
9. Jas. 2:14-17 (Emphasis, mine).
10. Matt. 12:38 (Emphasis, mine).
11. Acts 4:18-20 (Emphasis, mine).

only find yourselves fighting against God."[12] Isn't it amazing how accurate the Scriptures actually are? For, Christianity hasn't been stopped despite two-thousand years of persecution. Indeed, Christianity is from God, and its persecutors are constantly fighting against Him.

Love God and one another at all times. You don't have to beat someone over the head with your Bible to get them interested in Jesus. Just give them your time and love. You can plant the seed, but God will be the One to make it grow.[13] We can show that the Holy Spirit dwells inside of us by simply being around others who do not yet know Him.

On the Fifth Day

Once a year, my family and I travel outside of Reno to a neighboring state. Sometimes, we make the sixteen-hour drive to Denver, Colorado to visit my parents for Christmas. I'm always amazed at how different the landscape is from what I'm used to seeing. The terrain can change from flat and sandy, to green and mountainous in less than an hour. Dry and barren land can transform to marshes and lakes as far as the eye can see.

Much like traveling the roads of changing scenery, our lives morph and change as we grow older and gain more experience with our surroundings. We are all beautifully unique. God has designed us this way, perhaps so that life wouldn't become boring from the same people enjoying the same things all of the time. You were made exactly how God intended you to be. Jesus once encountered a blind man who had been blind from birth. His disciples asked Him, "who sinned, this man or his parents?" Jesus explained that neither him, nor his parents sinned, but he was blind so that the works of God could be displayed in him.[14]

I often wonder if the works of God displayed in those with disabilities are reflected in how we treat them. Do we love and care for them just as much as someone without a disability? After all, they are still made in God's image. Or, do we turn away from them, ignore their needs, and treat them like outcasts? I hope it's the former, but unfortunately, we've seen how cruel the world can actually be.

When you come across someone who is physically or mentally challenged, be sure and love them just the same as God loves you. Despite their outward deformity, their heart might be perfectly intact.

---

12. Acts 5:38 (NIV).
13. 1 Cor. 3:7 (Emphasis, mine).
14. John 9:1-3 (Emphasis, mine).

On the Sixth Day

The weather is nice today as my kids and I load up into the car for a day of wonder and enchantment. I used to believe that the only way my kids would be happy is if I spent money on them. As I grew older, I realized that they simply wanted to spend time with me. They were just as happy spending time together going for a walk, or riding our bikes, as they were at the ice-cream shop or bowling stadium, well almost.

My kids love to go to the park. As my older ones play on the swing set or teetertotter, my five-year-old daughter, Makayla searches for someone around her age to play with. It's always refreshing to see children of that young age not exhibiting prejudice or discrimination. They are simply happy to be able to spend time with someone that enjoys spending time with them as well. If only adults acted in this way.

The Bible tells us to: "Be completely humble and gentle; be patient, bearing with one another in love."[15] Before we cast judgement upon someone for looking or acting different than us, perhaps we should evaluate our own character and remove the plank that is in our eyes.[16] We must strive to be holy as God is holy.[17] But, realize that no one is born fully set apart in Jesus Christ. Sanctification is a lifelong process; we can always improve ourselves in some way.

If you struggle in certain areas of your life, pray that the Lord will help you remove the sin that plagues you and start living a life centered more on Him. The Holy Spirit lives inside of you to help you with this goal. I've found that when I stay focused on Jesus Christ, the other areas of my life that I struggle with begin to improve drastically.

On the Seventh Day

The warm breeze from the west blows in as ominous dark clouds encroach upon the valley. The smell of rain is in the air as the sound of thunder can be heard in the distance. Children hurry inside to protect themselves from the elements as neighbors close their windows to avoid the rain water getting inside.

In the Old Testament, God differentiates between intentional sins and unintentional sins *(such as a sinful reaction to someone)* by the sacrifices He required for each one. Indeed, the Hebrew people did sin unintentionally

---

15. Eph. 4:2 (NIV).
16. Matt. 7:5 (Emphasis, mine).
17. Lev. 11:44 (Emphasis, mine).

and were required to offer a bull without blemish.[18] The punishment for deliberate sin was far greater, for it required the sinner to be cut off from the people of Israel forever.[19] Yet, under the New Covenant, we all are guilty of sin, both unintentional and intentional; we fall short of God's glory.[20] The offerings of the Old Testament were a foreshadowing of what was to come; the ultimate offering of Jesus Christ, who Himself, provided a once and for all sacrifice for the removal of our sins. For it was written long ago in the Psalms, "Sacrifice and offering you did not desire, but my ears you have opened; burnt offerings and sin offerings you did not require."[21]

Whether we sin intentionally or not, we still do so willingly. Even if we do not act upon our sinful thoughts, the thoughts themselves are considered sinful.[22] This is why no one is considered good before the Almighty Lord, until they come to faith in Jesus Christ. We must make a genuine effort to repent of our sins, not just physical sin, but mental sin as well.

On the Eighth Day

When I was much younger, my Sunday School teacher told me that God's grace can be defined as: "something given that is not deserved." Perhaps, because we were only twelve or thirteen years old, this general definition was a satisfactory one. Yet, as I got older and deeper into my theological studies, I discovered that grace is not only something that we don't deserve, but it's something that we cannot come to salvation without.

God's grace is a beautiful thing, for without it, we would not be able to respond positively to the gospel message. In fact, the faith we have to believe in Jesus Christ, is itself, a gift from God.[23] Without God's grace, we would be forever separated from Him.

Our flesh is at naturally enmity with God, even from birth. Take, God's requirement to obey your mother and father, for instance.[24] No one has to teach us how to disobey our parents. I have several children and can attest that they all have done things I've told them not to do, and they have all gotten upset with me when I've grounded them for breaking the rules. If you don't believe me, simply observe any two-year-old child and you will

18. Lev. 4:2-3 (Emphasis, mine).
19. Num. 15:30-31 (Emphasis, mine).
20. Rom. 3:23 (Emphasis, mine).
21. Ps. 40:6 (NIV).
22. Matt. 15:19 (Emphasis, mine).
23. Eph. 2:8 (Emphasis, mine).
24. Eph. 6:1 (Emphasis, mine).

soon discover that they are quick to get into mischief and slow to accept the consequences of their actions.

Our sinful nature, inherited from Adam, results in our natural disobedience to the Father as well. This is where the enemy does the most destructive work; in our flesh. It's easy to continue in sin if you tell yourself you'll never be able to resist it. This happens because the enemy has already got you right where he wants you; far away from God. Yet, God has given us a new Spirit who can overcome the sin of the first Adam.[25] So, rebuke the slanderous devil that tries to separate you from the Creator. You deserve to live a life free from the burdens of sin.

On the Ninth Day

The morning awakens to the sound of birds chirping in the distance. The sunrise appears in the east as the dawn breaks. Another beautiful day is upon us as we enjoy the opportunity to worship God once again. I am always grateful for the ability to enjoy another day.

Patience is a virtue, at least that's what they say. The Bible tells us, "A hot-tempered person stirs up conflict, but the one who is patient calms a quarrel."[26] How patient are you in your interactions with others? In addition to the ministry, I also drive limousines and town cars for a local transportation company. Often times, I have to wait in the vehicle for hours while the client visits family or eats dinner. At first, it was hard to wait, sitting in a vehicle for hours on end, but as I grew in patience, I found it to be a time of relaxation. I would pass the time thinking about life's challenges, family bills, or the future. After spending some time in thought, I would listen to my Bible app from my phone, read a book, or study for an upcoming college exam. If we focus on the opportunities instead of the challenges, we will find our attitude towards patience begin to improve immensely.

Patience can also help with people in our lives that might tend to annoy or bother us. My first year of college was not only faced with academic challenges, but also learning how to work in groups with other students of various personalities. One student in particular, had great faith and trust in Jesus Christ, but tended to ramble on and on without letting anyone else get a word in edge-wise. Many of us found ourselves avoiding him at all costs, but as I thought about it, I realized that God loves him just as much as He loves everyone else. So, I decided to embrace him like Jesus would. We're still good friends and remain in touch to this day.

25. Rom. 8:10 (Emphasis, mine).
26. Prov. 15:18 (NIV).

On the Tenth Day

Mother's Day

Mothers are a true blessing. Without them, none of us would be here. I remember a time, long, long ago, when my mother would take me in her car to run various errands around town and I would sing along to Fleetwood Mac, The Eagles, Journey, and other 80's songs that came on the radio. As I grew older, my mom would help me with my homework assignments, support me in my music, and cheer me on at my sporting events. She was someone that I could always confide in when I felt upset or afraid.

My mother worked hard all of her life. As a single mom, she first found employment when she was just over twenty years old with the Lakeport Office of Education. Once we moved to Sparks, Nevada, she worked various retail jobs and then decided to go back to college and earn her Associates Degree in General Education. Later, she pursued a career with the school district in Denver, Colorado, helping mentally challenged young adults find local employment. She held that job until she retired a few years ago.

Although God chooses to reveal Himself as, *The Father* in Scripture, He does also care for us as a mother would care for her children. The Lord once said, "As one whom his mother comforts, so I will comfort you; you shall be comforted in Jerusalem."[27]

I hope that you take the time to say thank you to your mother for all that she has done for you. Many mother's sacrifice their time, energy, finances, and bodies to give to their children. Like my mother did, my wife Lisa goes to school full time, works overnights at the hospital, helps our children with their homework and cooks for all of us. We are so blessed to have her in our lives. I'd like to say thank you, to my mom, and my wife for always being there for me. I love you both with all of my heart.

On the Eleventh Day

Thunder storms blow in from the west this afternoon as the dark clouds cascade over the valley below. The smell of rain is in the air. The dry region longs for rain like an arid desert in the scorching heat. Surely, God is in control of the weather. So many of His chosen people were dependent upon the rain to produce crops and sustain life. Though He gets little credit now for providing life-giving elements essential to our survival, we are still

---

27. Isaiah 66:13 (ESV).

dependent upon Him every minute of every hour. Don't hesitate to trust in Him and remain encouraged, for the righteous are never forsaken.[28]

It's amazing how far a little encouragement can go. I received encouragement throughout my youth from certain friends and family members that helped me to persevere through the hard times. Yet, I didn't receive as much support as many of my friends seemed to get from their parents. This led to many nights of frustration, and a feeling as though I wasn't intelligent enough to make proper life decisions. As a result, I now tend to be over-encouraging with my children and people that I care for.

The Bible says that "God is our refuge and strength, a very present help in trouble."[29] These are strong words, for God, Himself is encouraging us to keep moving forward. Not long after my break-up with my ex-wife, I slipped into a deep depression. I allowed the enemy to enter my mind and make me feel as though life wasn't worth living. Yet, through it all, I kept my eyes focused on God. I asked Him to listen to my heart and not my mind, for surely, He knew my heart was for Him. As I prayed one evening lying in bed, I asked Him not to give up on me; He never did.

On the Twelfth Day

Sometimes, we may feel as though no one is there for us in our times of trial and tribulation. I have certainly felt alone at times, myself. Yet, all throughout history, God's children have felt this same way. Perhaps you had a rough childhood and were not very close to your parents? Israel's great King David once said, "Though my father and mother forsake me, the Lord will receive me."[30] Indeed, David felt this way too.

The beauty of God's word is that there is always something written that pertains to our current situation of blessings and curses. Even though technology has advanced since biblical times, our need for love, acceptance, hope, financial security, and encouragement has remained the same. Therefore, we must remain faithful to God, who provides all of these things for us.

Observe the animals and birds of the air. Do they appear to constantly worry about where their next meal will come from, or do they simply live their lives knowing that their creator has already provided for them and will continue to provide for their offspring? God once asked Job, "Who

---

28. Ps. 37:25 (Emphasis, mine).
29. Ps. 46:1 (ESV).
30. Ps. 27:10 (NIV).

provides food for the raven when its young cry out to God and wander about for lack of food?"[31]

If you feel distant from those around you or feel as though no one seems to care about what is going on in your life, realize that God has never left you. He is listening to you right now and has already determined a plan of action for you, if you choose to accept it. Even though life is full of challenges, I remain faithful that the Lord has me right where He wants me in this season of my life. I shall not worry about tomorrow, for God is my rock and my refuge; I will never be shaken.[32]

On the Thirteenth Day

The skies are still dark as I awake to write another day's entry for the world to read. The silence and solitude of the evening gives way to the quietness of the dawn. Only the sound of the clock ticking can be heard in the background, along with the tapping of my fingers upon the computer keyboard. These are the times in which the Holy Spirit likes to speak to me.

Spending time in seclusion with God is very important. Did not Jesus go into the mountains alone to pray, free from distraction and interruption?[33] I had never realized the power of time alone with the Holy Spirit until I experienced it myself, long ago while praying for my home to be cleansed of any evil spirits that might inhabit it. After saying a prayer, using olive oil, and casting out the evil from each room, window, and opening to the outside world, I finish with the Lord's prayer. If I'm successful, I feel a calming brightness of the Lord's presence. If I'm really successful, I feel the Holy Spirit send tingles all over my body, from my head down to the tips of my toes. Thank you, Lord, for reminding me that you're still there.

Try and make the effort to spend time alone with God each day. I know it's hard when you have small children around the house who need something from you constantly, but it can be done if you make the effort. I like to wake up early and spend time reading God's word, praying, meditating, and journaling. Perhaps, you are a night person and would rather stay up late after the kids are in bed to unwind and rest in the Lord? Either way, it will truly build your relationship with the Holy One, simply by making time to listen to what He has to say. We're only on this earth for a short while before

---

31. Job 38:41 (NIV).
32. Ps. 62:2 (Emphasis, mine).
33. Matt. 14:23 (Emphasis, mine).

we answer to the King of kings. Wouldn't you prefer He say to you, "Well done, good and faithful servant?"[34]

On the Fourteenth Day

Anyone who has children knows how dependent they can be upon their parents or guardians. My children are such blessings to me, yet they always need questions answered, something material to possess, and a lot of my time. Perhaps, they are simply reflecting the dependency that we have upon our loving Father in heaven.

In my early twenties, I was so excited to get away from my parents and live on my own, that I worked whatever jobs I could to support myself independently. My younger, and much smarter sister, Krisstin, stayed at home and attended college full-time, of which she graduated, then went immediately back for her master's. She later found a great job in Southern California, got married, and had a beautiful baby boy named, Noah. Why couldn't I do everything in that order? I decided not to go to college right out of high school. Instead, I got married, had my oldest son, Collin, made poor decisions, got divorced, had my second son, Nathan, worked two and three jobs to survive, got involved in a slew of unhealthy relationships, repented, came back to the Lord, and then met my beautiful, smart, and loving wife, Lisa. I then went to college, had my other three beautiful children, served the Lord, and now enjoy the blessings God has given me. Maybe God wanted me to experience the storm, so I would appreciate the sunshine.

We all face trials and setbacks in life. Mine might have seemed like a lot, but I assure you there were many other challenges that I didn't list. Perhaps you'll read about them in a sequel. Whatever the enemy tries to throw your way, realize that the Lord is always there to help you get through it. Therefore, do not be grieved for the joy of the Lord is our strength.[35] I wouldn't trade my experiences for anything, because what I've been through has only made me stronger. I have greater faith in Jesus Christ because I've lived to tell about it.

On the Fifteenth Day

Looking up at the clouds, I have a sense of peace and tranquility as they move slowly through the atmosphere. The blue background of the sky is

---

34. Matt. 25:23 (Emphasis, mine).
35. Neh. 8:10 (Emphasis, mine).

like the color of Lake Tahoe before the afternoon winds disturb the waters. We know that God dwells in all places,[36] but I like to think He prefers to remain in our hearts.

Heaven is a fascinating subject. The Bible doesn't tell us a lot of details about heaven, but it does assure us that the unrighteous will not enter into the kingdom of heaven.[37] Jesus ascended to heaven on a cloud and will descend back to the earth on the great day of judgment.[38] Those who have faith in Jesus Christ will be spared from the place of weeping and gnashing of teeth.

It's always exciting to read or hear of someone who has had a near-death experience and lived to tell about what they saw. Most of them experience a grand staircase towards white light, some of them are greeted by Jesus Christ, Himself! Others see loved ones who had long since passed away, and still others see only darkness. Have you seen the light of Jesus in your life?

One of my beloved parishioners, Jeannine, had suffered the loss of her aged husband Harry, many years ago. As he was lying on the bed in their bedroom, she noticed his spirit in the form of his body lift out of his body and ascend towards heaven! Being 89 years old, and of sound mind, Jeannine had no reason to make such things up. Surely, God allowed her to see His glory displayed in her husband at the time of his passing. Be confident that Jesus Christ has already secured a place for you in heaven. In fact, you don't have to travel far to get there. The kingdom of heaven is already at hand.

On the Sixteenth Day

As the earth begins to warm up this morning, the river sparkles with the reflection of the sunshine. The creatures who dwell in the holes and burrows of the earth come out to enjoy God's creation once again. The golden fields of wheat blow gently in unison as the birds of the air fly overhead.

A few weeks ago, I took notice of a homeless man sitting at the bus stop in front of our church. I had just boughten some breakfast and decided to offer him some of it. He was so overjoyed at the fact that I would make such a gesture that he kept thanking me profusely. As I went inside to set up for church, I thought, maybe he could use a drink and some money as well. So, I found a five-dollar bill in my wallet and gave it to him, along with a cold soda to wash down his breakfast with. Again, he thanked me, and I

---

36. Ps. 84:1 (Emphasis, mine).
37. Matt. 5:20 (Emphasis, mine).
38. Acts 1:9/Mark 13:26 (Emphasis, mine).

left saying, "May God bless you." He returned the blessing as I walked away with tears in my eyes.

It's hard to explain, but sometimes the Holy Spirit compels us to the point of breaking down emotionally. I believe that every Christian has the gift of discernment available to them if they ask for it. It's interesting, in some cases, I'm not compelled to help people that appear to be homeless, yet in other cases, the Spirit compels me so much that I cannot ignore it, and I help out in any way I can.

When you help someone in need, the reward is greater for you than for the one you help. I can guarantee that you will feel good inside for making someone else happy. We should take care of those less fortunate than us. God has blessed us in so many ways that it would be selfish to not pay our blessings forward. "Whoever is generous to the poor lends to the Lord, and he will repay him for his deed."[39]

On the Seventeenth Day

Not long after my wife and I were married, along came my beautiful son, Brett. We were renting a large home in northwest Reno at that time and had plenty of room for a family of three. My wife was working at a local hotel, and I had a small cleaning business and worked part-time as a bell captain. Everything was going great, and then . . . Lisa lost her job.

The recession and housing crisis of 2011 hit . . . and hit hard. Jobs were scarce, and I was lucky to have more than one, yet it wasn't enough income to support us. We ended up downsizing to a small apartment and Lisa decided to go back to college to pursue a career in the medical field. It was a very stressful time for us financially.

We all have times in our lives in which the burdens placed upon on us feel like more than we can bear. The Lord is willing to take our burdens on Himself. King David once wrote, "Cast your burden on the Lord, and he will sustain you; he will never permit the righteous to be moved."[40] Jesus Christ takes so much weight off of our shoulders. He has already paid the price for our anxiety; therefore, place your worries upon Him.

It's easy to get caught up in the overwhelming responsibilities of life, yet with God's grace, our hard work will overcome any trial or temptation that is laid before us.[41] Be encouraged friends, you are not facing life's hardships alone. Remain strong in faith and trust that the Lord has a reason

---

39. Prov. 19:17 (ESV).
40. Ps. 55:22 (ESV).
41. 1 Cor. 15:10 (Emphasis, mine).

you are experiencing burdens. Many of God's most cherished patriarchs had faced hardships in their lives at one time or another; many will face burdens in the future as well. God loves you, so don't worry about what you will eat, your body, or what you will wear. Life is more than food, our bodies, and our clothes.[42]

On the Eighteenth Day

I used to feel as though I needed to control everything around me. If I wanted something to go a certain way or to my benefit, I certainly tried to control the circumstances leading up to the event. After experiencing several setbacks in my life, I realized that I cannot control everything around me; I can barely control myself. The times that I let go and let God run my life were the times that I had the most success. When we try and go against God's plan for our lives, we always experience repercussion. This is where Satan gets a foothold, when we stop trusting in God and start trusting in ourselves to overcome the world's temptations.

The Bible tells us that God forms the light and the darkness; He is the author of good and of calamity.[43] Certainly, God is in control of everything. In theological circles, this can refer to "God's omnipotence," or that God is *all-powerful*. There is nothing that happens under the sun that God does not already know will take place. The great debate, of course, is if God predestined every event to happen, or do we have free-will within His master plan. Personally, I believe it's a combination of both. Whichever side of the great debate you fall on, we can all agree that we cannot handle life's challenges alone, we are dependent upon our Lord and Savior to overcome the demons that exist among us.

When I drive clients around at my limousine job, I rely heavily upon my GPS to navigate my course. Some clients I had taken home several times before, yet I always felt more comfortable knowing that I was being guided safely to my destination. When you feel like life is spinning out of control, pray to the Lord and ask Him to give you direction. His aim is always true, and His guidance will never take you off course.

---

42. Luke 12:22-23 (Emphasis, mine).
43. Isa. 45:7 (Emphasis, mine).

On the Nineteenth Day

It's hard to believe that summer is just around the corner. I remember cold winds and the snow falling down like it was just yesterday. I live in a region of the country that experiences all four seasons. Though we live in a desert climate, Northern Nevadan's experience rain and snow during the winter months thanks to the nearby Sierra Nevada Mountain range.

Much like the various seasons of each year, our lives experience diverse seasons as well. God might be testing us in a certain season of our life, only to reward us in another. Like many of you reading this, I too faced several obstacles at one point or another during my life. I've faced insecurity, to issues with self-confidence, issues with bullies, issues with promiscuity, issues with family, relationships, academics, and employment. Yet, through it all, I've kept my eyes focused on the Lord and allowed Him to guide me in my journey of blessings and curses. I made it through some tough times, and so will you.

The Apostle Paul once wrote:

> Five times I received from the Jews the forty lashes minus one. Three times I was beaten with rods, once I was pelted with stones, three times I was shipwrecked, I spent a night and a day in the open sea, I have been constantly on the move. I have been in danger from rivers, in danger from bandits, in danger from my fellow Jews, in danger from Gentiles; in danger in the city, in danger in the country, in danger at sea; and in danger from false believers. I have labored and toiled and have often gone without sleep; I have known hunger and thirst and have often gone without food; I have been cold and naked. Besides everything else, I face daily the pressure of my concern for all the churches. Who is weak, and I do not feel weak? Who is led into sin, and I do not inwardly burn?[44]

Certainly, if Paul could experience all of these things and still remain eager to proclaim the Gospel of Jesus Christ, trust in the Lord, and endure until the end, then so can you and me. We're only in this season of our lives for short while, so make the most of the time you have on earth to become a better reflection of Jesus Christ. You'll be so glad that you did.

---

44. 2 Cor. 11:24-29 (NIV).

On the Twentieth Day

The clouds cast shadows upon the earth below as the summer heat begins to set in. The flowers of the earth reach towards the sun as they come into full bloom. Children play outside at the park or swimming pool, passing the time away and making memories that they will look back on many years later.

Are you at a point in your life where you feel as though all of your goals have been achieved, or that you have become the person you always envisioned you would be; kind, caring, giving, slow to anger, faithful, loyal, strong, successful, beautiful outside, beautiful inside, intelligent, hard-working, loving, patient, the perfect weight, the perfect height? No? well don't worry, I haven't either.

We tend to want things in our lives in a finished or perfected form, almost immediately. Yet, God is in no hurry to see that you have everything you've asked from Him. Abraham and Sarah waited many years before they had their first son, and when God finally revealed that they would have a child, thereby allowing them to become the father and mother of many nations, Abraham could hardly believe it.[45] What we expect to happen often does not happen in the way we expect it to, yet it doesn't mean that God won't give us what we ask for, it may just be reserved later for His timing and purposes.

When some of the people of Jerusalem tried to seize Jesus, no one was able to lay a hand on Him because His hour had not yet come.[46] Perhaps, you are trying to seize your moment in this life but have been prevented from doing so? Don't let that stop you from reaching your goals. It may just be a matter of time before God opens the right door for you to walk through.

On the Twenty-First Day

The rain slowly pours down as the morning begins. Puddles of warm candescent water begin to emerge on the cold ground below. Children frolic in the fields, enjoying the change of season and the wonder of God's creation. Have you looked out at the beauty of the world lately?

Too often, we seek the admiration and vindication of our peers. Attempting to prove that we are right at all times based on the world's standards can be an ever-cumbersome endeavor. How many times have you attempted

---

45. Gen. 17:15-17 (Emphasis, mine).
46. John 7:30 (Emphasis, mine).

to show your value to someone, only to be ridiculed or made to feel that you weren't that great after all? A former co-worker of mine called me the other day saying that she had driven an executive around earlier that afternoon and he had complimented her on her driving ability. Excitedly, she told the managers of the company that she had just received a compliment on her smooth driving. Yet, instead of congratulating her for a job well-done, they mocked that fact that she was "smooth" as opposed to skilled.

Sadly, I've seen this type of discouragement time and time again. When I worked as a swimming pool manager, many years ago, we used to have a department director who was very old-school in his management style. He would only critique and yell; never compliment or encourage. One day, I vented my frustration upon our maintenance man, who was working on a newly installed pump in the boiler room. His reply was, "You don't need a pat on the back, your paycheck tells you you're doing a good job." Perhaps that is true, but everyone deserves a compliment for a job well-done once in a while.

The Bible tells us not to seek the approval of men, but rather, seek the approval of God.[47] At the end of the day, mankind is unable to venerate us. God alone marks you approved in Christ Jesus and that is all the justification you need.

On the Twenty-Second Day

As the warm weather increases, many people find their way to the great Truckee River that stretches from Lake Tahoe, through Reno, and to the east. The great rivers of the world were created at the beginning of time.[48] Indeed, water has been a part of life since the creation. Water has the power to sustain life, heal, and even destroy.

When the sun is shining, it's easy to forget about our friends who have nowhere to live. Too often, we think of solutions for housing the homeless when they are already sleeping by the river in the cold weather. How truly wonderful it makes us feel when we help someone in need. Jesus said, "But when you give a feast, invite the poor, the crippled, the lame, the blind, and you will be blessed, because they cannot repay you. For you will be repaid at the resurrection of the just."[49]

Last year, my dear friends, Pastors Bill Muck and Angelo Austria set out on a mission to discover what the homeless actually experience as they

47. Gal. 1:10 (Emphasis, mine).
48. Gen. 2:10-14 (Emphasis, mine).
49. Luke 14:13-14 (ESV).

traverse a lonely city that often humiliates and rejects them. They spent a week living on the streets, learning, communing, listening, and caring for those who cannot otherwise care for themselves. Living a life full of denigration and squalor, Pastors Bill and Angelo experienced first-hand what it was like to feel alone and rejected by society. This is why the homeless are so important to God. If you have ears, listen to what the Spirit is saying.

Indeed, the homeless will always be among us. If the Spirit prompts you to help someone in need, please do not ignore His message. There is a reason for everything, and God certainly has His reasons for inspiring you to help someone in their time of desperation. Reach out to the needy today and be blessed because of it.

On the Twenty-Third Day

The evening approaches and darkness covers the land. It's as quiet as the dawn. The iridescent light of the crescent moon penetrates through the clouds as nocturnal creatures adorn the skies above. The world seems silent now, if only for a moment, and I find myself alone again with only my thoughts and the Holy Spirit to occupy my time.

Over the centuries the nations of the world have had many kings and rulers. The position of the king was much like the position of our president and was in place to govern the country and serve the people. King David was one of the greatest kings of all Israel, yet even David found himself caught up in sin. David made mistakes, just like us. Yet, David had a heart after God's own heart,[50] just like us.

Throughout history, God has used both the righteous and the unrighteous to advance His purposes. Pharaoh's heart was hardened, yet did he not eventually let God's people go? God is glorified in all good things, therefore whatever you do, do all to the glory of God.[51] Even our bad intentions can be used for good in God's sovereign plan.

Too often, we focus on governmental figures and how they are running the country contrary to how we want it run. We take hardline political positions, yet are we not still commanded to love our neighbor as ourselves?[52] Though we currently submit to an earthly ruler, we are governed eternally by a heavenly ruler: that ruler is Jesus Christ.[53] Our president runs the nation, but Jesus Christ runs the kingdom. Therefore, ultimately, it makes no

---

50. Acts 13:22 (Emphasis, mine).
51. 1 Cor. 10:31 (Emphasis, mine).
52. Lev. 19:18 (Emphasis, mine).
53. Rev. 19:16 (Emphasis, mine).

difference for us if the earthly ruler is one that we like or one that we do not like. By accepting Jesus Christ into our lives, we have already secured our place in the kingdom of heaven.

On the Twenty-Fourth Day

Just the other day, I felt so overwhelmed by life that I let the enemy fill my mind with doubts. I was dwelling upon the fact that I had a Greek test the next day, a sermon to write before Sunday, one-hundred plus pages to read for a graduate level course, and two of my friends wanted council for their loved ones who had recently passed. On top of that, I hadn't slept much because my wife and kids were sick, and I wanted to care for them. The great prophet, Jeremiah once said:

> But blessed is the one who trusts in the Lord, whose confidence is in him. They will be like a tree planted by the water that sends out its roots by the stream. It does not fear when heat comes; its leaves are always green. It has no worries in a year of drought and never fails to bear fruit.[54]

If we place our trust in the Lord in all circumstances, He will always come through for us. Abraham was considered righteous because of his faith;[55] Abraham had trusted that the Lord would provide a substitutionary sacrifice for Isaac, and He did.

We must not fear when the heat of life comes our way. God gives us what we can handle. I made it through my reading, my wife's sickness, counseling my friends, and I even got a ninety-five percent on my Greek exam. Through placing our trust and faith in the Lord, Jesus Christ, we will always succeed in everything we do, and we will never fail to reap the fruit of our labors.

On the Twenty-Fifth Day

The plants have come back to life from their state of death during the winter season. Lilies and roses begin to bloom as the sunshine pours down upon them and the fresh water from heaven quenches their thirst. Life around us is beautiful; you'll notice if you take the time to observe it.

---

54. Jer. 17:7-8 (NIV).
55. Rom. 4:3 (Emphasis, mine).

Like the flowers that were once dead, but now alive again, we too can be restored by the Lord of Hosts. The Psalmist asked for restoration of Israel; that the face of the Lord would shine down upon them.[56] We are all in need of restoration during some point in our lives. I pray that God restore us as a nation, that division would cease, and that we would continue to love each other despite our political differences. I ask that God restore our love for one another. Satan has caused too much hate and deception in this world. I pray that God will restore you back into a right-relationship with Him. Satan's goal is to separate us from the Father. We must be active in our quest to be united in Christ.

Perhaps you have found yourself distant from God? Though we often run from Him, He never runs from us. He is always there, whether we take the time to notice or not. God created us and said that it was *very* good.[57] The love of the Father for us is un-comprehendible, and without judgement, preconditions, or restrictions. God is love.[58] Therefore, we must show our love for Him by studying His Word, praying constantly, spending time in solitude with Him, and reaching out to another brother or sister in Christ when we are facing hardships or setbacks. God gave us the ability to think, love, be strong, and be courageous. There's no reason to let the devil prevent us from loving God or each other. In the end, love wins.

On the Twenty-Sixth day

The mist of the morning can be seen high in the mountains as travelers traverse the windy roads in the hopes of arriving safely at their destinations. The eerie feeling of the fog can stir up all kinds of thoughts as our minds begin to cast doubts upon what is real and what is imaginary. We might see something out of the corner of our eye that was once not there, or hear sounds that have been long since forgotten.

While the Bible does mention the word "ghost," it's hard to pinpoint an instance in which the ghost is referenced as a deceased loved-one. Certainly, king Saul conjures up the deceased prophet Samuel through the power of a medium, but does not Scripture tell us, "Do not turn to mediums or necromancers; do not seek them out, and so make yourselves unclean by them: I am the LORD your God."[59] Therefore, was the appearance of Samuel really Samuel, or something pretending to be Samuel?

56. Ps. 80:19 (Emphasis, mine).
57. Gen. 1:26-31 (Emphasis, mine).
58. 1 John 4:8 (Emphasis, mine).
59. Lev. 19:31 (ESV).

Popular reality shows try and romanticize the idea of psychic phenomenon; however, prohibitions against witchcraft and seeking the aid of spirits are even mentioned in the New Testament. Paul, himself, cast out an evil spirit from a woman fortune-teller.[60] Therefore, do not be fooled into believing that mediums can send you messages from your long-lost grandparents or loved ones. The dead in Christ are alive in Him once again and enjoying His presence.[61]

If you are grieving the loss of someone close to you, fear not, for if they have accepted Christ into their lives, they are in a much better place than we are. We are dead to our sins and alive in Christ because Jesus has already conquered death at the cross. Nothing can separate us from the love of the Father.[62]

On the Twenty-Seventh Day

Who has been influential in your spiritual life? I was sitting on my recliner the other day enjoying the many memories of those who had made such a powerful impression in my life. My liturgical exposure and formal introduction to Christianity came from my dear friend, Rev. Mike Patterson at the young age of ten. My charismatic influence and revelation of Scripture were not only inspired by the Holy Spirit, but also by my beloved friend and mentor, David Quinn, and my passion for spiritual formation and care were spurned by the infamous, Professor John McKendricks. I guess good things do tend to come in threes.

Mentors have existed throughout time and in all civilizations. Surely, God used someone to bring you to church, or to spark your interest in His Holy Word. The Apostle Philip once came across a eunuch who was reading a scroll of Isaiah. Led by the Spirit, Philip asked the eunuch if he understood what he was reading? The eunuch admitted that he could not understand what he was reading unless someone was available to guide him. After Philip revealed the power of the story of Jesus Christ, the eunuch couldn't wait to be baptized.[63] Philip was sent by God to open the eunuch's eyes to the gospel.

Like Philip, we too are sent by God to enter into someone's life. We often think of missionary work happening in a far-off region or distant land, yet people right here, right in the very town you live in, need Jesus Christ

---

60. Acts. 16:16-19 (Emphasis, mine).
61. 2 Cor. 5:8 (Emphasis, mine).
62. Rom. 8:39 (Emphasis, mine).
63. Acts 8:26-35 (Emphasis, mine).

in their lives. Perhaps, a close friend is struggling with something devastating, or someone of faith has fallen into temptation, or maybe it's someone that you barely know who has yet to hear the gospel message? Don't worry about why or where God will send you, just know that God *will* send you to advance His good purposes.

On the Twenty-Eighth Day

One of the fruits that make up the collective *Fruit of the Spirit*, is the fruit of self-control. It's very easy to tell someone else that they need to practice better self-control, but how easy is it for us to practice it ourselves? From personal experience, my guess is, not so easy. Yet, it is possible if we ask the Father to empower us in the Holy Spirit to resist temptation when it rears its seductive head in our lives.

We must choose self-control because we must choose Christ over the world.[64] The Apostle John tells us, "Everything in the world—the lust of the flesh, the lust of the eyes, and the pride of life—comes not from the Father but from the world."[65] Therefore, everything that tempts us comes from the world. Whether it's the delicious ice-cream that you cannot live without eating every night, or the more serious temptation of sexual immorality, pornography, and lust, the three enemies of the world are conjoined together in an attempt to separate us from the Father. Yet, fear not, for if God is for us, who can be against us?[66]

In order to overcome temptation and develop self-control, we must be honest with ourselves about our weaknesses. Perhaps, you have a weakness of over-indulgence while eating food? Ask the Lord's forgiveness and that He helps you to overcome it. Perhaps you struggle with patience and are quick to anger? By admitting that you have challenges in this area, both God, and your brothers and sisters in the faith can work with you to help you overcome your spiritual strongholds.

We all need help in our Christian walk sometimes. It's ok to reach out and ask for help. God is always there to help us in our time of need, so take the time to talk with Him today.

---

64. Mark 8:36-37 (Emphasis, mine).
65. 1 John 2:16 (NIV).
66. Rom. 8:31 (Emphasis, mine).

On the Twenty-Ninth Day

As the clouds move through the blue and crimson sky, the sun sets elegantly in the west. The world seems to stand still as God's creation gets ready for the evening. The bluebird and raven fly overhead as the wind gently blows through the trees. Have you enjoyed a good sunset lately?

When I first began preaching, I would listen to popular preachers on the radio and wish that I could sound just like them. I longed to have the passionate zeal and cadence of Billy Graham, or the soft-spoken, yet hard hitting message of Tim Keller, or even the exclusive accents of Ravi Zacharias or Alistair Begg. Then God began to reveal to me that I had my own style and it was just as effective as any of those preachers. I might not have the vast audiences that they have, but what I do have, God uses to further His kingdom.

We had a young Asian lady attend our church service along with her five-year-old son for the first-time last week. She was fairly shy and quiet during the service, but after the service was over, she gave me the best compliment. She said, "You were really great; you were on fire." I must admit, I did feel the Holy Spirit's presence during that service just a little bit more than I had in the past; to Him I give full credit. I can always tell when the Holy Spirit takes over, because I rarely need to look at my sermon notes.

God will use your specific gifts to advance His purposes. We never need to compare ourselves to someone else. Each of us was made by God in a wonderful and distinct way.[67] No two people are exactly the same. Even twins have different personalities; therefore, enjoy the way God made you, for there is no one else in all the earth or all the heavens that shares in your uniqueness.

On the Thirtieth Day

It's important to pray for our leaders. Not only for our leaders in the church, but also for our leaders in our nation. The great prophet Daniel prayed on behalf of Israel to repent of their sins; taking the blame for the nation upon himself during the Babylonian captivity.[68] In so doing, Daniel acted as an intercessor who prayed for those who disobeyed the Lord.

We too must intercede on behalf of those who profess to be Christians yet have turned away from the Lord. At the church I serve for, we pray each Sunday on behalf of our brothers and sisters around the world and for the

---

67. Ps. 139:14 (Emphasis, mine).
68. Dan. 9:1-19 (Emphasis, mine).

repentance of those who have separated themselves from the Lord through their sinful behaviors.

The Lord is a merciful and forgiving God. If not, wouldn't we all be destined to Hell for our transgressions? When someone wrongs us, we must forgive them as God has forgiven us. Jesus tells us, "If you forgive other people when they sin against you, your heavenly Father will also forgive you. But if you do not forgive others their sins, your Father will not forgive your sins."[69] Indeed, forgiveness is important.

When our nation's leaders make mistakes, they need forgiveness as well. Everyone makes mistakes because everyone is not perfect. We might traverse this land with good intentions, yet sometimes the way that appears to be right actually leads to death.[70] Therefore, practice obedience to the Lord regularly. If you find yourself going off-course, pray that the Lord of Hosts will restore you back to Him. There is a better road that leads to life, through the doorway of Jesus Christ.

On the Thirty-First Day

Pentecost

The Festival of Shavuot

Well, we've come to the end of May. How did you do in your walk with Christ this month? Do you feel closer to Him, or further away? Do you hear His voice, or do you only hear silence? Do you sense the presence of the Holy Spirit, or have you lost touch with Him? I truly pray that my words of encouragement will penetrate the deepest parts of your mind and soul, and also help you to realize that many of us face similar challenges in this life. I've just been blessed by making the effort to get to know my Lord and Savior more deeply through His Words, His presence, and from spending time with Him.

Today, we celebrate Pentecost. Pentecost was originally a feast to celebrate the revelation of God to Moses at Mount Sinai. The Book of Leviticus tells us, "From the day after the Sabbath, the day you brought the sheaf of the wave offering, count off seven full weeks. Count off fifty days up to the day after the seventh Sabbath, and then present an offering of new grain to

---

69. Matt. 6:14-15 (NIV).
70. Prov. 14:12 (Emphasis, mine).

the Lord."[71] Therefore, we commemorate Pentecost on the fiftieth day following the Sabbath.

Much like the Spirit of God revealed God's words to His people at Mount Sinai, the Spirit of God under the New Covenant reveals the Word of God in a deeper and more powerful way to those who have accepted His Son as their personal Lord and Savior; giving them the ability to witness the Gospel to the ends of the earth.[72]

Jesus said that He would send an advocate; the Spirit of truth, to be with us forever.[73] When you feel as though you are all by yourself in this world, realize that you are never alone. The mighty power of the Holy Spirit dwells inside of you forever, and no one can take that away.

---

71. Lev. 23:15-16 (NIV).
72. Acts 1:8 (Emphasis, mine).
73. John 14:16-17 (Emphasis, mine).

Chapter 6

"Obedience"

The Month of June

On the First Day

THE SUN SHINES BRIGHTLY over the city as the open fields begin to flourish with life. The lush, green grass is growing at a rapid pace while the neighbors do their best to groom it. A thunderstorm can be heard in the distance; threatening dark clouds make their way overhead as they burst open with the latter rains.

Jesus is the light in the darkness of our lives. His light cannot be hidden. We carry on Jesus' light through the power of the Holy Spirit who dwells inside of us. Long ago, God separated light from darkness;[1] therefore, we must let our light shine before others so that they might see our good deeds and glorify our Father in Heaven.[2]

God the Father is also light. In Him there is no darkness. He is the light that overcomes the darkness. This is why Satan is so active at night, because our sins are hidden in the darkness. If the sins that you are committing, you wish not to commit, then it is no longer you who are committing them, but rather it is the sin living within you.[3]

Shine God's light into the hearts of those around you. You don't need to go out of your way to accomplish this. Simply being in the presence of someone who is living in darkness will speak volumes. The world takes notice when something as powerful as the presence of the Holy Spirit is in their midst. You are ambassadors for Christ Jesus; you have a flame inside of you that can never be extinguished.

---

1. Gen. 1:4 (Emphasis, mine).
2. Matt. 5:16 (Emphasis, mine).
3. Rom. 7:15-20 (Emphasis, mine).

On the Second Day

I love serving people. Most of my secular jobs have been in the service industry. At the age of twenty-one, I began working in the hotel business as a bellman and valet attendant, and later found employment as a home furniture salesman. Having a natural heart for people has helped me to build great relationships with both co-workers, and clients. And, I even made a few dollars doing it.

In life, we have to be willing to set boundaries. One of my co-workers once said, "Don't let people mistake your kindness for weakness." Sadly, every employer seems to have at least one person on staff who tries to do this. When I worked as a lifeguard at the age of sixteen, I would often find myself cleaning the locker rooms by myself because no one felt the need to help me; even though it was their job as well. Perhaps, my insecurities back then made it easier for me to be taken advantage of. Fortunately, as I got older, I became more confident in myself and my abilities.

As a pastor, I find myself eager to help everyone that needs me, but much like my experience as a lifeguard, I often begin doing more than I can handle. The Apostle Paul tells us, "Each one should test their own actions. Then they can take pride in themselves alone, without comparing themselves to someone else, for each one should carry their own load."[4]

Therefore, if you find that you are taking on more than you can handle, or that you are carrying the load of both you, and someone else, stand firm and tell the respective party that you need to focus on God and yourself right now and will be happy to help them out later where you can. Allowing yourself to get burned out will be of little benefit to anyone.

On the Third Day

Another beautiful day is before us as we look to glorify the Father once again. The brilliance of the sun's light reflects upon the moon as it shines throughout the night, lighting our path in the most luminous way. Are we not beautiful reflections of the Father's light as well?

Obedience is very important to the Lord. When God rescued Moses and the Israelites from their captivity in Egypt, He told them, "Now if you obey me fully and keep my covenant, then out of all nations you will be my treasured possession. Although the whole earth is mine."[5] Indeed, even

---

4. Gal. 6:4-5 (NIV).
5. Ex. 19:5 (NIV).

despite their disobedience, God's mercy was so great that He still gave them chance after chance to return to right-standing before Him.

I know from first-hand experience how difficult obeying God's commands can actually be. I mean, who can actually keep track of all six hundred and thirteen commands given by God during Old Testament times? I have some good news for you; you only need to remember these two: Love God with all of your heart, mind, soul, and strength; and love your neighbor as yourself. There is no greater command than these.[6]

You see, if you keep these two commandments, then you will automatically keep the rest of the requirements of the law, because the law will then be written on your heart.[7] I realize obedience is not a natural thing for us; believe me, I've been there, but we must try. When we face our creator on judgment day, will it make a good defense if we say, "I decided it was easier to disobey God than to obey Him, so I chose the former?" The more that I obey these two commandments, the further I separate myself from sin. The less I obey these two commandments, the further I separate myself from God. Which path are you taking?

On the Fourth Day

Many millennia ago, kings were established to rule and reign over the people of the land. Prior to this time, God had used the great prophets to oversee the land and speak on behalf of Him to His people. However, God's chosen people began questioning the true intentions of the prophets, and decided they wanted a king to rule over them like all the other nations had.[8]

This displeased the Lord, for He was ruling over them from the beginning. Samuel warned the Israelites that they would surely be forced to pay taxes to the king, give the king their property, women, men for war, livestock, bakers, choice goods, and other material possessions. Yet, the Israelites refused to listen and still demanded a king, so the Lord gave them what they wanted.[9] They soon ended up with king after king; some were great leaders, such as David and Solomon, yet others did evil in the Lord's eyes, such as Ahab and Ahaziah.

Sometimes, when we don't listen to the Lord, He will give us what we want to remind us that our dependency should be upon Him instead of

---

6. Mark 12:29-31 (Emphasis, mine).
7. Rom. 2:15 (Emphasis, mine).
8. 1 Sam. 8:1-4 (Emphasis, mine).
9. 1 Sam. 8:19-22 (Emphasis, mine).

upon the world.[10] We don't always understand the Lord's ways, but I assure you, they are without fault. Human beings will always have a motive for what they do, because we have flesh that is tainted from the fall. Yet, God is without ulterior motives, because He is pure in all ways. God's motivation is love, and everything He does for us He does with that in mind.

When you feel as though you cannot live without something; that the material possession you *must* have needs to be bought at any cost, remember to ask yourself what is motivating you to have it? Are you desiring it to glorify the Lord, or are you desiring it to glorify yourself? In all things you do, do it with your whole heart, as working for the Lord and not human masters.[11]

On the Fifth Day

The warm evening is inhabited by all kinds of people from all walks of life. Rich people, poor people, people of all races and ethnic backgrounds, people of all genders, single people, married people, young people, and old people. We are all beautiful occupants of this earth that God has given us.

King David was anointed as king by the prophet Samuel at a very young age. He displayed the characteristics that God was looking for in someone that should have an earthly leadership position. He was strong, kind to others, wise, humble, made mistakes, but asked for forgiveness, sang to the Lord, obeyed the Lord, and prayed to the Lord regularly. Does the leader of the company you work for exhibit these characteristics?

God saw in David a foreshadowing of a future king who would reign forever. Therefore, The Lord established a covenant with David.[12] This king would have all of David's strengths, yet none of his weaknesses. He would be a servant to all, a powerful healer, a great preacher and teacher. Indeed, He would be like no other man before Him. He was none other than, Jesus Christ.

Like us, David had his share of sins. He once sent Uriah into war so that he would be killed by the opposing army.[13] Yet, David still had a heart after God's own heart. How can this be? This is due to the fact, not that David sinned, but that David had genuine repentance from his sin. We too must genuinely repent and turn back towards the Father when we sin. If our hearts are fashioned after God's own heart, we will gladly turn away from

---

10. Ps. 81:11-13 (Emphasis, mine).
11. Col. 3:23 (Emphasis, mine).
12. 2 Sam. 7:12-16 (Emphasis, mine).
13. 2 Sam. 11:14-17 (Emphasis, mine).

our sins and be reconciled back to the Father through our faith in His Son, Jesus Christ.

On the Sixth Day

Jesus Christ atoned for our sins by shedding His blood on the cross as a covering for us. In the Old Testament, God instructed Moses and the Hebrews to place the blood of an unblemished lamb over the top of the doorframes and doorposts of their homes in order that they would be passed over by the death angel and their lives be spared.[14] In this same way, we have the blood of the unblemished lamb covering us because of our faith in Jesus Christ. We need not worry about death, for death no longer has any power over us.[15]

God has always required a sacrifice to atone for sin. The sacrifice to atone for the sins of the Israelites was first consecrated by the high priest once a year in the Most Holy Place of the Tabernacle.[16] Yet, Jesus Christ was able to atone for our sins *once and for all* through His death and resurrection. This is because mankind owed a debt to God and it had to be paid by someone who was not a debtor. Angels couldn't do it because they are not human; regular human beings couldn't do it, because they still owed the debt. Therefore, the only one who could satisfy what God required had to come from someone that was both God and a sinless human: that someone was Jesus Christ.

Are you actively practicing obedience to God on a daily basis? Are you enjoying the blessings that God has given you? I make a habit of thanking God every day for the things I have in this life. I try and thank Him for both the blessings, and challenges in my life, as I know He has a reason for providing me with both. If you don't thank Him for anything else, thank Him for your eternal salvation that was bought at a price. The price of a life that was paid for due to our transgressions.

On the Seventh Day

About six months ago, I got a text from a good friend of mine whose father was in hospice and had only a few weeks to live. He asked if there was any way that I could put together a Bible study on death and dying and teach it

---

14. Ex. 12:23 (Emphasis, mine).
15. 1 Cor. 15:55 (Emphasis, mine).
16. Lev. 16:32-34 (Emphasis, mine).

to his family as soon as possible. I had a guest lecture I was conducting that week on Pneumatology, and a Greek exam to study for. Perhaps, in my own lack of faith, I thought that I might not have enough time before he passes to meet with them, but I went ahead and committed to a time and day, trusting that the Lord would work it out. As it turned out, my instructor canceled my Greek exam, and my lecture went over well because I had prepared my notes a few weeks prior and just had to review them.

After a few days, The Holy Spirit gave me a great study on death and dying that addressed both believers and non-believers alike. I covered ghosts, and mediums, and everything in between. Thanks to the Holy Spirit for guiding my words, I only needed to look at about half of my notes. The rest was taught from my heart and my own experiences.

When we feel overwhelmed in life, remember that God orchestrated these events at the beginning of time. He puts people in our path knowing that something we will say will alter their course and lead them to Him. Out of the fifteen people at that Bible study, three reached out to me to learn more about Jesus Christ. Perhaps, they would have never thought to seek Him if I had made excuses for myself and not shown up that night. God's work is not finished in you; therefore, be confident of this, that He who began a good work in you, will carry it to completion until the return of Jesus Christ.[17]

On the Eighth Day

As the summer months continue, the warm weather prompts the squirrel and chipmunk to store food away for the coming winter months. Storing up various nuts and grains will truly have paid off when the trees are bare during the cold season.

Much like the natural instincts of animals to store away food for the winter, we too must prepare for untimely events that might take place in our lives. Joseph was elevated to the second highest position in all of Egypt because he correctly interpreted Pharaoh's dream about seven years of plenty followed by seven years of famine.[18] During the seven years of plenty, Joseph stored up warehouses full of fruits, vegetables, crops, and grains. His father and brothers were eventually reunited with him in Egypt due to the fact that there was no food in their homeland because of the great famine.

---

17. Phil. 1:6 (Emphasis, mine).
18. Gen. 41:25-36 (Emphasis, mine).

Jesus tells us that no one but the Father, knows the day or the hour of His return.[19] Therefore, we must always be prepared for Him when He comes back. You do not want to be caught trying to fill your lamps with oil, while the great marriage celebration is taking place. It's possible that as you return, after having been gone from seeking to know Him, that He will answer the door and say, "I do not know you."[20]

I cannot stress enough the importance of building your relationship with Jesus Christ while you still have time. Tomorrow is never guaranteed for us, and we do not know when Jesus will come back; therefore, always be on guard; be watchful for the great day of the Lord. We don't want to be among those who were waiting until the last minute to get to know Him. By then it may be too late. Are you prepared?

On the Ninth Day

King Solomon was considered one of the wisest kings in all of history. The Lord's hand was on him in so many ways. When approached by two prostitutes who each claimed the other had killed their newborn baby, he suggested they cut the child in half and give a piece to each of them. Don't worry, the baby wasn't harmed at all, because Solomon knew that the true mother would not allow her baby to be killed and instead, would rather give it to the false mother.[21]

Solomon later wrote the Book of Proverbs in which his wisdom flourished in writing. Through the divine inspiration of God Himself, King Solomon warns about something that we all can relate to, at least indirectly if not directly. That topic is a dirty, four-letter word called, "lust." Indeed, Solomon knew of Satan's deception and enticements well, for His father David had first-hand experience with lust when he first noticed Solomon's mother, Bathsheba bathing.[22]

Proverbs chapter five, warns us men, not to be intoxicated with another man's wife.[23] Solomon says, "Keep to a path far from her, and not go near the door of her house.[24] These are very wise words, for in my past, even I found myself easily tempted when going near the home of a woman who was in a marriage covenant with someone else.

19. Matt. 24:36 (Emphasis, mine).
20. Matt. 25:10-13 (Emphasis, mine).
21. 1 Kgs. 3:16-28 (Emphasis, mine).
22. 2 Sam. 11:2-4 (Emphasis, mine).
23. Prov. 5:20 (Emphasis, mine).
24. Prov. 5:8 (NIV).

Satan will use careless thoughts to build upon. Sooner or later, if you let these thoughts control your actions, you will find yourself giving into temptations far worse than you could ever imagine. In this particular example, lust in men is the culprit; however, Satan does not discriminate between men and women, race, or economic status. Satan's goal is to separate us. His goal has always been to separate us. Listen to what the Spirit has to say.

On the Tenth Day

The dawn breaks as the sun slowly rises. Mankind enjoys the cool air of the summer morning as they walk their dogs along the river near downtown. I stop into my favorite coffee shop near the river and order a mocha as I peer out of the large glass windows at the cars that drive slowly by.

Aesthetics have such an impact on our experiences. Whether it's sitting in front of a warm fireplace during the cold winter months or staring out at the vastness of the ocean in the middle of July, powerful things happen to our senses when we are in the midst of tranquil surroundings.

The early church struggled with the veneration of icons. On the one hand, God forbids any images to be made of Him or of anything in heaven above.[25] Yet, we know that He instructed Moses to carve out cherubim's in gold.[26] How can we reconcile the two? God forbid the Israelites to carve out images of Him because He knew that they would turn and worship the image as an idol.[27] Whereas, the Cherubim adorned the ark as a sacred decoration that was to be admired, not worshiped.

We too, must be careful not to turn images we create into idols that we worship. Other religions worship statues and idols made of stone, yet what can inanimate objects accomplish in the lives of their worshipers? Surely, they cannot dwell inside of their worshiper or help guide them in their quest for sanctification. Can they die for their worshipers and forgive their sins? Do they offer their worshiper salvation? Jesus Christ is the living Word because He is intimately involved in every aspect of our lives. He is the only God worthy of our worship.

---

25. Ex. 20:4 (Emphasis, mine).
26. Ex. 25:18 (Emphasis, mine).
27. Ex. 20:5 (Emphasis, mine).

On the Eleventh Day

Sometimes, we may find ourselves questioning God's intentions. If God loves us so much, why is there cancer, famine, diseases, and homelessness? Why do some people flourish who have turned from God, and others suffer who are faithful to God? Why did I survive, yet my close friend didn't?

When I was watching the memorial service of President George H.W. Bush on the news, I was moved by two things: 1) his capacity to honor his country and its citizens, regardless of political affiliation and 2) that he took the time to write five to ten notes per day to check in on people that he knew. George H.W. Bush questioned why he had survived being shot down by the enemy during World War II; he found his answer much later in life. Bush would later become a Texas representative in Congress, Ambassador to the U.N., Chairman of the Republican National Committee, and President of the United States.

The early disciples had a plan orchestrated by God to advance the kingdom of heaven. The Lord chose the most unlikely people to act as His ambassadors, and spread Christianity to the ends of the earth. With honor and grace, these brave men, and many since, have given their lives for the sake of us, whom would later reap the harvest of the seeds that they had once sewn.

We may not know what God has planned out for us in the future, but we can be confident that He does have a plan for us. The impact you make in someone's life will have a great ripple effect, like a rock gliding across a lake of glass. Never take your life for granted. There is a purpose for you that you may only notice many years later after looking back at your life and realizing why God kept you alive.

On the Twelfth Day

The beautiful landscape of the Sierra Nevadas is home to many different people. Some are here to enjoy the serenity of the great lake that is nestled high on top of the mountains. Others come to prosper economically. Still, others move here to retire and enjoy the four seasons that Northern Nevada has to offer them. Wherever you call home, take the time to look outside at what the Lord has created. You might just be surprised at what you see.

Honesty is very important to God, despite the fact that the world might tell you otherwise. When we start with a small lie, it will eventually lead to a bigger lie, and sooner or later it will ultimately lead to habitual lies. Therefore, we must be honest with ourselves and one another.

During the time of the Old Testament, moneychangers and merchants would use scales to weigh the goods or products sold against the counter-weights. Of course, the more the items weighed, the more they cost. Corrupted merchants would use fake counter-weights for the scales that they used. This upsets the Lord very much for Proverbs says, "The LORD detests dishonest scales, but accurate weights find favor with him."[28]

Much like honest merchants, we too must find favor with the Lord in our work. In all things, have integrity, honesty, compassion, and a sense of pride. Your character will be reflected in the outcome of your deeds. If you always cut corners, or take advantage of others, God will surely judge you for it. When I take on a task, I try to do it to the best of my ability because I am not just working for the world, but I am working for God, Himself. If you do your best in all things, you can find joy even in failure. The beauty of the cross is that we can cast all of our burdens there and immediately feel the weight lifted off of our shoulders.

On the Thirteenth Day

It's never too late to turn from your sins and come to salvation in the Lord, Jesus Christ. The Bible says, "He is patient with you, not wanting anyone to perish, but everyone to come to repentance."[29] If you are reading these words and feel as though your heart is longing to learn more about Jesus Christ, then make the time to get to know Him. Find a good Christ-centered, faithful friend, or Christian small group that you can join and learn about Christ from the priesthood of believers.

Though the Lord is patient, Satan will use that patience to his advantage. If we repeatedly turn away from God, we might reach a point of no return because our hearts have grown too cold, much like the criminal on the cross who said, "Aren't you the Messiah? Save yourself and us!"[30]

A good friend and co-worker once told me he was going to wait until he retired to investigate religion. Saddened by this, I began to ask God to intervene. After much prayer, I was happy to discover that he enjoyed a book on heaven that I'd given him, and he even purchased a Bible to read and ask me questions from! God is great, indeed!

Many people in the East during the second and third centuries, would wait until they were literally on their death beds to bring in a priest to baptize them. This wasn't necessarily because they all came to Christ at their

---

28. Prov. 11:1 (NIV).
29. 2 Pet. 3:9 (NIV).
30. Luke 23:39 (NIV).

dying moment, but rather, that they wanted an excuse to live a sinful life up until their final breath. Do you think God was fooled?

If you are "on the fence" with your faith, don't delay. Don't let Satan take advantage of God's patience with you and lead you into eternal devastation. The kingdom of Heaven is at hand! Will you be a part of God's kingdom today?

On the Fourteenth Day

It never ceases to amaze me how God uses us to advance His purposes. I went to coffee this morning with a lady who was about to lose her children in a custody battle with her ex-husband because she had recently lost her job and was staying with friends until she could get on her feet again. In the process of counseling her, I discovered that God was giving me words of encouragement for her that I hadn't thought of myself.

Shortly after we parted ways, I walked towards the door to leave and behold, my dear friend and colleague, Will was sitting there by himself and we began to engage in great conversation. I hadn't seen Will in over a year, so it was great to catch up. He was set to graduate in a few weeks with a BA in Bible and Theology and struggling to choose a master's program. Being a Registered Nurse already, he could do either, a Master of Nursing, a Master of Counseling, or my personal favorite, a Master of Divinity Degree.

I could sense his challenge in choosing the right path. Then, I thought about it for a moment and realized that no matter what path he chose, God was with Him. I had this same type of dilemma when deciding which church I would try and serve at when I started Bible College. I could remain where I was; although, I was extremely stressed out and unhappy with the way the church leadership was running the church, or I could pray that God would open up another door for me to walk through. God chose the latter for me. You see, God wants us to be happy as well as obedient. If we simply suffered through life doing things we didn't enjoy doing, then what would be the point in having faith that God will provide something better for us?

God has a plan for each and every one of us. Sometimes, you have to go through trials first, before you realize that you will eventually end up exactly where God meant for you to be.

On the Fifteenth Day

The grandfather clock rings twice as I awake from my evening slumber. My wife is asleep next to me in bed and I find myself in prayer to the Lord as I wake up to the illumination of my cell phone from notifications that have long since passed.

I really didn't sleep well at all last night. Scrolling through Facebook, I took notice of a young lady who posted that she was going to commit suicide. Not knowing her personally, I read through the comments to see if anyone was able to reach out to her to prevent such a tragedy. Unfortunately, no one was able to get her to respond. Something prompted me to get out of bed and reach out to her directly. That something was the Holy Spirit.

I'm glad I listened to God and intervened. When we were messaging back and forth, I couldn't get her to reveal her address to me so that I could send an ambulance for her. After reaching out to three other church leaders, my friend Michael responded. Together, we were able to break through to her and get her the help she needed. I took some criticism for involving another pastor into the situation, but God had an obvious plan for both of us to be involved. She actually related better to Michael than to me. Everything has worked out so far, and this young lady is getting the treatment she needs for her depression and is in the process of changing her living situation.

It's important to have accountability partners with you during serious interventions. This is where I should have heeded the advice of my, much wiser, Christian leader. Scripture tells us, "Let the wise hear and increase in learning."[31] Everything turned out okay in this situation, but I've certainly heard of things not going well, and no witnesses were there to verify or deny the claims. The enemy is always scheming to harm us; therefore, we must always be on guard.

On the Sixteenth Day

Have you ever wondered why forgiveness is available to us? Shouldn't God just expect us to do everything right? Yet, if we *could* do everything right, then there would be no need for forgiveness. Indeed, the Lord knows we cannot, not sin;[32] therefore, He provides a way for us to be forgiven; ultimately, in Christ Jesus, and situationally, by asking for forgiveness and through genuine repentance of our sins.

In ancient times, the Hebrew people would establish a covenant, or promise with each other by splitting an animal in two and putting each piece of the animal on the ground. The first person would do a figure eight around the pieces, followed by the second person doing a figure eight around the pieces. This was like saying, "If I don't uphold my end of the covenant, let

---

31. Prov. 1:5 (ESV).
32. Eccl. 7:20 (Emphasis, mine).

this happen to me!" And, vice versa. You might remember, that during God's covenant with Abraham, Abraham was actually put into a deep sleep in which he couldn't walk through the pieces to fulfill his end of the covenant. God moved through the pieces in the form of a smoldering pot, but Abraham could not move, he could only watch a vision of this happening.[33]

Abraham could not go through the pieces to uphold his end of the covenant because God knew that Abraham's ancestors would not be able to fulfill their part of obedience to God. In essence, God was saying, "If I don't uphold my end of this covenant, let this happen to me . . . And if you don't uphold your end of this covenant, let this happen to *me*. And, it did, at the cross.

If you find yourself slipping into sin once and a while, it's not the end of the world as long as you ask for forgiveness. God knows we still have flesh, which is why He sent His Son to die for us. If we could become sinless ourselves, then Christ died for nothing.

On the Seventeenth Day

The mind is a powerful thing, and often something that the early Greek philosophers would connect with the soul. When I was taking undergraduate courses at Multnomah University, the Philosophy professor, Dr. Gurney, used to pray for us before each class thanking the Lord that He gave us minds to think with, and hearts to love with.

My son, Brett, has such a brilliant mind. At the age of six, his I.Q. was tested at 136. He would ask me question after question about everything from who God is, to how the human body works, to engineering, physics, and astronomy. Like Brett, most of us have inquisitive minds. God has given us great minds to understand His word; therefore, we, along with the power of the Holy Spirit can certainly discern lies that we hear or read, from the truth.

My Early Church History Professor, Tony Slavin would often say, "Don't be too hard on the early church Fathers for their beliefs, they might not have been wrong, we might be." This is so true. Though we do have powerful minds, God's mind is far greater holding the mysteries in whom are hidden all the treasures of wisdom and knowledge.[34]

I once came across a Facebook posting in which scientific evolution and the big bang theory were clearly advocated for. I couldn't help but respond that someone (thing) had to cause the big bang, if there even was a

---

33. Gen. 15:17-18 (Emphasis, mine).
34. Col. 2:3 (Emphasis, mine).

big bang. Logically, creation cannot create itself. I was so quick to prove my adversary wrong, that I found myself in constant banter with virtual non-believers and didn't take the time to understand why they believed the way that they did. Perhaps my arguments just provoked them to argue back.

Our minds and hearts are beautiful tools that God gives us to enlighten others with *His* knowledge; not impress ourselves with ours.

On the Eighteenth Day

As the clouds begin to form over the valley, a cool mist in the air can be felt. The distinct aroma of rain makes its way towards the city as the thunderstorms begin to rumble above. Like a flowing river, the winds of change blow swiftly past as I embrace the day that God has planned for me.

Have you ever been in competition with someone for a leadership or management position? My guess is you have, especially if you've lived on this earth for a while. We tend to be naturally competitive creatures.

Moses was a great leader, but his job could be very stressful at times. He once encountered opposition to his leadership by Korah and the sons of Ruben. They were upset because they felt that all in the congregation were holy and didn't understand why it was that Moses and Aaron were in charge. So, Moses decided to have them both meet in the morning and let God choose between them; the one that God drew near would be considered the holy one to lead His people. As soon as Moses finished declaring that the Lord would surely kill the evil men of Korah by un-natural means, the ground opened up and swallowed them, with all their households and all the people who belonged to Korah![35]

Often times, we long for positions of power within our careers or communities, but make sure God's hand is the one guiding you. If you try and remove someone from their sovereign appointment, you might just find yourself fighting against God. When I was younger, I thought that being a leader would be the best thing in the world, until I actually became one. Not only did I have to learn to *lead* people, I also had to learn to *relate* to people. I think that sometimes we make things harder on ourselves than they have to be.

---

35. Num. 16:1-35 (Emphasis, mine).

On the Nineteenth Day

Have you ever been to the ocean? Its beauty and power are truly something to marvel at. My younger sister decided to get married on one of the beaches of San Luis Obispo, California. As I peered out at the waves, took in the vastness of the water, and could smell the saltiness of the ocean, I began to realize just how big our God truly is.

Salt has a lot of symbolism in the Bible. It can be used to preserve something, add flavor, purify something or someone, or even used in punishment for disobeying the Lord.[36] Through the covenant of salt, all of the contributions made to the Lord through Aaron, including the firstborn man and animal were redeemed back to the Lord.[37]

I'm not a big fan of eating sushi. My wife loves sushi, so reluctantly, I'll tag along every once in a while, but when I actually do eat fish, I prefer them to be cooked. Have you ever wondered why the ocean fish we eat don't taste overly salty? I mean, sushi, before it becomes sushi, spends its entire life swimming in an ocean full of salt. It has salt all over its body, in its gills, in its lungs. The fish quite literally breaths the salt! Yet, when the restaurant prepares it for us to eat, it doesn't taste that salty.

This takes place because even though the fish spends its whole life surrounded by salt, the salt doesn't consume him. Therefore, even if we spend our entire lives surrounded by sin, the sin does not have to consume us, because we have Christ Jesus as our redeemer. Like the covenant of salt in the Old Testament, God establishes a new covenant with us through the death and resurrection of Jesus Christ. All we must do is put our trust and faith in Him and we too will be preserved from the sin that tries to overtake us.

On the Twentieth Day

I've always enjoyed participating in or listening to a lively conversation. Many years ago, while working in the transportation industry, we had this exuberant character named, Joseph. Syrian by descent, Joseph was always the life of the party. He could talk on and on about any subject, but he mostly enjoyed telling driving stories of when he was younger. Everyone loves Joseph.

Sometimes, when we want to be the center of attention, we lose sight of the fact that the person we are conversing with wants to speak as well. My oldest daughter, Michelle speaks very quietly and thoughtfully. Sometimes

---

36. Gen. 19:26 (Emphasis, mine).
37. Num. 18:1-19 (Emphasis, mine).

she has to think about what she is saying, even after she begins saying it. Her less than patient older brother, will often start talking before Michelle can finish her sentence, so I'm constantly reminding him that he has to wait until his sister finishes what she's saying, before I'll listen to his plethora of questions about the world and everything in it. Their interaction reminds me that conversations are best practiced with dialogue, not monologue.

I have even had professors and church leaders who want to talk so much that they will begin to respond to my questions or statements before I can finish with useful and pertinent information. Solomon tells us, "To answer before listening is a folly and a shame."[38]

Therefore, take the time to listen to one another in godly love. Your brother or sister in Christ may be trying to communicate with you in deeper ways than you realize, but because you keep interjecting into the conversation before they can finish their thought, they get discouraged and may stop speaking altogether. No one, that I've ever heard of, got upset because someone listened to them too much.

On the Twenty-First Day

Father's Day

Father's Day is a time in which we pay tribute to our fathers for working so hard to ensure that we have a good life, food to eat, a roof over our heads, and material possessions. At least, that is what my stepfather helped to provide for me, and my younger brother and sister as we were growing up.

My stepfather and I didn't have a great relationship when I was younger. Perhaps, his lack of affection or sarcasm helped to contribute to ill feelings on my part. However, he is very intelligent, has been there for me when I really needed him, and always had a dependable, high-level government job which provided well for our family.

As the years went by, I started becoming more insecure and less confident in myself or my abilities. I found security and compassion in the church, and for that, I am forever grateful. Yet, something inside was always needing more, and I allowed myself to be entertained by alcohol and promiscuity. It wasn't until later, when I asked God to help get me back on the path of a healthy relationship with Him, that I finally broke free from Satan's strongholds, returned to the church, and experienced financial success.

I'm happy to say that my stepfather and I have a much better relationship today; perhaps, even a great relationship. This is because I put God first

---

38. Prov. 18:13 (NIV).

in everything that I do, which helps to improve my relationship with not only Him, but with others as well.

If you haven't had the best relationship with your earthly father, you're not alone, so don't give up. Give it some time. Work on building your relationship with your heavenly Father and see what happens. God and His angels are in your corner. You might be surprised by the outcome. I certainly was.

On the Twenty-Second Day

Back in college, we had a guest speaker who was the senior pastor of a charismatic church in the area. I remember he spoke about dealing with people who claimed to have prophetic messages from God, or spoke in tongues without an interpreter, or tried to get leadership positions in the church, regardless if they believed in the present gifts of the Spirit or not. Yet, one thing he emphasized more than once was that he has always had a good name and reputation in the area.

When I hear people proclaim that they have a great reputation, I automatically think that they are just saying that because the opposite is actually true. However, having a good name is biblical. Proverbs tells us, "A good name is more desirable than great riches; to be esteemed is better than silver or gold."[39]

When I was in the Air Force, many years ago, I had a friend in basic training who told me that our work reflects who we are. In other words, if our work is sloppy, people will judge us to be sloppy. If the work we do is above and beyond what is required, people will associate us as a person who goes the extra mile at all times. If we do everything at the last minute (which is my biggest pet-peeve), then people will label us as procrastinators. If we show compassion for one another, people will see the Spirit of God inside of us.

It's important to work hard at everything you do. Take pride in your work. Because of our brokenness, society is quick to label people in certain ways. Do you want to be known as the person who always oversleeps, shows up late, does half the job, and could care little about someone else? Or do you prefer to be known as the person who always does their best, cares about him or herself, and has compassion for others? Which reputation do you choose to live up to?

---

39. Prov. 22:1 (NIV).

On the Twenty-Third Day

If you've been reading this devotional consistently, you may recall the day when I talked about giving to the Lord and how when I was down to my last dollars, I gave to the church in faith, regardless of my financial situation. You may remember that I had $2,300.00 deposited into my bank account a few days after that.

That lesson wasn't just about obedience, but it was about trust as well. We can be obedient to the Lord but still lack trust in Him. Or, we can be trusting in the Lord, but not be obedient which allows Him to *be* trusted.

When I lived in Las Vegas with my ex-girlfriend, I was not that happy. Sure, the money I made was great and I had a nice rental home in Henderson, but I never felt like I was advancing in my walk with Christ. In fact, I felt quite the opposite. My ex enjoyed the party life and was always out drinking. Sexual temptation was all around and easily accessible. I remember praying to the Lord to get me out of the toxic relationship that I was in. I lacked the faith and obedience to listen to what the Lord was saying to me, until finally, after three years of struggles and setbacks, I placed my trust in God to guide me to a better place. That was when a position opened up at a hotel in Reno that was full-time, with benefits, and paid well enough that I could support myself.

Faith, trust, and obedience all go hand-in-hand when serving the Lord. The Bible tells us that, "Those who know your name trust in you, for you, Lord, have never forsaken those who seek you."[40] I find that the more obedient I am, the more the Lord blesses me. The more that the Lord blesses me, the more trust I have in Him. And, the more trust I have in Him, the more faith I have that He will always be there to guide me, no matter what choices I make in this life.

On the Twenty-Fourth Day

Evenings, for me, can seem so relaxing sometimes. After a hard day of work or school, it's nice to come home, unwind, and spend time with my wife and kids. Last night, I took the kids around the block on their bikes as I walked behind them with my daughter, Makalya (she was on a small scooter). As I journeyed through the neighborhood with them, I realized that I was constantly looking for potential dangers that might come in their path. Dangers such as oncoming traffic, loose dogs, other bike-riders, or

---

40. Ps. 9:10 (NIV).

bumps in the road. I suppose most parents try and protect their children in the same ways.

As we get older, we go through an adolescent stage in which we are not quite adults, but not quite children either. Sometimes, by the way he talks to me, I wonder if my son is already a teenager, even though he's only ten years old. As we grow, we learn important lessons along the way. Some are proactive on the part of our parents; Some lessons are due to the consequences of our actions; but, regardless of how we learn things in our lives, God is always there to help guide us. Just because bad things happen, doesn't mean that God has abandoned us. Perhaps, He was giving our adversary the free-will to make a better choice.

If you've struggled with your past or are currently in a situation that you don't want to be in, pray to God that He will deliver you from your enemies, both physically and spiritually. Perhaps a more powerful prayer than that, would be to pray that your enemies turn from their sins and accept Jesus Christ into their hearts. If they do this, they will surely feel remorse for what they've done to you and repent of their sinful behavior at the same time. This is why Jesus tells us to bless those who curse us and to pray for those who mistreat us.[41]

On the Twenty-fifth Day

We've all heard the phrase, "Live each day like it's your last." Yet, I would prefer to say, "Live each day like it's your last chance, while on this earth, to get to know Jesus Christ." A bit longer than the common phrase but filled with more meaning. That might change your perception of what living a complete life, truly is. No longer is the focus on ourselves and what makes us happy, but the focus is on Jesus Christ and how we can please Him.

This paradigm shift is an essential one. For, eternal life is the knowledge of God, and Jesus Christ whom He sent.[42] We're only on this earth a short time compared to the endlessness of eternity. A good illustration is this. Picture a long rope, perhaps two-hundred feet long. Now, picture a quarter-inch of black electrical tape wrapped around one end of the rope. You have the image in your mind? Ok, now envision tying off the end of the rope with the black electrical tape and unwinding the rest of the rope around your backyard. The tapped end represents our time on this earth; whereas, the rest of the rope represents eternity.

---

41. Luke 6:28 (Emphasis, mine).
42. John 17:3 (Emphasis, mine).

We are so concerned with what other people think about us, that we forget that it's what God thinks about us that matters. Unfortunately, the two may not always line up, because God doesn't judge us based on our possessions, looks, or earthly achievements, God judges us based on our hearts.

Sadly, my stepmother passed away last December from a long battle with cancer. Since she was a believer, I hope that she made time to get to know more about Jesus Christ before she passed. Certainly, she will have time to get to know Him in heaven. Therefore, if you find yourself concentrating too much on your earthly achievements and not enough on your heavenly achievements, change your pattern. Tomorrow is never guaranteed.

On the Twenty-Sixth Day

The wind blows through the trees this afternoon as the long swaying branches move back and forth like the pendulum of a grandfather clock. The cool air brings relief to those who have basked in the dry heat of the day. The swimming pools are full of children as the neighborhood ice cream truck passes by.

We should have confidence in our abilities and gifts. Yet, too much confidence can lead to us soliciting compliments from people instead of receiving them willingly. We then begin to turn our acknowledgement of a job well done into an idol that we set up for ourselves that longs to be worshipped. This is why Paul says, "May I never boast except in the cross of our Lord Jesus Christ."[43]

To Christ goes all of the credit, because through the Holy Spirit come all of our gifts.[44] If we credit ourselves with our gifts, then we do not acknowledge the One who died on the cross to send us the Holy Spirit. Not all of us have the same gifts; but, collectively, we make up all of the gifts that are available to us. This enables the church to function in unity and to serve all of mankind regardless of their needs.

I have actually sent people who wanted to go to my church to another church instead because their personal spiritual growth and needs would be met better there. Similarly, I have been blessed with members of Christ's body whose needs are best met from the church where I serve.

All of us are unique; therefore, all of us have different needs and desires. Yet, in Christ, we all have one Spirit. Be sure and thank the Lord for dying on the cross for us. Without Him, there would be no one worthy enough to boast about.

43. Gal. 6:14a (NIV).
44. 1 Cor. 12:11 (Emphasis, mine).

On the Twenty-Seventh Day

The skies are bright blue this morning as the sun makes its way overhead, casting shadows on the inhabitants below. The river is filled with all kinds of wildlife as children gather near the headwaters to swim. There's something about the brightness of the atmosphere that puts my mind in such a great mood.

I met with my biblical studies professor, Jay, yesterday to go over the details of team teaching an upcoming Pauline Epistles course with him. I've been so blessed to be able to teach at the college level as a teaching assistant for so many great professors over the past few years. I pray that the Lord will help me inspire someone in ministry the way that my professors have inspired me.

Sound biblical knowledge and teaching is mentioned a few times in Scripture. Paul, while in Macedonia, encourages his young student, Timothy, to oppose false teachers who want to be teachers of the law, but do not know what they are talking about. Paul instructs Timothy to oppose them with a pure heart and sincere conscience.[45]

When we teach others, we must be diligent to take the time to pray that the Holy Spirit illumine the Scriptures for us. We must invest hours in study and research of sound biblical doctrines. After all, we are representing God's Word, and it must be handled delicately. Before I began my formal studies at an evangelical seminary, I tended to believe whatever anyone told me about Scripture that sounded good. Jesus uses allegory in many of His parables, so there's a place for allegory in Scripture, but it must be exegeted properly. Scripture always interprets Scripture; therefore, if what someone tells you is symbolic or allegorical, look to see if Jesus, or one of the biblical authors has already explained it, and let the Holy Spirit be your guide.

On the Twenty-Eighth Day

Missionary work is vital for the continued growth of the church. The Apostle Paul set out on three missionary journeys during his lifetime. He was generally known for preaching a law-free gospel. One can pick up on the contrast between grace and works in several of his letters. He also promoted unconditional love and unity between Jews and Gentiles. Paul encouraged his churches to spread the gospel message through faith to all the ends of the earth. It's amazing how much he did in the name of Jesus Christ, that we still feel the effects of today.

---

45. 1 Tim. 1:3-7 (Emphasis, mine).

Mission work does not have to be conducted strictly overseas. In fact, North America needs missionaries just as much as any other country. Realizing this to be the case, other countries actually send missionaries here to preach the Gospel of Jesus Christ to us! According to the Bible, we should all be missionaries, whether at home or abroad. Jesus tells us to: "Go into all the world and preach the gospel to all creation."[46] I've found that I don't even have to leave my home to evangelize. God sends me people to share the gospel with on nearly a daily basis. It's up to me to be obedient to God's call on my life and share the good news with them.

If you feel that someone you know could benefit from hearing the story of Jesus' birth, life, death, and resurrection, don't be afraid to share your story with them. Our personal testimonies of how we came to faith in Christ are very powerful tools that open up the lines of communication. Every one of us has a unique story and experience to share. No two stories are exactly alike. God will place someone in front of you that needs to hear His plan of redemption. Perhaps, you have yet to accept Christ into your heart and need to hear the testimony of someone else? God knows that as well. This book may just be the water for the seed that God has planted in you. After all, you are reading this at this very moment, aren't you?

On the Twenty-Ninth Day

It's still dark this morning as I walk into work to pick up a client from south Reno and drop him off at the airport. The streets are quiet as I make my way towards his house, which is about 30 minutes outside of town. I never know who I'll pick up, what conversation will be had, or how the interaction will go. I guess that's why I love meeting new people. They're all different, and you never know what you'll get.

Today, I had a great conversation with an African-American gentleman who said he grew up poor in Compton in the 1960's and experienced segregation, crime, and all kinds of other setbacks. Yet, despite his conditions growing up, he refused to let his circumstances affect his future. He joined the Navy, worked for a large distribution company and advanced up the ladder to the level of director. He paid for all of his kids to go to college, is almost retired, happily married, and lives in an affluent part of the city.

We talked about everything from church, to politics, to how to raise your kids. You'd be surprised how much you can cover in a thirty-minute drive. One thing that he mentioned that I really appreciated was a road trip that he took his eighty-three-year-old father on so that they could talk and

---

46. Mark 16:15 (NIV).

bond together before he passed away. He was able to thank his father for raising him in such a respectable way and even shared some great memories with him during their three-day adventure to the Dakotas.

The Bible tells us to train up a child in the way he should go and even when he is old, he will not depart from it.[47] We don't have to be products of our environment. If you feel like you are in a place that you don't wish to be, you can change it. God will help you get there, and I'll be praying for your success.

On the Thirtieth Day

My wonderful English professor, Kathe, has been teaching English for many years. She's taught at several colleges and universities, including the one I attend. In fact, she helped me earn my English minor a few years ago during my undergraduate studies at Multnomah University in Reno, Nevada.

Kathe is one of the hardest working women that I know. She has a full-time law practice, serves at her church, does volunteer work, and has a professorship, not to mention a wonderful husband, children, and several grandchildren.

One day, she decided to resign from teaching and focus more on her church and family. In her letter, she mentioned that she felt the need to be obedient to what the Lord was asking from her. Without hesitation, she decided that the Lord's desires had to come before her own.

This is a great lesson for all of us to follow. So often, I would attempt to go about life in a way that best suited my desires or financial needs. Yet, when I was obedient to the Lord's call for my life, He still provided for my desires and financial needs. We sometimes fail to look at the forest of our lives and instead, stay focused on what's happening in the trees. God has a bigger plan for you than you know. Stay obedient to Him and allow His plan to play out.

The Bible says, "And this is love: that we walk in obedience to his commands. As you have heard from the beginning, his command is that you walk in love."[48] Therefore, if we love the Lord, we should walk in obedience to His commands. You may ask, "How am I supposed to remember all that He commanded?" Fear not, for His commands are written on your heart. If you show love for both Him, and His creation, you are already practicing obedience to the Father.

---

47. Prov. 22:6 (Emphasis, mine).
48. 2 John 1:6 (NIV).

Chapter 7

"The Goodness of the Lord"
The Month of July

On the First Day

The warmth of the sun is like a warm blanket that has just come out of the dryer. The lilies reach towards the bright, golden rays for nourishment as the children play carelessly in the front yard. The fountain sounds so serene as I sit on my front porch contemplating life and the blessings God has given to me.

The goodness of the Lord is unmeasurable. The Lord is good to all and He shows mercy towards all of creation.[1] When I reflect back on some of the opportunities that God has given me, I am always thankful for them. Without God's goodness, I wouldn't have any of the things that I cherish so much: a beautiful family, a great church leadership position, a secular driving job that works around my other commitments, success in school, an income to provide for my wife and kids, and the list goes on and on.

When we pray, it is important not to ask the Lord for a bunch of things. Like someone once told me, "God is not Santa Clause." Indeed, the Lord already has our future planned, for He knew us before we were formed in our mother's womb.[2] To have success in this life, we simply need to walk in obedience and stop resisting the plan He already laid out for us. You might ask yourself, "How do I know what His plan is?" If you discover that challenges and barriers oppose your decisions at every turn, then the chances are good that He has a different plan for you.

1. Ps. 145:9 (Emphasis, mine).
2. Jer. 1:5 (Emphasis, mine).

On the Second Day

The green pine trees overshadow the cello brown earth below as the marvelous blue bird makes his nest in the tall branches above. Time seems to stand still as I look out at the glass-like surface of Lake Tahoe; remembering the days of long ago when I had little care or worry about the ins and outs of day-to-day life.

We had an extremely busy winter season at my transportation job. The early morning hours, in conjunction with church and school, started to take its toll on me, to the point that I sought employment at a hotel-casino in hopes of working a regular, part-time shift. The transportation manager and I had a great conversation over the phone, and he assured me that he could work around my school and church obligations, so I set up a time to sit down and meet with him later in the week.

I happened to be driving a client from Reno to Lake Tahoe that same evening and had a long time to think about the pros and cons of switching employment. During the hour and a half drive back to Reno from South Lake Tahoe, I began to question whether or not changing jobs at this point in my life was a good decision. After much back and forth, it was the Holy Spirit, who gave me the spiritual reason- perhaps the most important reason- which hadn't occurred to me until later that evening.

As I reflected back on the many jobs I've had in the casino industry, I came to realize that every casino that I had worked at (starting at the age of twenty-one) involved meeting women who would eventually disrupt my family life, as well as my relationship with Jesus Christ, every single one. Perhaps, the evil spirits of greed, lust, and anger, that inhabit those buildings had left me vulnerable to the temptations of lust and fornication. You can only wade in deep water for so long before you become exhausted and drown, so I decided against changing jobs.

On the Third Day

Have you ever noticed that the more rules are imposed on us, the more likely we are to break them? When I was a teenager, my parents had a rule that we could only have ice-cream one night a week. Yet, my brother and I would stay awake until after my parents fell asleep, and then raid the freezer, stashing our empty ice-cream bowls under our beds. My sister never had the same craving for ice cream. Perhaps, that's why she is still thin today.

The Apostle Paul would often contrast God's grace with mankind's works when writing to a church during his missionary journeys. He once asked rhetorically, "Why, then, was the law given at all? It was added because of transgressions until the Seed to whom the promise referred had come."[3] We might ask, how do our sins and the giving of the law reconcile themselves? Why give us laws that no one can obey?

God knew that we could not keep the law, yet sin was in the world before the law was given. Despite the fact that sin was not charged against anyone's account prior to the law, sin still existed because death still reigned from Adam to Moses.[4] Therefore, the law was a reminder that God had led his people out of Egypt and expected obedience from them. If they weren't sure as to exactly what God expected from them, they could refer back to the law for clarification. The other reason the law was given was for our transgressions. We cannot live up to God's holy standards; therefore, we are dependent upon the One who was righteous in every way. God does not consider us righteous through our works of the law, but rather, through our faith in Jesus Christ who gives us the gift of God's righteousness once we accept Him into our hearts. In this way, it is not our flesh that God sees, it is our hearts for His Son that His law is now written upon.

On the Fourth day

Independence Day

Independence Day is here, for those of us in the United States. Many of the early settlers were escaping England's religious unity between church and state. Even after the Reformation, England continued to try and control its people through religion and fear. This is why the founding fathers were sure to include a separation between church and state in the Constitution of the United States of America.

During the first century, Rome had much control over the Middle East. Despite random persecution of Christians, the authorities that existed had been established by God. Not a popular notion in today's divisive culture, yet the Apostle Paul knew that whoever was appointed to lead God's people, was surely foreknown by God, Himself. One can always debate whether God uses rulers as a result of disobedience, such as the Israelites being ruled over by Assyria, Babylon, and Persia, or if God simply appoints a ruler to advance His purposes, regardless of how they govern the people. I suppose the outcome is still the same. Maybe, that is why Paul tells us to subject ourselves to government authority?

3. Gal. 3:19a (NIV).
4. Rom. 5:13-14 (Emphasis, mine).

Ultimately, when God is displeased with the way His people are being ruled over, He will remove that ruler. This has happened all throughout history, and I imagine it won't stop until the ultimate ruler, Jesus Christ, has returned to reign with the saints, over all of God's creation.[5]

Whether you are a Republican or Democrat, do not be afraid to respect those whom God has chosen to lead us. If Jesus tells us to, "love your enemies and pray for those who persecute you,"[6] how much more should we love and pray for those who lead us?

On the Fifth Day

The darkness in the world has always bothered me. Evil spirits love the darkness, for their deeds can remain hidden. I used to drive home from work late at night near downtown and could see people on the streets manifesting the evil that dwelt within them. Whether they were yelling out obscenities, shooting drugs, involved in gang activity, or prostitution, my Spirit, like that of other believers, has the ability to discern good spirits from evil ones; one of the many gifts God has blessed me with.

As the time of Jesus' return draws closer, the enemy is ramping up his goal of separating us from our creator. He will use all kinds of tactics: logic, reasoning, relativism, pagan worship, coexistence, acceptance of society's morals, and the like. Yet, we must not be deceived by this. If you have ears, listen to what the Spirit has to say. Satan has always been deceptive, right? So, why should he stop now, especially when he is so close to losing his power? It's not an easy battle, and you will surely have setbacks, but keep pressing forward. Never give up on your desire to form a strong relationship with Jesus Christ through faith and obedience to Him. Satan was once cast down from heaven for trying to become like God.[7] Ever since then, Satan has tried to convince us that we can be like God as well.[8]

Sometimes, I wish my current self could go back in time and talk to my younger self. I would warn him of the dangers of giving in to sin, the earthly and heavenly consequences of my actions, and the people that would get hurt along the way. But, I can't. I can only try to be a better Christian, husband, and father today than I was yesterday. The good news is that God will never give up on you, so be sure not to give up on you either.

---

5. Rev. 20:4 (Emphasis, mine).
6. Matt. 5:44 (NIV).
7. Ezek. 28/Isa. 14 (Emphasis, mine).
8. Gen. 3:5 (Emphasis, mine).

On the Sixth Day

The wind is blowing clouds in from the west as the atmosphere echoes thunderous sounds from above. Seeking shelter from the rain, my kids and I scramble to reach the car and head home for the evening.

Like a child who seeks the safety of a parent in the time of storm, the Lord is a safety net for all who grasp onto Him. The Lord is good, a stronghold in the day of trouble; he knows those who take refuge in him.[9] When we place our trust in Him, we need not worry about the storms of life, for they will certainly pass, and we will remain victorious in Christ Jesus.

Every time that I worry about life, work, school, or the church, God reassures me through the Holy Spirit that I'm not going through this life alone. Did not the Holy Spirit come to help guide Christ's followers and the Apostle Paul throughout his mission to witness Jesus Christ to the people of Judea, Samaria, and to the ends of the earth?[10]

The Holy Spirit will guide, council, convict, and prevent us from getting too far away from the Father. Therefore, pray to the Lord and ask the Holy Spirit to guide your life in a positive direction. I've always relied on my faith to help me make wiser choices. The more I trust the Lord and seek His guidance, the better choices I make.

Satan wants us to constantly worry about our future, our goals, and our decision making. Worry is indeed a result of the fall, which is why the Apostle Peter tells us to cast our burdens upon Christ.[11] If you are worrying too much about something, place your worry at the foot of the cross and enjoy the weight off of your shoulders. You'll be glad you did.

On the Seventh Day

There are many false teachers in the world. Those who teach that money is God's way of rewarding those who obey Him, to those who preach that Jesus is simply a prophet of God, and not God, Himself. Have you ever noticed that most "prophets" on television insist on money being sent in towards their ministries?

I was once visiting a non-denominational church that my friend attended, and they happened to have a guest speaker who claimed to be a prophet of God. He had many people in the audience who would come up and he would pray for them and some would claim to be healed and some

---

9. Nah. 1:7 (ESV).
10. Acts 1:8/ Acts 16:6 (Emphasis, mine).
11. 1 Pet. 5:7 (Emphasis, mine).

would pass-out after he laid his hands on them and so forth. Naturally, the first thing he did after his sermon and healings was to ask for those in the audience to "sew a seed" for their future prosperity. "Do I have someone willing to sew a seed of $5,000.00?" He would ask, and sure enough someone would. I'll never forget how his eyes seemed to pop out of his skull after he saw a check for that amount. He assured the person that they would have wealth in the next three months. Of course, they were in the same financial position as they were in before they gave him $5,000.00. Actually, they were in a worse financial position because now they had $5,000.00 less than they had before.

The Apostle John tells us, "I say this because many deceivers, who do not acknowledge Jesus Christ as coming in the flesh, have gone out into the world. Any such person is the deceiver and the antichrist."[12] Meaning, that if someone claims to be a Christian, yet denies that Jesus is God incarnate, then he or she is a deceiver. Even if they profess Christ as their Lord, they can still deceive us with their intentions. Do not trust anyone like this. Place your trust in Jesus Christ and allow the Holy Spirit to discern the godly people from the ungodly ones.

On the Eighth Day

Have you ever taken the time to observe how many beautiful colors there are in the world? The water of Lake Tahoe contains several shades of blue. The sands of the earth range from bright white to mocha brown, with every shade in between. The skies exhibit deep blues, crimson reds, royal purples, and golden yellows. Color is obviously important to God and we are blessed to have a world with colors in it.

The four colors used in the tabernacle were: red, white, purple, and blue.[13] Nothing that God used for construction was there by chance. Everything, from the building of Noah's Ark, to the tabernacle has a meaning behind it. The scarlet red signifies Jesus' blood and atonement for us. The white symbolizes purity in Christ and the resurrected body. The purple represents the kingship of Jesus and His eternal reign, and the blue represents God's presence with us at all times just like the sky is blue and God's presence is with us between the sky and the heavens.

I love to plan things. In fact, I sometimes plan too far in advance and then realize I probably should have waited a bit longer. Nonetheless, planning ahead is generally a good idea. When we take a family vacation, or

---

12. 2 John 1:7 (NIV).
13. Num. 4:6-13 (Emphasis, mine).

when I plan out my school assignments for the semester, there's always a sense of accomplishment when I've been able to stick to my plan and reap the benefits of my labors.

The Lord plans things as well; He leaves nothing to chance. Therefore, how much more has He designed a meaningful plan for your life? When you look up at the heavens, remember that there is a supreme designer that took the time to create everything around us. This intelligent designer spoke life and creation into existence. Everything, including us, has its proper place and pre-determined action in the sovereignty of God.

On the Ninth Day

I really enjoy reading. I once read about the well-known theoretical physicist, Albert Einstein. Albert Einstein spent most of his life trying to unify all theoretical scientific properties and equations into one consistent theory called, "The Unified Field Theory." His premise was that all things in nature happen in a predetermined way and nothing happens by chance. This is actually similar to the hard-lined determinism view that would argue that everything is predetermined or predestined by God and we have no choice in the matter, even to the smallest details of our lives.

Einstein was forced to change his position in 1939 because upon analyzing thought experiments of particles bouncing off of one another, there was, the thought of if you measured particle "A", its distance would match that of particle "B" even if they were millions of miles away from each other. To Einstein's dismay, quantum mechanics had an uncertainty principle within itself which says that it is not possible to know both the precise position and momentum of a particle at the same moment. Thus, there was, what Einstein liked to call, "spooky action at a distance" that could not be explained.[14]

So, all this to say that, even though God has a plan and sovereign design for everything, we cannot always figure it out. We can only grow in our relationship with Him. Some things we most certainly have a choice in, yet there still remains a sovereignty to God's character. We can choose to accept Jesus or not to, just like a particle can choose to end up somewhere that cannot be calculated by science. Despite Einstein's self-proclaimed agnostic view of religion, even he admits that only a God could design the universe in such a way to have things organized, and yet still remain mysterious.

---

14. *Encyclopedia Britannica*, 15th ed., s.v. "Unified Field Theory."

On the Tenth Day

I'm not sure why, but for some reason God likes to wake me up at 4:00 a.m. to reveal things to me. Perhaps, I'll get to sleep-in once I'm in heaven. This morning I kept getting this message in my mind saying, "I Am." Despite the evil that is currently playing out in the world today, *I Am* is still with us. *I Am* knows exactly what's going on and is still in control, and *I Am* will always be with us.

I Am, or *"YHWH"* is an action word; a Hebrew verb. Even though the name YHWH is etymologically difficult to explain, to a Hebrew audience it may have translated very much like: *He who causes that which is to be*. *I Am* is also past, present, and future. God refers to Himself as *I Am* in the book of Exodus, but the Hebrews referred to Him as, "You Are." God said to Moses, "I AM WHO I AM" . . . "Say this to the people of Israel, *I Am* has sent me to you."[15]

Samson's father, Manoah, encountered an angel of the Lord prior to Samson's birth who told him that his wife could not drink wine or eat anything unclean.[16] When enquiring from the angel what His name was, the angel of the Lord replied, "Why do you ask my name? It is beyond understanding."[17]

Even I need to be reminded that YHWH is beyond comprehension and is still in control. I think we often forget that we are not going through this life blindly. Our Father in heaven gives us strength through His son, Jesus Christ. We can trust that whatever challenges we face, God is controlling the outcome. If we are blessed, we should give thanks. If we are challenged, we should give thanks. Give thanks in all things, for the Lord is in control.

On the Eleventh Day

Beautiful colors fill the sky as the sun begins to set over the valley. I always enjoy watching the sunset beyond the Sierra Nevada Mountains while the atmosphere cools off and brings relief to those of us who work outdoors in extreme heat. Or, perhaps you've spent time in your yard or garden today and look forward to the cooler evenings in which you can sit on the front porch and enjoy watching people walk by.

There's an extreme contrast between faith and works. Works tells us to "do" salvation; faith tells us that salvation is done in Christ Jesus. Some may

---

15. Ex. 3:14 (ESV).
16. Judg. 13:6 (Emphasis, mine).
17. Judg. 13:18 (NIV).

use their salvation as a license to keep sinning. One might ask, if I believe in Christ, and I have been forgiven for my sins, then should I be allowed to sin without repercussion; should I sin even more so that I can be forgiven more? The Apostle Paul addresses this issue in his letter to the Romans:

> What shall we say, then? Shall we go on sinning so that grace may increase? By no means! We are those who have died to sin; how can we live in it any longer? Or don't you know that all of us who were baptized into Christ Jesus were baptized into his death? We were therefore buried with him through baptism into death in order that, just as Christ was raised from the dead through the glory of the Father, we too may live a new life.[18]

We are saved from God by God. Jesus saved us from the eternal consequences of sin, but not the earthly and heavenly consequences of sin. Because of the fallen nature of the world we live in, evil still exists among us. Just because we have accepted Jesus Christ into our hearts, doesn't mean that we no longer have to worry about transgressing. In fact, Satan will often try harder to tempt those who are close to God, in an effort to get them to fall away.

When we become Christians, it's not as though we now have a license to keep sinning, but rather the result of becoming Christians is that we want to be done with sinning and be closer to Jesus Christ.

On the Twelfth Day

Addiction comes in many forms. It can be sexual, drug or alcohol related, or something that is psychologically comforting such as watching tv, gambling, or eating too much. I've known several people who have, or still do, suffer with addiction in their lives. I also know many believers who were freed from their addictions once they accepted Jesus Christ into their lives.

The Apostle Peter tells us, "They promise them freedom, while they themselves are slaves of depravity—for people are slaves to whatever has mastered them."[19] Indeed, once you allow the temptation to gain momentum and become something more, you've basically allowed the sin to master you. Addiction works in a similar way. Most people focus on the chemical or psychological aspect of addiction but fail to address the spiritual problem with addiction.

---

18. Rom. 6:1-4 (NIV).
19. 2 Pet. 2:19 (NIV).

If I have an alcoholic beverage once in a while, chances are good that I won't become addicted to alcohol. On the other hand, if I go out every single night and drink alcoholic beverages, I have a very high chance of becoming addicted to alcohol. Why? Because our bodies get used to functioning with a foreign substance in them to the point where our bodies become dependent upon that substance to function: Hence, substance abuse and addiction.

So, why go there in the first place? Addiction and idolatry go hand-in-hand. Soon, you begin to worship the addiction without even realizing it. Paul tells us, "You cannot drink the cup of the Lord and the cup of demons too; you cannot have a part in both the Lord's table and the table of demons."[20] The Lord is jealous in this way for good reason. He wants to keep you safe and keep you healthy. That was the way He originally designed us. If you are struggling with addiction, please seek help. There are several Christian counselors in the community that would be more than willing to talk to you and/or lead you in the right direction to better your life.

On the Thirteenth Day

As the clouds slowly drift past, I look up in awe of the beautiful tapestry God has painted for us to enjoy. Each day of cloud formations is unique. The raindrops could have been evaporated from any of the great lakes or oceans. Yet, God has designed the earth in such a way that we can be fully sustained by it.

Defending our faith is very important, especially in a world where everyone wants everyone else to agree with them. The idea of religious co-existence sounds great, and it's not a new concept. God told Abraham that He will make a great nation out of Ishmael's descendants, just as He had done for Isaac's descendants.[21] Yet, God's everlasting covenant was made with Isaac and his descendants.[22] Therefore, not every religious belief can be the correct one. This is where studying Christian apologetics can be of great value.

The Apostle Paul tells his young apprentice: "Timothy, guard what has been entrusted to your care. Turn away from godless chatter and the opposing ideas of what is falsely called knowledge, which some have professed and in so doing have departed from the faith."[23] Gnosticism in Paul's time

---

20. 1 Cor. 10:21 (NIV).
21. Gen. 17:20 (Emphasis, mine).
22. Gen. 17:19 (Emphasis, mine).
23. 1 Tim. 6:20-21 (NIV).

was the precursor for the New Age movement that we see today. Paul was dealing with these heresies in his day, and the Jews had to deal with them even before Jesus walked the earth.

Do not let the devil deceive you. There *is* something called absolute truth, and an absolute moral standard. The standard is found in God, Himself. This is why once we accept His Son, Jesus Christ into our hearts, we have moral accountability. Christians will still sin, but they now have a conviction from the Holy Spirit.

On the fourteenth Day

Thinking back to 1986, when I was only ten years old (a long time ago, I know), I remember attending a small Lutheran Church in my little town of Sparks, Nevada. The church only had about fifty or so members who filled the entire sanctuary. We would meet every Sunday at 9:00 am and sit with the rest of the adults in the congregation. After the service, which mainly consisted of Holy Communion, we would break out into our Sunday school classes for an hour until the eleven o'clock service began.

I really enjoyed attending Lord of Mercy Lutheran Church. I have so many great memories of my time there. I actually have four or five of the former members from thirty years ago as Facebook friends. God's presence was clearly felt from the start of the service to the finish and we didn't dare misbehave at all during service.

My best friend, Paul was there with his family each week, and I very much enjoyed spending time with them at church and afterwards for brunch. After some consideration and baptism classes, I decided that I should be baptized as I felt in my heart that Jesus Christ was God's only son and died for my sins. I felt the love of Jesus Christ all around me; something that I was missing at home.

Jesus was once sitting with some of the disciples when a Pharisee named, Nicodemus came to visit Him. During their conversation, Nicodemus asked, "How can someone be born when they are old?"[24] Clearly not understanding what Jesus meant by being "born again." When we accept Jesus Christ into our hearts, we get a second chance. No longer do we have solely a physical birth, of which we will someday physically die, but now, we also have a spiritual birth, one of which we will never die.

---

24. John 3:4 (NIV).

On the Fifteenth Day

The warm rain cascades across the plains as the earth absorbs the water. Like an athlete who desperately needs liquid after perspiring all of the water and saline from his body, thirsty plant roots are replenished by God's own provisions.

The Lutheran tradition, and many other high church faith traditions, focus the majority of their services around Holy Communion. Communion is a weekly celebration and remembrance of what Jesus participated in with His disciples at the last supper. Indeed, Saint Luke tells us that we should break bread together every time we gather.[25] Some churches celebrate communion monthly, and some celebrate it even less frequently.

Holy Communion was always a powerful experience for me. At the time, I didn't know the doctrinal differences between transubstantiation, consubstantiation, or remembrance, but in hindsight, I would agree that Jesus' presence was amplified for me during the experience, perhaps even due to a corporate communal mindset and liturgical aesthetic.

The Apostle Matthew recalls the event for us:

> While they were eating, Jesus took bread, and when he had given thanks, he broke it and gave it to his disciples, saying, "Take and eat; this is my body." Then he took a cup, and when he had given thanks, he gave it to them, saying, "Drink from it, all of you. This is my blood of the covenant, which is poured out for many for the forgiveness of sins. I tell you, I will not drink from this fruit of the vine from now on until that day when I drink it new with you in my Father's kingdom." When they had sung a hymn, they went out to the Mount of Olives.[26]

During a Jewish Seder, several cups are placed at the table. The cup that Jesus drank from here, was just one of those, yet it had great significance. The cup that Jesus drank from was reserved for Elijah, of whom the Jews thought was the promised Messiah. No one, except for Jesus had sat in Elijah's seat or drank from his cup since Moses began celebrating the Passover.

---

25. Acts 2:42-47 (Emphasis, mine).
26. Matt. 26:26-30 (NIV).

On the Sixteenth Day

Being a part of a community is so rewarding, especially if that community is faith-based. I took so much pleasure in meeting after class with my professors and colleagues at Multnomah University. We discussed and debated a wide-range of theological topics, yet we always had respect for a fellow student or professor's point of view. In this way, we were unified on areas of agreement, and still honored the faith traditions of those with whom we couldn't find agreement.

The Apostle Paul tells us that the body is made up of many parts.[27] I'm confident that this is how God intentionally designed His church. No single person living on this earth has all of the answers to life's questions, or the skill set to deal with every possible situation. Yet through a community of believers, we can offer a combination of the spiritual gifts to help others in need and advance God's kingdom.

The Bible reminds us of how the early church practiced community:

> All the believers were one in heart and mind. No one claimed that any of their possessions was their own, but they shared everything they had. With great power the apostles continued to testify to the resurrection of the Lord Jesus. And God's grace was so powerfully at work in them all that there were no needy persons among them. For from time to time those who owned land or houses sold them, brought the money from the sales and put it at the apostles' feet, and it was distributed to anyone who had need.[28]

In this way, we, too should realize that everything we have belongs to the Lord. Our spiritual gifts belong to the Lord, our material possessions belong to the Lord, and the Holy Spirit that dwells inside of us belongs to the Lord; therefore, we should share what belongs to the Lord with others. How much greater would this world be if everyone had that mindset?

On the Seventeenth Day

Grey skies cover the landscape as the birds fly overhead. Looking towards the horizon, I see streams of God's light shining through the darkness. As the clouds move, more light shines through. Like a young child who grasps

---

27. 1 Cor. 12:12 (Emphasis, mine).
28. Acts 4:32-35 (NIV).

on tightly to his mother's hand, I grab hold of the hope that is given to me through the death and resurrection of Christ Jesus.

When I was younger, I had many fears. Fear of my stepfather, fear of neighborhood bullies, fear of failing, and fear of the unknown. It wasn't until I was saved that I realized I was not alone. I now had the power of the Holy Spirit within me to give me courage during my fearful encounters. Was I still nervous or afraid at times? Of course, yet now I had the strength and tranquility to know that everything would work out alright in the long run. Even as I entered into adulthood, I sometimes found myself in compromising situations, yet every time that I can think of, the Lord gave me the words to say to help defuse the situation and bring calm to the uncomfortable atmosphere.

Just last week, one of my parishioners, Jeannine, was sharing with us that, before she was saved, she once had a man hold her hostage at gunpoint. Yet, God was still looking out for her because she was able to talk him out of harming her. God often intervenes for us even before we accept Him into our hearts; therefore, how much more will He intervene for us once we have accepted Jesus into our hearts? King David once said, "The Lord is my light and my salvation, whom shall, I fear? The Lord is the stronghold of my life of whom shall I be afraid?"[29]

When you face adversity, hostility, or the other evils of this world, know that you have a helper who dwells inside of you. Having the gift of the Holy Spirit will help you to persevere through any challenge that you might face.

On the Eighteenth Day

I'm sure that you've noticed by now, that I've tried to include a doxological piece to most of the entries in this devotional. I usually begin the day with glorifying God as seen through His creation. Whether it's admiring the beauty of Lake Tahoe, the pine trees of the Sierra Nevada mountains, or beautiful flowers and vegetation that surrounds my home, creation itself reminds me that there is a creator.

In the beginning, God spoke life into existence; creating even the light itself.[30] Similarly, Jesus speaks life into His hearers during the Sermon on the Mount.[31] Like a brilliant artist who creates a glorious masterpiece, one can logically deduct that if there is a creation, there must be a creator. Just take

29. Ps. 27:1 (NIV).
30. Gen. 1:1-3 (Emphasis, mine).
31. Matt. 5:2 (Emphasis, mine).

the time to look around you. Have you noticed that every part of creation influence, or sustains something else? Every member of the food chain has a way to survive, the earth has different seasons that spring life back into itself after a cold winter. Houses and shelters are made from the very wood and elements found within the earth. God provided, and still provides everything we need to maintain life. It's we, who damage the earth by not taking care of it. Moses tells us not to pollute the land in which we live.[32]

God created everything that can be found in nature. Some people try to combine God and nature, yet God is fully independent of His creation, otherwise He would have to answer in some way to the very nature that He created. The next time you go for a hike, walk, bike-ride, or look out of the window of your home or favorite coffee shop, remember who created the scenery that you enjoy looking at so much; it surely didn't create itself. Therefore, give God the honor and glory He deserves, for there is no one like Him in all of the universe.

On the Nineteenth Day

The summer rain falls down as the great Truckee River displays its whitewater rapids that descend from Lake Tahoe, through downtown Reno, and eventually make their way into Pyramid Lake. Thanks to the heavy snowfall this past winter, the lake is back to normal level and we can enjoy pleasures of a drought-free summer.

Some of you might wonder why Jesus had to die on a cross. True, that it was the common form of Roman capital punishment in Jesus' day, yet Paul was beheaded, and many of the Jews who broke God's Law were stoned to death. We find our answer in the book of Deuteronomy:

> And if a man has committed a crime punishable by death and he is put to death, and you hang him on a tree, his body shall not remain all night on the tree, but you shall bury him the same day, for a hanged man is cursed by God. You shall not defile your land that the Lord your God is giving you for an inheritance.[33]

Because Jesus took on the entire sin of the world at the cross, He had to answer to God's Law in a way that would represent the appropriate punishment for a Jewish person who had violated it. Always remember, that nothing in the Bible is there by accident or mistake. Every word of poetry, story, and letter has a specific meaning and purpose.

---

32. Num. 35:33 (Emphasis, mine).
33. Deut. 21:22-23 (ESV).

Jesus took on the wrath that God should have unleashed upon us. Today, we're much more likely to encounter people who do not even believe there is a God, let alone what commandments of His that they have broken. In ancient times, and really up until the Enlightenment period, most people didn't question God's existence, they simply chose to follow their own selfish desires instead of what God had wanted for them, and what Jesus had given His life for. I guess not much has changed in our generation, only now we deny that there even is a God that we have to answer to. I'll continue to pray for our generation to move away from the darkness, and into the light.

On the Twentieth Day

Every once in a while I'm asked about my thoughts on Christians and dating. Having much experience with dating throughout the years (although, not during the past twelve years that I've been married), I can only encourage you to try and find someone that loves and cares for you and who also loves the Lord.

We are not always equally yoked in our relationships. In fact, my wife only had exposure to the Buddhist belief system before she met me. Yet, I knew that God had put us together for a reason, and eventually, she came to accept Jesus and Christianity. I always encourage believers to lead by example and not bombard others with their beliefs. We are just seed-planters in the grand scheme of things. We cannot save anyone or force anyone to come to faith, so there is no need to be overbearing about it. We can evangelize more effectively if we tell people of the gospel message and allow God to do the work, for God is the one who makes the seed we planted grow.[34]

The Apostle Paul tells the Corinthians, "Do not be misled: 'Bad company corrupts good character.'"[35] It's important to realize that if you seek out someone who doesn't believe in God, then you might be corrupting yourself in the process. King Solomon was obsessed with pagan women and allowed himself to become corrupted with their beliefs after he married them.[36]

While God may join you together with someone who is not a believer, there is a difference between an agnostic view of God and the worshipping of foreign gods. If you find you are dating someone who is against your beliefs, it may be better to cut your ties, lest you be corrupted by theirs. Placing God first will always yield a great relationship with others.

---

34. 1 Cor. 3:6 (Emphasis, mine).
35. 1 Cor. 15:33 (NIV).
36. 1 Kgs. 11:1-8 (Emphasis, mine).

On the Twenty-First Day

The amber sky breaks into the dusk as the sun sets over the mountains in the west. The warmth of the summer air blows gently across the valley like the heat that emanates from a wood burning fireplace in winter. The stars become more visible as the illumination of the moon reflects the sun's light half a world away.

Last winter, I had the pleasure of driving a wonderful, godly woman named Katherine from Squaw Valley, California to the Reno Airport for a flight that she had to catch to San Francisco. One thing that I enjoy about the transportation industry, is that in most cases, you never know who you will be transporting until you greet them.

Katherine was very friendly and conversational during our hour or so drive to the airport. We spoke about everything from education, to Christianity, to early stage cancer testing that she was helping to develop. In fact, in 2004, Katherine was the first patient in the world to use the Oncotype DX test to guide her chemotherapy treatment decision. Standard assessments indicated that chemotherapy would be necessary for her treatment, but because of the Oncotype DX test results, she and her physician made the decision to forgo chemotherapy and its side effects.[37]

It always amazes me when I take the time to pay attention to who God has predestined to have enter into my life. The Lord does everything intentionally knowing that the outcome will benefit both people. It's kind of like the old television series, Highway to Heaven. God uses us to advance His purposes just like He did with the angel of that T.V. series. Look back on your life; were there people that you helped? Were there people that helped you?

On the Twenty-Second Day

I really enjoy sharing the Bible and its message with people. In fact, it's probably one of the most fulfilling experiences that I could have in a given day. I actually have several passions. My first is my Lord and Savior, Jesus Christ, second is my wife and children, and third is music and teaching. I used to enjoy martial arts but have been out of practice now for many years.

Having a passion in life is important. What gets you up in the morning and excited about the day ahead? What keeps you up at night thinking about all of the possibilities that your ambitions could yield? Do you have

---

37. Young, "Precision Medicine While Saving Health Care Costs."

something or someone that you think about constantly and cannot get out of your head? That obsession is probably your passion.

Along with my passion for teaching, comes the students that I can hopefully inspire through the power of the Holy Spirit to achieve their dreams in life and who in turn, will inspire someone else. This is the idea behind discipleship. As a disciple of Jesus Christ, one can expect some type of personal sacrifice to be given. In the West, it may involve a sacrifice of time or treasure, in the East, it may involve the ultimate sacrifice, the one that has been given since the first century by many of the martyrs.

Jesus once said, "Whoever wants to be my disciple must deny themselves and take up their cross and follow me. For whoever wants to save their life will lose it, but whoever loses their life for me and for the gospel will save it." [38]

Discipleship is more than simply teaching someone about Jesus Christ, it involves sacrificing our time and energy into loving someone as Jesus has loved us. By doing this, everyone will know that you are His disciples.

On the Twenty-Third Day

I once wrote the chorus to a song that went like this:
And if all that I know can be seen in bright colors,
And the love for my brother hasn't faded away;
Then tomorrow may show that I had to start over,
And the pain that we suffer can be lifted away.

Because it's now that I see that the love for each other,
Can be stronger than ever if we want it to be;
Because the fear deep inside is that no one would love us,
But He's standing above us and that's all that I need.

The idea behind the song is that if we claim to love each other, it shouldn't matter what we look like, or what our economic status is, or if we choose to dress a certain way. The Bible intentionally addresses diversity. The Apostle Paul tells us that "Here there is not Greek and Jew, circumcised and uncircumcised, barbarian, Scythian, slave, free; but Christ is all, and in all."[39]

---

38. Mark 8:34-35 (NIV).
39. Col. 3:11 (ESV).

The kingdom of heaven is comprised of every tribe and tongue, from every nation.[40] There is no prejudice in the kingdom of heaven, the only requirement is that you believe in Jesus Christ. We should be reflecting on earth what is already taking place in Heaven. This is why the Lord's Prayer proclaims, "Your kingdom come, your will be done on earth as it *already* is in heaven."[41]

The kingdom of heaven is already at hand for those of us who place our faith and trust in Christ Jesus. Therefore, we should be loving everyone that is a part of the kingdom, as well as everyone who is not. It's never too late to turn from your prejudgments of people and love them as Christ loves them, for love covers a multitude of sins.[42]

On the Twenty-Fourth Day

Sometimes, I'll make the thirty-minute drive east of town to the house I owned once with my ex-wife. As I drive through the old neighborhood, all of the past memories come flooding back into my mind. Some are great memories, but many are not so great. I suppose that is why we divorced at the young age of twenty-two.

Marriage is not easy. Anyone who has been married for more than five years can attest to that. It takes work. Often times, we are not willing to put in the effort required to sustain a healthy marriage. We may be selfish in our approach to the relationship, or we may have thought that things would be different once we married someone we cared about.

Statistically, the divorce rate is above fifty-percent in the United States. This means that out of every ten people, including pastors, at least five will have been divorced. It's important to think about the repercussion of divorce, especially if children are involved. In some situations, such as domestic abuse or infidelity, divorce may be inevitable, but it's always best to try and work out the issues in your marriage and save divorce for a last resort.

The Apostle Paul gives some godly advice in this matter: "To the married I give this command (not I, but the Lord): A wife must not separate from her husband. But if she does, she must remain unmarried or else be reconciled to her husband. And a husband must not divorce his wife."[43]

Perhaps, Paul knew that divorce has devastating consequences. Certainly, Moses allowed for divorce, but as Jesus said, that was due to the

---

40. Rev. 7:9 (Emphasis, mine).
41. Matt. 6:10 (Emphasis, mine).
42. 1 Pet. 4:8 (Emphasis, mine).
43. 1 Cor. 7:10-12 (NIV).

Israelites' hardness of heart.[44] So, if you are having trouble in your marriage, seek out a Christian counselor who can make an assessment from a distance, pray to the Lord, and try to reconcile if at all possible.

On the Twenty-Fifth Day

The morning breaks as the golden sky gives way to a blue horizon, blanketed with white clouds. Flowers of all colors adorn the ground and God's creation awakes to another brilliant day ahead. The hills and valleys pay tribute to the One who created them; time stands still for just a few moments as I take it all in.

My dear friend, Frank, is a co-worker of mine in the transportation business. A few years ago, Frank told me that he was waiting on looking into religion until after he retired. I immediately thought to myself, what if he passes away or Christ returns before he retires? As time went on, he would ask me various things about the Bible and Scripture. It was always a pleasure to answer his questions to the best of my ability.

A few months ago, Frank called me and asked which Bible translation he should purchase because he wanted to read the Bible cover to cover. After explaining the various translations and the history behind them, he settled on an NIV study Bible. Last I spoke with him, he was reading the book of Joshua and had a lot of questions about it.

Something amazing happened to Frank once he started reading and pondering over God's word. He was beginning to notice that certain things in his life were not happening to him by chance, but rather, by divine appointment. I told him that because he is making an effort to build a relationship with God, God is building a relationship with him as well.

The prophet Jeremiah once revealed a command from God who said, "Obey me, and I will be your God and you will be my people. Walk in obedience to all I command you, that it may go well with you."[45] Because of Frank's obedience, things are going well for him; because of his efforts to get to know Jesus Christ, things will continue to go well for him.

On the Twenty-Sixth Day

I worked as a lifeguard for most of my teenage and young adult years. I was promoted to the swimming pool manager around the age of nineteen

---

44. Matt. 19:8 (Emphasis, mine).
45. Jer. 7:23 (NIV).

and was responsible for the staffing, training, scheduling, and budget of the swimming pool: a lot to take on for someone of such a young age, now that I look back on it.

One day, I was downstairs in the mechanical room with the maintenance worker who was painting some of the old pipes and valves. Having been frustrated that my boss was upset with me because we went over our budget for the fiscal year, I commented, "You know, it would be nice to get a pat on the back once in a while. It would be great if he would just tell me that I'm doing a good job, instead of always criticizing everything." Tom turned to me and said, "Your paycheck tells you that you're doing a good job."

Though at work we are rewarded for our efforts financially, it's important to realize that as believers, we are also rewarded for our faith spiritually. The author of Hebrews tells us:

> Let us hold unswervingly to the hope we profess, for he who promised is faithful. And let us consider how we may spur one another on toward love and good deeds, not giving up meeting together, as some are in the habit of doing, but encouraging one another—and all the more as you see the day approaching.[46]

When we encourage one another in love, we move towards a better relationship with our fellow believers, and with God. When we are faithful to Jesus Christ, He is faithful to us. Take the time to meet with a brother or sister in the faith and encourage them to remain strong, despite what they see happening in the world around them. We are in the world, but not of the world. Through faith and perseverance, we can overcome any obstacle that the enemy throws at us. I want to encourage you my friends, that this life is only temporary; therefore, continue to focus on the eternal, for this life may be over in the blink of an eye.

On the Twenty-Seventh Day

I love to talk about Jesus Christ. I talk about Him at least once a day and twice on Sundays, but I believe that even Jesus prefers that we use evangelism in a way that connects best with our listeners.

For example, I have many Buddhist and Muslim friends, who believe in Jesus as a historical figure or prophet, but not as being God. Instead of trying to prove that Jesus is God to them, I find common ground that we can agree upon such as the virgin birth, or the miracles that He performed while He walked the earth, or the many prophesies that predicted a Messiah

---

46. Heb. 10:23-25 (NIV).

would come to save God's people from their sins, etc., and allow them to recognize the supernatural behaviors that He exhibited for themselves.

Evangelism is not only important for the Christian, but also commanded of us to do by Jesus Christ, Himself.[47] However, sometimes to reach people with the gospel, we must humble ourselves and respect their cultural traditions and practices. I remember, several years ago, in my course on World Missions, the professor said that every time he traveled to other countries to spread the gospel message, he had more success by dressing like the people he was talking to and immersing himself in their culture, than if he dressed like a twenty-first century American who refused to learn their culture or language.

The Apostle Paul once said, "I have become all things to all people so that by all possible means I might save some. I do all this for the sake of the gospel, that I may share in its blessings."[48] This doesn't mean that we compromise the core essentials of our faith to win people over to Jesus Christ, but it does mean that we evangelize in such a way that also respects the culture and traditions of those we are trying to reach with the gospel message.

On the Twenty-Eighth Day

The tranquility of the summer evening brings peace to my soul as the sun descends over the Sierra Nevada mountain range near my home in Reno, Nevada. Like a prism of beautiful colors, the sky above turns from yellow, to blue, to purple, and then to red. As the clouds clear out from the breath of the wind, the amber troposphere begins to darken, and the moon and stars shine with brilliantly reflected light.

I had the pleasure of watching George H.W. Bush's funeral service on television last year and was taken aback by the fact that he took time out of his busy day to write notes by hand to those that he cared about and who served with him during his presidency. He even wrote letters, up to twenty or more per day, to people who didn't hold his same political opinions. It was his way of keeping in touch with people and letting them know that he was thinking about them.

I decided, not long ago, to follow President Bush's example and reach out to people on my Facebook friends list whom I wouldn't normally reach out to. You would be amazed at how responsive and positive people were; simply from taking the time out to tell them that they have value and that I was praying for them. My beautiful high-school friend, Janna, was very

---

47. Matt. 28:18-20 (Emphasis, mine).
48. 1 Cor. 9:22-23 (NIV).

appreciative when I reached out to tell her that I was thinking about her, and her husband and kids, and that I was also praying for them.

It takes only a moment to tell someone that they are important to God, and by extension, are important to you as well. Won't you take just a few short moments and reach out to someone you don't normally interact with, and let them know that they are loved and that they have value? It will surely bless you more than it blesses them.

On the Twenty-Ninth Day

I really don't like flying. I mean, don't get me wrong, it is convenient and statistically the safest way to travel, but something about being high in the air and not being able to control anything doesn't sit well with me. At least when I drive, I'm the one doing the driving. I suppose there has to be a level of faith in the pilot that he will get us to our destination safely. Perhaps, even more faith must be placed upon the aircraft mechanics that they will check over the engine and essential components of the airplane to ensure that nothing is unsafe before takeoff.

Many things in this life require our faith. Flying in an airplane requires some level of faith for sure, but we also put faith in physicians, faith in our managers, and faith in our family. Even scientists must have faith that their theories of earth's creation are true, since they cannot go back in time and reproduce it. In this way faith and trust go hand-in-hand. Ultimately, our faith in Jesus Christ led us to accept Him as our Lord and Savior.

The Bible defines faith as, "The assurance of things hoped for; the conviction of things not seen."[49] You may ask, "how can we have faith in something we can't see?" Well, let's take the wind for instance, or gravity. We do not see the wind because it's transparent, but we do see the effects that the wind has on various things. We notice the leaves moving when a breeze comes through the trees, we might see the dust from the road upheave and fly into the sky, or we may simply feel air blowing on our faces during a windy day. Similarly, we do not see the force of gravity, for it is not recognizable in and of itself; yet, we certainly notice when gravity is removed, such as in water or in outer space.

As Christians, it is essential that we put our faith and trust in Jesus Christ. God has already overcome the world, let's trust in Him that we can overcome any temptations we face.

---

49. Heb. 11:1 (ESV).

On the Thirtieth Day

The sun encroaches upon the top of the sky as the birds overhead fly by in a V-formation heading towards the refreshing lake below. The summer heat is in the triple digits this year. It's nice to get some relief at the local swimming pool, where my kids splash around and play with the other neighborhood children.

Growing up, I didn't feel a close connection with my parents, though we are much closer now that I'm an adult with children of my own. I enjoyed the escape from home by visiting my grandparents on my mother's side and my other grandparents on my stepfather's side. They both made me feel special and were a very important part of my childhood. I look forward to the day I can see them again in heaven.

Family is important to God as well. The Apostle Paul tells us:

> Children, obey your parents in the Lord, for this is right. "Honor your father and mother" (this is the first commandment with a promise), "that it may go well with you and that you may live long in the land." Fathers, do not provoke your children to anger but bring them up in the discipline and instruction of the Lord.[50]

We all have had a parental figure of some-sort, at some point in our lives. So, Paul's words apply just as much to us as they do to our own children. Paul was reminding the Ephesians that one of the ten commandments is us to honor our father and mother.[51] Yet, how are we honoring them here in the West? Do we take care of them when they get older or, do we put them in a retirement home and visit them when it's convenient for us? These are all things to think about when it comes to family. Are you showing godly love to your children as well as to your parents? After all, they did love us enough to take care of us for so many years.

On the Thirty-First Day

We've made it to the end of July. How did your month go? Did you take the time to recognize the goodness of the Lord this month? He is so gracious. If I took the time to record every single situation that He has helped me with in my life, there wouldn't be enough pages to contain them all.

As we finish out this month, I'd like to touch on the area of fasting a bit. This is actually a discipline that has so many benefits when practiced, but so

---

50. Eph. 6:1-4 (ESV).
51. Ex. 20:12 (Emphasis, mine).

hard to initiate. Fasting first appears in the Bible around the time of Moses during the Hebrews' forty years in the wilderness. God commanded the Israelites to fast once a year on the Day of Atonement.[52] Scripture also tells us that Moses was with the Lord for forty days and forty nights and ate no food. It was during that time that the Lord wrote the Ten Commandments.[53]

Jesus fasted Himself, for forty days and forty nights during the temptation in the wilderness.[54] This allowed Him to gain victory over the devil's temptations, for we know that Jesus was genuinely tempted. This gives us hope that when we are facing temptation, we too can fast to help strengthen our Spirit for battle with the enemy. Catholic Priests will often fast for many days before engaging in the deliverance of someone tormented by evil spirits. This is because they know that replacing food with prayer yields great results.

I encourage you to make an effort to fast on a somewhat regular basis. You may have to start out with a partial fast, supplemented by snacks at first, but as you progress in your fasting, you will begin to notice that the Lord will start communicating with you in a more clear and vivid way.

---

52. Lev. 16:29-31 (Emphasis, mine).
53. Ex. 34:28 (Emphasis, mine).
54. Luke 4:2 (Emphasis, mine).

Chapter 8

"The Light in the Darkness"
The Month of August

On the First Day

THE LIGHT IN THE world overcomes the darkness. Light existed before darkness, therefore the darkness can never overcome it. Long ago, light and darkness were separated in order to contrast God's goodness from Satan's evil. Evil does not like the light because its deeds are easily exposed. Therefore, be the light in this dark world for all to see. God's Word is a lamp for our feet and a light for our path.[1]

We all deserve a pat on the back once and awhile. Although, if we begin to expect it from our good deeds, then it's no longer a praise in the name of the Lord, but rather, it becomes an idol that we constantly try and live up to. This can be dangerous because it can inflate our egos as well as turn us into boasters. Scripture tells us to, "Let another praise you, and not your own mouth; a stranger, and not your own lips."[2] By letting others recognize the light in us, we no longer have a need to brag about ourselves to earn the favor of the world. The Holy Spirit acknowledges our accomplishments for us.

It's important to honor the Lord by working hard, living ethically and morally, and keeping Jesus' commandments. Always remember that you are a chosen people, a royal priesthood, a holy nation, God's special possession, that you may declare the praises of him who called you out of darkness into his wonderful light.[3]

---

1. Ps. 119:105 (Emphasis, mine).
2. Prov. 27:2 (ESV).
3. 1 Pet. 2:9 (NIV).

On the Second Day

The intense heat continues to prevail through the summer season. I read somewhere that this summer was the hottest summer on record for Northern Nevada. Thankfully, sporadic thunderstorms do bring a little relief to the parched land. Fortunately, we had a heavy snow-fall last winter which helps to keep both the reservoirs, and Lake Tahoe full. Lake Tahoe is the main source of water for us, here in the valley.

For the past six or seven years, I've been getting my haircut once a month or so, by my favorite hair dresser, Stephanie. Excitedly, she tells me all about the successes and challenges that she faced during the previous month. In turn, I tell her all about my triumphs and challenges, as well as my love for the Lord. One thing I admire about Stephanie is that she works very hard at running her own hairdressing business, despite having to raise young children by herself, and she does it with such a great attitude. Too often, I encounter people who claim to have hardships, but they fail to change their situation.

God will help us to persevere, but we also have to make the effort to better ourselves and our circumstances. The Bible says, "You need to persevere so that when you have done the will of God, you will receive what he has promised."[4] You see, we are not alone in our journey through this life, but we have to endure, work hard, and persevere to succeed. If we are faithful and just, God will surely help us through any obstacles that may come our way.

If you face challenges with motivation, reach out to a friend or pastor who can help to encourage you. Perseverance of the saints involves the saints participating in the perseverance. God will always be there to help you get through it, and He will always be there to pick you back up when you fall.

On the Third Day

Fear is an emotion that we all experience to some degree. When I was much younger, I was afraid of my parents, most adults, and some of my classmates. As I grew older, I feared the intangible; things like loss of employment, fear for my children and what they might experience in life, loss of a relationship, debt, etc. I suppose most of us have these concerns at some point in our lives.

---

4. Heb. 10:36 (NIV).

The fear of the Lord is a different kind of fear that we experience amongst each other, and as being a part of God's creation. It's more of a healthy fear, if you will. King Solomon once wrote, "The fear of the Lord is the beginning of knowledge; fools despise wisdom and instruction."[5] In this sense, if we fear the Lord, and the eternal consequences of our actions, we begin to become wise in the way that Solomon was. Godly wisdom is far greater than earthly wisdom, for Godly wisdom will result in eternal life; whereas, earthly wisdom will result in eternal death.

The Apostle Paul once told young Timothy, "For the Spirit God gave us does not make us timid, but gives us power, love and self-discipline."[6] Indeed, the Holy Spirit will allow us to overcome our fears of the world and the enemy. No longer must we fear the devil for he was defeated at the cross. Death no longer has mastery over Christ; death no longer has mastery over us.[7]

The only fear we need to have in this life is fear of the consequences of our sin. If we have accepted Christ into our hearts, then we no longer need to fear the eternal consequences of sin, but we do need to fear the earthly and spiritual consequences of sin.

On the Fourth Day

The warmth of the sunshine falls down upon my skin as the breath of life fills my lungs once again this morning. I think that we often take life for granted. Just when we think our life is going bad, we can point to someone else who is far worse off than we are.

One thing I love, love, love about people is that God made them all different. Some are go-getters, some are idle, some are large, and some are small, some are emotional, and some are not, some are talkative, and some are silent. I could go on and on, but the point is that we are all unique for a reason.

The Apostle Paul says, "For we are God's handiwork, created in Christ Jesus to do good works, which God prepared in advance for us to do."[8] And, what better way to do good works, than with the fellowship of believers. King Solomon once wrote, "Two are better than one, because they have a good return for their labor: If either of them falls down, one can help the other up."[9]

5. Prov. 1:7 (ESV).
6. 2 Tim. 1:7 (NIV).
7. Rom. 6:9 (Emphasis, mine).
8. Eph. 2:10 (NIV).
9. Eccl. 4:9-10 (NIV).

I've fallen down plenty of times in my life. It's always nice to have a brother or sister in the faith reach out to me for comfort and council. I try and pay that forward by meeting regularly for coffee with friends and co-workers who are struggling with something. I find that I really don't have to say much during our time together. Sometimes, the best thing I can say is to say nothing at all. God will use those moments to help encourage one of His children through another one of His children. We are the instruments that God uses to advance His will. Always remember that you have a fellowship of believers of all faith traditions who should be reflecting the light of Christ by caring for you when you are down.

On the Fifth Day

The beautiful mountains stand high above the valley as the fields below flourish with existence. Mankind is enjoying walks with pets as the sprinklers bring fresh water to the grassy lands that they inhabit. Fresh apples swing softly in the trees as the summer wind blows ever so gently from the west.

We are so fortunate to have a forgiving and merciful God. Time after time, the ancient Israelites turned from the Lord and abandoned His commandments. Yet, time after time, the Lord forgave them and allowed them to prosper. This is not to say that there weren't disastrous consequences for their actions. The Lord once told the prophet Jeremiah, "You have rejected me," declares the LORD. "You keep on backsliding. So, I will reach out and destroy you; I am tired of holding back."[10] And, indeed He did. Soon after, the Babylonians ruled over the Israelites, followed by the Persians, Greeks, and ultimately, the Romans.

Through all of the Israelite's captivities, there always remained a remnant; one who would keep the chosen people of God from perishing completely. God orchestrated all these events to take place in order to preserve the lineage from the tribe of Judah, which would ultimately lead to the birth of Jesus Christ. You might recall that Ruth (a Moabite) and Boaz (the kinsman redeemer from the tribe of Judah) eventually married and had a son named Obed.[11] The name Obed may not ring a bell, but surely you recognize the name of Obed's son, Jessie. And, I'm quite certain you recognize the name of Jessie's son, David. This is why Jesus is both king and high priest. His priesthood comes from the order of Melchizedek, which preceded the tribe of Levi. His kingship comes from the line of David, who was from the

---

10. Jer. 15:6 (NIV).
11. Ruth 4:13-17 (Emphasis, mine).

tribe of Judah. And, His deity comes from His eternal relationship with the Father and the Holy Spirit.

On the Sixth Day

I try and avoid engaging with those who I don't agree with on social media, yet the double-edged sword of social media is that everyone has a voice. As we divide more politically, those voices tend to show less compassion for each other as human beings. I'm becoming more convinced that Satan, himself is behind social media, since it tends to divide more than it unites; just like Satan.

I once saw a post that said ministers should not be paid for ministry because Jesus was not paid for His ministry. It's true that Jesus was not paid directly for His ministry, but He was certainly supported by people who gave money to His ministry. If He wasn't, why did He have a treasurer?[12] Therefore, financial responsibility has its place, even in the Bible. Jesus even paid taxes; out of a fish's mouth, nonetheless.[13]

In my early twenties, I used to be quite careless with spending. If I saw something I wanted, I bought it, and usually on credit. Eventually, my credit cards maxed out, and not only could I not afford to make the monthly payments, I also could not afford to pay for much of anything else. Ultimately, my credit took a huge hit, and I ended up making arrangements with bill collectors to pay off my debts in smaller payments. Through the grace of God, and my wife's excellent accounting skills, I have settled all of my past debts and over time, my credit has gone from poor to excellent.

If you find yourself struggling with finances, I encourage you to seek out the help of a financial advisor or credit counselor. Sometimes, we get behind with our bills, but that doesn't mean that we can't recover. The Lord will help you every step of the way, so don't give up. He certainly hasn't.

On the Seventh Day

The clouds roll over the valley as the thunderstorms loom overhead. The rain brings a refreshing smell to the area and the parched vegetation rejoices at its presence. The sky roars with noise as the water from the clouds pours down.

---

12. John 13:29 (Emphasis, mine).
13. Matt. 17:24-27 (Emphasis, mine).

I can honestly say that I have very few, if not any enemies in this world. The people that I have wronged, I've asked forgiveness from, and the people who have wronged me, I have forgiven. Forgiveness is a powerful process in which the Lord is intimately involved. When we forgive someone, we are not telling them that what they did to us was okay, but rather, that what they did to us is no longer holding us prisoner; that what they did to us is now for God to decide if they are genuinely repentant and deserve *His* forgiveness.

The Apostle Peter once asked Jesus how many times he should forgive his brother who sins against him. Assuming that up to seven times was enough to satisfy God, Peter responds as such. Jesus replies, "Not just seven times, but seventy-seven times!"[14] Therefore, we should forgive each other many times, not just a few.

How should we ask God for forgiveness? The Old Testament gives us a great example, "If my people, who are called by my name, will humble themselves and pray and seek my face and turn from their wicked ways, then I will hear from heaven, and I will forgive their sin and will heal their land."[15]

If we ask God for forgiveness from our sins in humble fashion, He will indeed forgive us. It is more important to receive God's forgiveness than to receive forgiveness from mankind; although, both are ideal. Pray to God to forgive your sins and enjoy eternal life without consequence.

On the Eighth Day

We often tend to take our freedom for granted. Perhaps, because we've always grown up in a nation that has freedoms, we don't think about what it would be like if we didn't have them. Certainly, the Jews were not free while under Roman rule from around the time of Alexander the Great until Constantine. Yet, they still maintained the hope that the Messiah would come and restore Israel back to its place of prominence as it was during the time of King David.

Freedom to practice your faith without worry of persecution, freedom to disagree with the government, and freedom to choose your career path and future spouse, are all things that we have in the West that others do not have in other countries, yet there is a far greater freedom that we experience, and that is the freedom from sin.

Jesus Christ once said, "Very truly I tell you, everyone who sins is a slave to sin. Now a slave has no permanent place in the family, but a son

---

14. Matt. 18:20-22 (Emphasis, mine).
15. 2 Chron. 7:14 (NIV).

belongs to it forever. So, if the Son sets you free, you will be free indeed."[16] We are actually prisoners to our sin, not able to escape its eternal consequences; not able to free ourselves from its condemnation, yet through faith in Christ Jesus, we are set free from our sins and therefore we are no longer prisoners to them.

I always laugh when I hear someone say that Christians are hypocrites because they speak out against sin, yet they sin themselves. The truth is, we all sin, whether we are Christians or not. If we say that we don't, we only deceive ourselves and the truth is not in us.[17] The difference is, that as believers, we have the Holy Spirit who helps to prevent us from sinning, and who also convicts us when we do. We are no longer imprisoned by our sins, but now have an advocate and high priest in heaven who has paid the price for them.

On the Ninth Day

The bedroom windows are open this evening, which allows for the fresh summer evening air to blow lightly in. As I lay in bed, I can hear the sound of the downtown train go by as the thoughts of long ago return to my mind. God's light shines in the shadows of the secret place within, that no one else can penetrate.

I've been blessed to have had many great friendships over the years. My best friend Paul is a great man of God, loving father, and former military officer. As you might have read in a previous devotional, Paul was actually the person who introduced me to church when I was around nine or ten years old. His passion for the Lord, as mine, has never ceased. We still keep in touch, though not as often, since he currently lives in Japan.

Another good friend of mine, Tony, has always supported me emotionally and spiritually. We first met at a local hotel where we both worked as bellmen. We also share a love for playing music. Tony is a very seasoned drummer, and, in the past, we would make time to jam together in the small corner room of Tony's apartment. Sadly, Tony's long-time girlfriend had passed away not long after we met. It was then that I realized how much love for God and others Tony actually had. I was honored to be invited to her memorial service.

King Solomon once wrote, "A friend loves at all times, and a brother is born for a time of adversity."[18] Indeed, I truly love my friends and I know

---

16. John 8:34-36 (Emphasis, mine).
17. 1 John 1:8 (Emphasis, mine).
18. Prov. 17:17 (NIV).

that they love me as well. Jesus said, "Greater love has no one than this: to lay down one's life for one's friends."[19] And, that is exactly what He did on the cross. So, in a sense, we are all considered Jesus' friends because He died to atone for the sins of the entire world.[20]

On the Tenth Day

Driving along the lonely streets of Reno, I often drive past so many people who are hurting emotionally, spiritually, financially, and physically. I wish I could help them all, but if I were to give all of my money to everyone who asked me for it, I would have nothing left for my church, or my own wife and kids, who depend upon me as well.

There's nothing wrong with prioritizing our finances and saving money. In fact, it's quite biblical to do so. The Bible tells us that "For the protection of wisdom is like the protection of money, and the advantage of knowledge is that wisdom preserves the life of him who has it."[21] However, if we have been blessed with an abundance of income, then we should be generous with it. The Apostle Paul tells us:

> Remember this: Whoever sows sparingly will also reap sparingly, and whoever sows generously will also reap generously. Each of you should give what you have decided in your heart to give, not reluctantly or under compulsion, for God loves a cheerful giver. And God is able to bless you abundantly, so that in all things at all times, having all that you need, you will abound in every good work.[22]

At my limo driving job, I often earn tips in cash. One day, I received around forty dollars from a client who already had a gratuity built into his account. As I was driving along one of the main boulevards on the outskirts of the city, I saw a young man on the corner with a sign asking for help. The amazing thing is, that I actually drove past him once thinking that someone else would help him. But, just then, the Holy Spirit whispered to me, telling me to turn around and give him what I had, so I did. Would you believe that the next client I drove to Lake Tahoe gave me a one-hundred-dollar bill in addition to what was already built into his account? God rewards those who love His children.

19. John 15:13 (NIV).
20. 1 John 4:10 (Emphasis, mine).
21. Eccl. 7:12 (ESV).
22. 2 Cor. 9:6-8 (NIV).

On the Eleventh Day

The amber sky begins to darken as the evening sets in. The clouds clear out as the crescent moon illuminates the world below. The breeze blows ever so gently as I sit on my front porch and enjoy God's creation.

My friends, Jim and Deanna, are always sending me encouraging messages on Facebook. Both have a love for the Lord, and both work hard at their places of employment. Jim once asked me for advice on preaching. He had a sermon and personal testimony to deliver to his church congregation the following week and may have been a little bit nervous. I told him that when I preach, I always say the same prayer; that the Holy Spirit's words, and not mine, would speak through me and reach out into someone's heart who needs to hear from Him. He thanked me and ended up delivering a great message.

You see, it's not really us who delivers God's message. I mean, it is us, but it's not. In the same way that the Apostles delivered God's message, that is, through the power and inspiration of the Holy Spirit, we too deliver God's message through the power and inspiration of the Holy Spirit. The Apostle Paul tells the church in Philippi to, "Be like-minded, having the same love, being one in spirit and of one mind."[23] Meaning, that there is an accord between all believers that involves the Holy Spirit, love, and like-mindedness.

As Christians, it's important that we utilize the Holy Spirit in love to deliver God's message to those who He intends to hear it. This is why it's so important to pray before we read Scripture or meet with someone to talk about our faith. This will ensure that it's not us speaking, but God Himself, speaking through us.

On the Twelfth Day

When I was in Bible college, I had a course on theology in which we studied what's known as, *Theology Proper*. Theology proper deals specifically with the being, attributes, and works of God. God has several attributes that He reveals throughout Scripture.

The Lord once passed in front of Moses and said this about Himself:

> I am a compassionate and gracious God, slow to anger, abounding in love and faithfulness, maintaining love to thousands, and forgiving wickedness, rebellion and sin. Yet I do not leave the

---

23. Phil. 2:2 (NIV).

guilty unpunished; I punish the children and their children for the sin of the parents to the third and fourth generation.[24]

Here, we learn something about God. He is compassionate and slow to anger, yet He does not leave the guilty unpunished. Some Christians believe that they have a license to sin, simply because they have faith in Jesus Christ, yet clearly God is just and leaves no sin unpunished. It's important to remember that just because we may be secure in our eternity, doesn't mean that we won't have some type of consequence for our sins.

The Apostle Paul tells us, "For we must all appear before the judgment seat of Christ, so that each of us may receive what is due us for the things done while in the body, whether good or bad."[25] So, there is no escaping our sins, yet there is forgiveness for our sins thanks to the ultimate sacrifice of Jesus Christ. Jesus knew no sin but became sin so that we might become the righteousness of God.[26]

If you are struggling with sin, know that you are not alone. All of us sin, if we are honest with ourselves. The goal is to keep working towards a sanctified life. No one is perfect, but we should always try and be better representations of the One who died for us.

On the Thirteenth Day

The heat of the summer permeates through the windows of my Volkswagen Jetta as I drive through Reno, getting ready to set up for church. The air conditioner is on full throttle and feels as cold as the walk-in refrigerated vegetable section at Costco. I can't wait until the fall season begins and the summer swelter subsides.

I've had several jobs throughout my life. Prior to my marriage with Lisa, I owned and operated a commercial cleaning business. I was able to start with a few apartments, then advance to the entire apartment complex, then I began getting more and more accounts to where I had to eventually hire a staff to help me. I built it up from one, to several residential and commercial accounts, then sold it right before the recession hit in 2008.

Through my cleaning company, I had a client, named Brian, who owned an internet café in downtown Reno. He sold his café around the same time that I sold my cleaning business and we decided to start a new internet café, coffee shop, and laundromat together. After securing a lease on an old

---

24. Ex. 34:6-7 (Emphasis, mine).
25. 2 Cor. 5:10 (NIV).
26. 2 Cor. 5:21 (Emphasis, mine).

run-down chiropractor's office, we transformed it (mostly by hand) into a trendy coffee shop and lounge.

Sadly, Brian and I didn't get along as business partners as well as we did as friends, and we eventually parted ways. He sold the business not long after that. After some years had went by, Brian asked if I was interested in another business with him, but I thought, I'd much rather keep him as a friend than have him as a business partner.

Sometimes, God puts us through an experience to see if we learn anything from it. In this case, I learned that friendship was more important than money. As a result, Brian and I are still good friends to this day.

On the Fourteenth Day

The mountains reflect the beauty of the Creator. Like an artist, God paints the sky on a canvas of blue every single day. Have you taken time to look at the clouds lately? I am always at awe when I take in the beauty of God's light shining through bulbous cloud formations. Like lost sailors at sea, God's light shines out from the emptiness of the waters and guides us safely home.

Jesus Christ is transformational in our lives. When I first met my dear friend, Eileen, she had just recently got out of an abusive relationship, a trafficking situation, and was attending a missionary church in town. I was amazed at how much perseverance she had, despite her rough past. Eileen gave her life to Jesus Christ and was forever transformed into His light. She is now over half-way finished with her undergraduate degree in theology and counseling, a successful beautician, a talented musician, and a wonderful mother to her children.

The Apostle Paul once proudly proclaimed, "I have been crucified with Christ. It is no longer I who live, but Christ who lives in me. And the life I now live in the flesh I live by faith in the Son of God, who loved me and gave himself for me."[27] When we accept Jesus Christ into our hearts, we are transformed in a way that only God can ensure. Christ, Himself is alive inside each one of us in the form of the Holy Spirit. We no longer have to succumb to the enemy; but, rather, we have already overcome his temptations through the faith we have in Jesus Christ.

The enemy no longer has power over us, because we have the light of the world inside of us. Even if we have set-backs in life, God is there to help us persevere because we can do all things through Christ who strengthens us.[28] If you struggle with thoughts that you aren't good enough or that your

---

27. Gal. 2:20 (ESV).
28. Phil. 4:13 (Emphasis, mine).

past has forever tainted your relationship with the Father, please know that He is still there with you; He is loving and guiding you in all that you do.

On the Fifteenth Day

God's sovereignty is something that even Jesus Christ could not escape. Before Jesus was about to be betrayed by Judas, He went to the Garden of Gethsemane to pray. "My Father, if it is not possible for this cup to be taken away unless I drink it, may your will be done."[29]

God's will applies to everyone and everything within creation. He first spoke order into chaos and ever since the fall, that order involves a natural circle of life. God told Adam, "By the sweat of your brow you will eat your food until you return to the ground, since from it you were taken; for dust you are and to dust you will return."[30]

Even though God knows our next move before we make it, from our perspective, we still have a genuine choice to go along with or to go against His will for us. You may recall the story of Jonah. We studied the book of Jonah in-depth for my graduate level Biblical Interpretation course. During the study, I couldn't help but notice that even the pagan sailors recognized God's will.[31]

Some may question if God's will is fair. To this I say, it's not fair, but it *is* just. It's important to remember that what we finite mortals deem as fair is not the same thing as what an infinite God deems as fair or just. Job found this out the hard way when he questioned God. We should try our best to remain faithful and obedient to God's Word. Those whom God considered righteous in the Old Testament still had sin because they were descendants of Adam, but they also had a love for God the Father and a willingness to please Him. We would be wise to do the same.

On the Sixteenth Day

My wife and I have been blessed to live in a nice neighborhood near a great school in a modest-sized home that accommodates us and our three children. We rent our home from my younger brother and his wife, and we have been fortunate to live here for over five years now.

---

29. Matt. 26:42 (NIV).
30. Gen. 3:19 (NIV).
31. Jonah 1:14 (Emphasis, mine).

Last February, our heater went out around 2:00 a.m. Frigidly, I got out of bed, put extra blankets on the kids, and grabbed my space heater from the garage. The thermostat on the heater went from sixty-eight, to sixty-seven, to sixty-six, and ultimately down to sixty-one before my brother (also, our maintenance man) could come over and repair it.

My younger brother, Justin has so many talents. At a young age, he could build several complex Lego formations. As he went into high school, he finished a computer certification with Microsoft and was taking college computer courses before he graduated. After high school, he opted out of going to college, but instead started a successful aquarium maintenance business and has been the owner-operator of it ever since. He married a talented CPA that works for Microsoft, and since they haven't had children yet, they enjoy traveling abroad quite often.

God blesses people like my brother, and my youngest son, Brett with intelligence, yet people may be too intelligent to realize that God is the one that gave them their gifts. King Solomon, quite wise himself, once said, "For the Lord gives wisdom; from his mouth come knowledge and understanding."[32]

There's a difference between intelligence and wisdom. Many people who are intelligent lack wisdom, and vice versa. Wisdom is the fear of the Lord and the consequences of our disobedience. If you are blessed to have intelligence, pray for wisdom as well. You will be so glad that you did.

On the Seventeenth Day

The river flows rapidly past the rocky terrain as tourists come down to enjoy some white-water rafting during the hot summer season. The water drifts eastward in a timeless motion as the jagged edges of the rocks beneath are smoothed over. God transcends space and time in a magnificent way, and much like the water, He is timeless.

The good news of Jesus Christ is that we are no longer eternally convicted of our sins; that through His death, burial, and resurrection, we are now considered righteous and have no condemnation before the Father. We are saved through our faith in Jesus Christ! This is great news indeed! Even the prophet Isaiah recognized the good news, some seven hundred and fifty years before Christ was born into the world: "How beautiful on the mountains, are the feet of those who bring good news, who proclaim peace, who

---

32. Prov. 2:6 (ESV).

bring good tidings, who proclaim salvation who say to Zion, "Your God reigns!"[33]

Jesus, Himself announced the good news as well by saying, "The time has come." He said, "The kingdom of God has come near. Repent and believe the good news!"[34] Repentance is important for how can we believe if we cannot even ask God for forgiveness and turn from our sins? Surely, the two go hand-in-hand.

It's important to remember to share the gospel message with everyone you encounter. Their very eternal lives are at stake. You don't have to have a degree in Theology or Biblical Studies to share Jesus' message. Simply giving your personal testimony of how you came to faith in Christ will speak volumes into someone's life who is searching for truth.

On the Eighteenth Day

God's love is truly unconditional. Unlike human love, that often expects something in return, God can love us without us doing anything in return for Him. When I was younger, I used to struggle with my emotions. My home wasn't really a place where I felt unconditional love. Instead, I found love without conditions in the church. My church family was so kind and made me feel very special. Eventually, I realized that they loved me because God first loved them.[35] Not long after I started attending church, I decided to get baptized there and publicly declare my love for Jesus Christ.

The prophet Hosea was told by God to marry someone who would not love him back, so he married a prostitute named Gomer. Gomer and Hosea had three children named, Jezreel, Not Loved, and Not My People.[36] The Lord did this in order to show Israel what it was like to Love someone who couldn't love them back. Indeed, the lack of love for God the Father can still be seen today.

Yet, God redeemed Jezreel, Not Loved, and Not My People the same way He redeems us, through the death of His only Son, Jesus Christ. We are now all considered God's people who have received His mercy, despite our transgressions. The Love of the Father is truly amazing in that way.

If you have someone in your life that needs your love, give it to them without conditions for the Father is very much involved with our lives each

---

33. Isa. 52:7 (NIV).
34. Mark 1:15 (NIV).
35. 1 John 4:19 (Emphasis, mine).
36. Hos. 1 (Emphasis, mine).

and every day. After all, He is a God, not of the dead, but of the living.[37] If everyone loved everyone else unconditionally, this world would be a much better place.

On the Nineteenth Day

Waking up this morning to the bright rays of the sunshine is a true blessing. I can remember back to a time in my life when I avoided the sun and preferred to be in the dark. Depression can do that to us; the devil can do that to us. Enjoy the sun while it's around you, but never forget that Christ is the true light. His light is reflected in everyone who believes in Him, and His light will never go out.

I have worked for many employers over the years and had several different types of jobs. I've worked for the government, in sales, in a restaurant, in a kitchen, in the funeral business, in education, in hotels, in transportation, in recreation, in security, in a warehouse, and in the ministry. Out of every job that I've had, I can remember several hot-tempered employees and managers, but very few even-tempered ones. I've had managers scream and yell at me in their offices over something very minor that we disagreed on. I've even had the owner of a company I worked for, threaten my life! Although, he did apologize to me after the incident.

The Bible tells us, "Do not make friends with a hot-tempered person, do not associate with one easily angered."[38] It's hard to work, or live with people that have anger issues. The stress of that environment can be too much to bear sometimes. Even people we love can burn with anger at times. The Lord certainly burned with anger over the disobedience of His chosen people, but there's a difference between human anger and godly anger. I've found that by being kind to all people, there's little for them to be angry at me about. Therefore, you can reflect God's light by simply showing love and compassion to those who clearly need it. Don't be afraid of their anger ruining your day. The Lord has you in their lives for a reason. You don't have to be best friends with them, but you still have to love them.

On the Twentieth Day

The bright blue sky is full of storm clouds as the evening thunderstorms begin to roll in. A dark atmosphere is like a freshly poured cup of coffee,

---

37. Mark 12:27 (Emphasis, mine).
38. Prov. 22:24 (NIV).

minus the cream. I sit and watch as the rain pours down rapidly, and pools of water begin to form on the cold cement ground below.

My oldest daughter, Michelle is a brilliant artist. At five years old, she could sculpt some of the most wonderful Disney characters, plants, fruits, and other inanimate objects with exact precision. When she was a few years older, she began to draw the cutest cartoon characters that looked like they should be in a children's book or on television. Now, she's nine years old and can paint, sculpt, and draw. My youngest daughter, Makayla, can sing on pitch to any song that comes on the radio (I did the same thing when I was her age, and I also played the piano). My son, Brett is gifted with a brilliant mind; we are so blessed to have such beautiful and talented children.

Like Michelle, many of us have God-given talents. We may not be able to draw or sing, but God uses our talents of teaching, preaching, healing, love, compassion, energy, empathy, kindness, gentleness, and the like to advance His purposes. The Bible tells us that everyone who is called by God's name, whom He formed and made, was created by Him for His glory.[39] Therefore, we all contribute our talents in a way that glorifies God.

I encourage you to use your talents and gifts to help advance God's kingdom. He chooses to use human beings as instruments who can speak into someone's life that needs to hear from Him.

> "We are all sculptors and painters, and our material is our own flesh and bones."
>
> —Henry David Thoreau

On the Twenty-First Day

Many years ago, when I served as a youth pastor for a large non-denominational church in Sparks, Nevada, one of the leaders defined God's grace as, something that is given that is not deserved. Indeed, the grace of God does have that component, but it's far more than that, for without it, we would all be judged based on the Law which no one can keep.

The Apostle John tells us, "Out of his fullness we have all received grace in place of grace already given. For the law was given through Moses; grace and truth came through Jesus Christ."[40] Perhaps, because Moses represented the Law, he couldn't have made it to the promised land. Instead, Joshua (aka: Yeshua) led the Israelites into Canaan.

---

39. Isa. 43:7 (Emphasis, mine).
40. John 1:16-17 (NIV).

We see the effects of God's grace manifest itself all around us on a daily basis. When I should have suffered long ago from the consequences of my sins, God's grace was there. When I was depressed and lonely, and ready to end my life, God's grace was there. When I felt as if I'd failed; time after time, having given into my temptations, God's grace was there. Indeed, "the grace of God has appeared that offers salvation to all people. It teaches us to say "No" to ungodliness and worldly passions, and to live self-controlled, upright and godly lives in this present age."[41]

Grace is a powerful gift that God gives freely to each and every one of us. We are abounding in grace because of the sacrifice made by Jesus Christ over two-thousand years ago. Thanks to a gracious God, we have been saved from our sins by the One who has conquered death. Praise and glory and strength and might be to God and the Lamb forever, amen.

On the Twenty-Second Day

Driving through the forests of Lake Tahoe reminds me of the times that I used to ride with my grandparents in the mountains of Northern California towards Redding. My grandfather had a workshop near the garage and would let me build small toys with him. My grandmother made sugar cookies and would take me with her to buy antiques in town. I have such great childhood memories of those earlier times.

The Lord is a healer. A great psalmist once wrote, "Praise the Lord, my soul, and forget not all his benefits; who forgives all your sins and heals all your diseases."[42] The Lord can heal us physically, but more importantly, He can heal us emotionally and spiritually. Jesus performed many miracles while on earth. I know that miracles still take place today, if we only had the faith of a mustard seed to believe in them.

Jesus once passed by a man blind from birth. Displaying the works of God in him, Jesus made mud, placed it on the blind man's eyes and told him to go in faith and wash in the pool of Siloam. Immediately after that, his sight was restored.[43] Jesus took the same earth that formed Adam and restored the blind man back to his original state of glory.

In the same way that Jesus restored sight to the blind man, our sight is also restored once we see the light of Jesus Christ at work in our hearts. The Apostle John once wrote, "Dear friend, I pray that you may enjoy good health and that all may go well with you, even as your soul is getting along

---

41. Titus 2:11-12 (NIV).
42. Ps. 103:2-3 (NIV).
43. John 9:2-6 (Emphasis, mine).

well."[44] Even if healing doesn't take place within our bodies, the true healing has already taken place within our souls.

On the Twenty-Third Day

Lord, I give you all of my heart, and my love for you and your creation will only strengthen with the passage of time. Like the serendipitous ways in which you choose the path set before us, the love you have for me is also unexpected. The Lord rescues us from certain eternal death and the consequences of sin; there is no greater love.

In Bible College, one of my favorite New Testament professors was Professor Bill Osgood. Having been taught at Trinity Evangelical Divinity School, Professor Osgood's lectures tended to be both intriguing and captivating. His knowledge of the historical Near East is greater than anyone I've ever met. The world is truly a better place because he is in it.

Over my six-year tenure at Multnomah University Reno-Tahoe, I've been blessed with sound theological teachings from many diverse evangelical and traditional perspectives. In addition to Professor Osgood, there are several other professors with various church traditions and backgrounds who bring a lot to the theological table. I feel as though this is where God had intended for me to be, among other diverse scholars who share in my passion of studying God's Word. The Apostle John once had a vision that a great multitude that no one could number, from every nation, from all tribes and peoples and languages, were standing before the throne and before the Lamb, clothed in white robes, with palm branches in their hands.[45]

In this way, we too should embrace our differences. Nobody has all of the answers. We are still being sanctified until the day the Lord returns, so it's important to remain scholarly, yet humble in our interpretation of Scripture. One day, all that we fail to understand will be revealed to us.

On the Twenty-Fourth Day

The dark and barren road that lays ahead of us has a light at the end. Though we sometimes travel through the darkness on this road we call life, we have hope in the assurance that Jesus Christ will be standing at the end of the road eager to embrace us and welcome us into His heavenly house.

---

44. 3 John 1:2 (NIV).
45. Rev. 7:9 (Emphasis, mine).

I have to admit that I don't always see eye to eye politically with my Christian brothers and sisters; however, I always respect their opinions, and love them as members of the kingdom of God. My friend, Bill and I attended seminary together and he has been a great friend through the years, despite the fact that we are from opposite political parties. Ironically, Bill ended up joining a Lutheran Church where my old Sunday School teacher and friend, Rev. Mike Patterson was serving as the Interim Pastor.

The Apostle Peter once said, "Honor everyone. Love the brotherhood. Fear God. Honor the emperor."[46] Even though, we may not agree with the decisions our government makes, we must honor the fact that those leaders were placed there for a reason. Either God is using them to punish us for our disobedience to Him, or God is using them to reward us for our obedience to Him. You'll have to decide on the perspective, but either way, God is still sovereign.

Jesus had compassion for everyone, regardless if they worked for Caesar, or if they were homeless and laying on the streets of Jerusalem. In the same way, we too must be compassionate towards others that we do not agree with. Satan is the one who causes division, so we need to remember that divisiveness is spiritual, not emotional. We must be united and of one accord when it comes to the gospel message. The Holy Spirit is available for us to use to reconcile with a brother or sister of faith whom we may have hurt by our political arguments.

On the Twenty-Fifth Day

Staring up at the stars really reminds me of how big our God actually is. Of all the gazillions of miles in outer space, there is only one Earth. Like outer space, the idea of heaven is often associated with something that exists in the skies above us. Yet, the Hebrew people identified three different heavens that exist in which God's presence can be found. Indeed, His omnipresence allows Him to dwell in all three.

The first heaven is the atmosphere in which the birds of the air fly. Jeremiah describes this as, "I looked, and behold, there was no man, and all the birds of the heavens had fled."[47] The second is the celestial or stellar heaven. God told Abraham, "Indeed I will greatly bless you, and I will greatly multiply your seed as the stars of the heavens and as the sand which is on the seashore; and your seed shall possess the gate of their enemies."[48]

---

46. 1 Pet. 2:17 (ESV).
47. Jer. 4:25 (New American Standard Bible).
48. Gen. 22:17 (NASB).

Finally, Paul tells the Corinthians, "I know a man in Christ who fourteen years ago was caught up to the third heaven. Whether it was in the body or out of the body I do not know—God knows."[49]

Jesus proclaimed that the kingdom of heaven was at hand because God's plan of redemption had reached its culmination in Jesus Christ through His death on the cross. Therefore, no longer is the kingdom of heaven somewhere that we must go; but, rather, it's something that we possess inside of us.

When we pray, we need not pray to the sky above, but to the Spirit inside of us. God dwells there just like He dwelt among the Hebrews in the wilderness. The Word became flesh and tabernacled with us two-thousand years ago, and now, the Word is still tabernacling with us through the power of the Holy Spirit.

On the Twenty-Sixth Day

One thing that I really appreciate about the Christian community, here in Reno, is that there is a genuine sense of love and excitement when it comes to interactions with fellow believers, regardless of their backgrounds or faith traditions. I'll never forget how much my dear friend and professor, Dr. Doug Vaughan, had encouraged me throughout my undergraduate studies. His love for others shines so brightly that it's like a radiant beam of light from a secluded lighthouse which penetrates through the densest fog of the ocean.

The friendly embrace of my longtime friend and Christian brother, Michael is another example of this type of Christian love. We are truly happy just to see each other and catch up on lost times. In fact, there isn't one person in my Christian circle that does not exhibit love and affection for each other.

The Apostle Peter tells us that love covers a multitude of sins.[50] Perhaps, this is God's way of allowing us to forgive ourselves for our transgressions. When we love one another, we represent the very best of Jesus Christ. There wasn't anyone on earth that Jesus hated. We are all broken in one way or another; some of us just hide it better than others.

I had the pleasure of counseling a married couple a few months ago who were having trust issues in their marriage. I told them that no relationship is perfect, but we can work towards being better husbands and wives for each other through building a stronger relationship with God. Too often,

---

49. 2 Cor. 12:2 (NIV).

50. 1 Pet. 4:8 (Emphasis, mine).

we prioritize work or earthly relationships over obedience to Jesus Christ. The times that I fell away from obeying Jesus were the times that I suffered the most, yet the times that I strengthened my bond with Him were the times that my work and relationships benefited the most.

On the Twenty-Seventh Day

Darkness comes over the land as the storm clouds roll in from the west. The parched land longs for the timeless water that was once created by God, rained down on Adam, fell into lakes and rivers, then evaporated back into the clouds again. This same water cycle has been happening since the beginning of time.

When one thinks of Hell, images of pitchforks, a red devil, and lakes of fire often come to mind. It is true that some Scriptures allude to this type of imagery for the place of torture, weeping, and gnashing of teeth. Yet, the Apostle Paul tell us that God will punish those who do not know God and do not obey the gospel of our Lord Jesus. And, that they will be punished with everlasting destruction and *shut out from the presence of the Lord* and from the glory of his might.[51]

Imagine being forever separated from someone that you love. No more interactions, no more hugs, no more spending time laughing together, talking together, crying together. This is exactly what Satan wants. When Adam and Eve sinned, it caused separation because no longer was Adam comfortable around his Creator. He went into a state of hiding and shame. Satan's goal has always been to separate us from God. So, while Hell may be full of sulphur and fire, the true Hell is being eternally separated from the Holy One.

You can have such a great relationship with God if you simply repent of your sinful ways and turn back to Him. Tomorrow is never guaranteed, so don't delay. If you haven't accepted Jesus Christ into your heart yet, I pray that you will realize how much He has done for you; that you can trust in Him even if no one else can be trusted. Jesus loves you unconditionally. Invite Him into your life today.

On the Twenty-Eighth Day

There is something common about all Christians. We all possess the Holy Spirit. Some extreme Pentecostal traditions hold to the fact that one must

---

51. 2 Thess. 1:8-9 (Emphasis, mine).

speak in tongues as proof of Spirit baptism, yet the Apostle Paul tells us that we are all baptized by one Spirit and given one Spirit to drink.[52] I consider myself Charismatic, for I have received several gifts of the Spirit at my own Spirit baptism, yet I would argue that the Holy Spirit does not limit Himself to distributing only certain gifts. The Spirit gives various kinds of gifts as He wills.[53]

One of the main functions of the Holy Spirit is to help us in becoming more Christ-like. He's the voice inside that convicts us when we sin, and He's the thought that gives us compassion to help someone in need. Jesus once said, "But the Advocate, the Holy Spirit, whom the Father will send in my name, will teach you all things and will remind you of everything I have said to you."[54] This is important, because without the Holy Spirit, we would not be born again. Jesus told Nicodemus: "Very truly I tell you, no one can enter the kingdom of God unless they are born of water and the Spirit. Flesh gives birth to flesh, but the Spirit gives birth to spirit. You should not be surprised at my saying, "You must be born again.""[55]

The Holy Spirit does so many things for us in our quest for sanctification. He helps guide and empower us, He allows us to witness the glory of Jesus Christ to the ends of the earth; He helps us understand the Bible, and He helps us understand each other. When you struggle with something of this world and question which way to respond, remember to pray that the Holy Spirit guide you in the right direction. You are not traveling through this life alone. God has sent The Paraclete to comfort and advise you in all spiritual matters.

On the Twenty-Ninth Day

As the month of August ends, the heat begins to taper off a bit. The winds start to blow in from the west bringing shade from the billowing clouds that linger above us. The light of the sun peaks through the trees as heaven reveals its glory.

One area in which most of us struggle is that of humility. Remaining humble regardless of the circumstance is not always easy. Take marriage, for instance. The old saying goes, "You can be right, or you can be happy." I must admit, I'm usually happy. Sometimes it's best to admit that we might

---

52. 1 Cor. 12:13 (Emphasis, mine).
53. 1 Cor. 12:11 (Emphasis, mine).
54. John 14:26 (NIV).
55. John 3:5-7 (NIV).

be wrong about something. Only God has every answer to every situation. We are finite and therefore have limited knowledge in certain areas of life.

The Apostle Paul encourages the Philippians to:

> Do nothing from selfish ambition or conceit, but in humility count others more significant than yourselves. Let each of you look not only to his own interests, but also to the interests of others. Have this mind among yourselves, which is yours in Christ Jesus.[56]

If everyone cared more about the feelings of someone else than they did about their own, there would never be arguments, power-struggles, jealousy, or envy of someone else's accomplishments. We would simply love the person for being made in the image of God. Sadly, the fall has disrupted God's plan for this type of harmony amongst each other. But, not to worry. God's plan of redemption has been in motion since Adam's transgression and will be completed at the great day of the Lord.

Building each other up often requires us to allow the glory to go to someone else. Did not John the Baptist lessen his influence so that Christ could gain more followers?[57] In this respect, we, too, must humble ourselves before God and allow the Holy Spirit to speak through others.

On the Thirtieth Day

Jesus was the one who committed no sins, yet He became sin so that we might enter into God's kingdom eternally.[58] Jesus is the light that shines out into a dark world. Jesus had both light and love; a godly love that is not hindered by malice or prejudice.

The birth of Jesus was foretold by many of the prophets. The book of Isaiah says:

> For to us a child is born, to us a son is given, and the government will be on his shoulders. And he will be called Wonderful Counselor, Mighty God, Everlasting Father, Prince of Peace. Of the greatness of his government and peace there will be no end. He will reign on David's throne and over his kingdom, establishing and upholding it with justice and righteousness from that time on and forever. The zeal of the Lord Almighty will accomplish this.[59]

---

56. Phil. 2:3-5 (ESV).
57. John 3:27-30 (Emphasis, mine).
58. 1 Pet. 2:22 (Emphasis, mine).
59. Isa. 9:6-7 (NIV).

Someone once told me that if God had flesh, He would look like Jesus, and rightly so, for Jesus is God. Jesus fulfilled everything written about Him in the Old Testament. In fact, Jesus Himself tells us that everything must be fulfilled that was written about Him in the Law, the Prophets, and the Psalms.[60]

The mystery of the Holy Trinity is perhaps something that will never be completely solved, yet the early church Fathers all came to an agreement upon the divinity of Christ. There is only one God, yet over the course of history, He has manifested Himself in three different ways. During the time of the Old Testament, God revealed Himself as YHWH. During the time of Christ, God revealed Himself as the Son. Finally, God reveals Himself today in the same way that He has since Pentecost, and that is in the form of the Holy Spirit.

Jesus Christ is fundamental to our faith as Christians. His teachings and love for others cross all religious, cultural, and ethnic boundaries. He is the Alpha and the Omega, and He will return soon to judge the living and the dead.

On the Thirty-First Day

Well, you've made it to the end of August. I hope that this month's devotional has been transformative and edifying to your soul. I thank you for your commitment to better your relationship with Jesus Christ, and I pray that you will continue on to further develop that relationship through prayer, Scripture, meditation, time in solitude, and time with fellow believers.

I once wrote an article for a local newspaper regarding whether or not "religion" makes people happier. I qualified my answer by stating that a saved follower of Jesus Christ should possess the fruit of the Holy Spirit, which includes joy. The Apostle Paul tells us that "The fruit of the Spirit is love, joy, peace, patience, kindness, goodness, faithfulness, gentleness, self-control; against such things there is no law."[61]

In terms of God Himself displaying joy, there are several Old Testament passages that demonstrate this attribute. The most transparent way in which we see this joy displayed is in others around us. The image of God is very prevalent in all of God's creation; therefore, if you find yourself unhappy as a result of the religion you practice, you must re-evaluate your religion.

In this sense, religion may or may not make people happier, but Christianity should certainly make people who practice it happier. The Apostle John

---

60. Luke 24:44 (Emphasis, mine).
61. Gal. 5:22-23 (NIV).

once quoted Jesus as saying, "These things I have spoken to you, that my joy may be in you, and that your joy may be full."[62] Indeed, Jesus' joy is in each and every one of us who profess Him as our personal Lord and Savior. No longer must we fear the world, for Jesus has overcome the world.[63]

May the Lord bless and keep you. May He make His face to shine upon you and bring you peace. May He comfort and guide you in all that you do.

---

62. John 15:11 (ESV).
63. John 16:33 (Emphasis, mine).

Chapter 9

"The Calm in a Time of Storm"
The Month of September

On the First Day

THE WINDS OF CHANGE blow slowly in as the seasons turn from summer to fall. The storms inside cannot compare to those that usher in the calming rains as I peer out my ordinary and double-paned window. Sometimes, emptiness and despair set in and the enemy gets the best of me.

I once felt that way: lonely and empty inside. As I spent time in my bedroom alone thinking of happier times, wishing my teenage years were past me, something, or should I say, someone, would always encourage me to continue on. That someone, was the Holy Spirit, who has never left my side, and never will.

I've always had a love for writing and playing music. One song that I wrote called, "The Calm Within the Storm" was on an album that I debuted at the Knitting Factory in Reno, Nevada in the summer of 2013. The lyrics speak of this time in my life. Perhaps they will speak to you as well:

> The night falls over me,
> It feels the best when I'm alone;
> Close your eyes and see,
> In your mind the strange unknown.
>
> If you realize,
> That you're never on your own;
> Then don't hesitate,
> To believe what you've been shown.
>
> Hold your head up high,
> Just be glad that you were born;

> Try and touch the sky,
> He's the calm within the storm . . .

On the Second Day

When I look back at all of the storms I've had to endure in my life, I'm happy to say that I made it through, fairly unscathed. Divorce, loss of employment, debt, depression, and other setbacks really tests one's character. Yet, in the end, I knew that I would still be standing, for God has always been there with me.

So often, we focus on the Apostle Peter's lack of trust in Jesus Christ as contributing to him sinking into the sea. Although, we forget that Peter still had enough trust to step out of the boat in faith towards Jesus who was waiting for him nearby. Sometimes, we have to step out of our comfort zones and trust that Jesus will be there to support us, to lift us back up when we give in to our temptations and begin sinking into an endless sea of sin.

We all face storms in our lives sometimes. In fact, Israel has never had a navy because they regard the sea as an evil place. The sea can be a place of chaos and darkness, but we have to keep in mind who it is that is sending the storm. When the Sea of Galilee was turbulent and fierce, Jesus was asleep down below. Frightened by the storm, the disciples woke Jesus up and requested His assistance. Jesus, in response, rebuked the storm, and the waves immediately calmed down.[1]

Similarly, the Prophet Jonah, was also asleep during a storm at sea, yet he could not rebuke the storm, because God, Himself had sent it.[2] In Jesus' situation, Satan was trying to prevent the spread of the gospel to the other side of the sea. In Jonah's case, the storm was appeased when Jonah was thrown overboard. Sometimes God sends storms our way to test our faith, and sometimes Satan sends storms our way to tempt us, which also tests our faith. Will you pass the test?

On the Third Day

The coolness of the night is apparent now as the summer heat has left us for another year. I enjoy the cool breeze blowing through my open window as the leaves begin to slightly turn red on the trees surrounding me.

---

1. Mark 4:35-41 (Emphasis, mine).
2. Jonah 1:4 (Emphasis, mine).

We are considered justified before God because of our faith in Jesus Christ. I can't tell you how many "on-the-fence believers" that I have counseled who almost always start off the conversation with something like, "I don't see why I have to believe in Jesus Christ to be saved, I haven't murdered anyone, I don't even swear that much, or sleep around." They always end their statement by saying, "I'm a good person; therefore, I deserve to go to heaven." I always have to remind them that Jesus said that "There is no one good, not one."[3] So, what does this mean for us? Because God requires atonement for sin that we, ourselves cannot sufficiently give, a substitute who lived an obedient life had to satisfy the penalty for our sins in God's courtroom.

The Apostle Paul tells us, "For all have sinned and fall short of the glory of God, and all are justified freely by his grace through the redemption that came by Christ Jesus."[4] Similarly, Paul's words to Titus were, " But when the kindness and love of God our Savior appeared, he saved us, not because of righteous things we had done, but because of his mercy . . . so that, having been justified by his grace, we might become heirs having the hope of eternal life."[5]

Therefore, it is not through any good deeds that we can perform in this life that will earn our entry into heaven, but rather, it's only through our faith and trust in Jesus Christ, who paid the price for us on the cross, so that we can spend eternity with the Father.

On the Fourth Day

A little kindness goes a long way in helping someone through a challenging situation in life. Kindness can be both gratifying and reciprocal. There have been so many people in my life who have expressed kindness towards me and others, that it's hard to only highlight a single experience.

One of my favorite God-fearing and kind persons, is my dear friend and colleague, Nathan DuPree. He was recently selected as a finalist for the City of Reno At-Large city council member seat. Despite the fact that he didn't end up getting the position, it struck me that he was so grateful for the tremendous support that was shown in terms of his character and knowledge of the city and the various youth programs within it. Nathan has a great heart and is always so happy just to see me. I can only hope that I emulate his kindness in a similar way.

3. Mark 10:18 (Emphasis, mine).
4. Rom. 3:23-24 (NIV).
5. Titus 3:4-5,7 (NIV).

Jesus once said, "Love your enemies, do good to them, and lend to them without expecting to get anything back. Then your reward will be great, and you will be children of the Most High, because he is kind to the ungrateful and wicked. Be merciful, just as your Father is merciful."[6] If we are to treat our enemies in such a way, how much greater should we treat our friends? I try and show kindness to everyone that I encounter because I never know what struggles they are facing.

The Apostle Paul once said, "By grace you have been saved, and raised us up with him and seated us with him in the heavenly places in Christ Jesus, so that in the coming ages he might show the immeasurable riches of his grace in kindness toward us in Christ Jesus."[7] Kindness on this earth is only a foreshadow of the kindness that is to come in the heavenly places.

On the Fifth Day

The sun sets beautifully in the west as the skies reflect God's glory with radiant rays of purple, yellow, and blue that are blended into the distended clouds. As I sit outside and watch the kids play in the front yard, I reflect back on my own youth and the great fun I had playing with the other neighborhood children in the late 1980's.

Jesus talks about the kingdom of God a lot in the New Testament. John the Baptist gives us some insight into the background of the first mention of the kingdom of heaven when he said, "Repent, for the kingdom of heaven has come near."[8] Jesus ushers in the kingdom of heaven with His birth. God's sovereign plan was about to unfold with Jesus' ministry, death, and resurrection.

In his letter to the Romans, the Apostle Paul states that "The kingdom of God is not a matter of eating and drinking but of righteousness and peace and joy in the Holy Spirit."[9] In this way, the kingdom is not a place of drunkenness and gluttony; but rather, the kingdom of God is a place in which our righteousness is brought to fruition in joy through the power of the Holy Spirit.

If you could have anything you wanted in this world that was non-material, what would it be? For me, I'm happy with loving others and being loved by God. Those are the essentials to the kingdom of heaven. What is your life's purpose? To make money? You'll never see a U-Haul behind a

---

6. Luke 6:35-36 (NIV).
7. Eph. 2:5-8 (ESV).
8. Matt. 3:2 (NIV).
9. Rom. 14:17 (ESV).

hearse because none of us are taking our possessions with us after this life is over. Therefore, work on your relationship with God and others. Do that, and your reward in heaven will already be paid in full.

On the Sixth Day

I've been to several leadership conferences since I've been a pastor. I've also had several leadership courses at both the undergraduate, and graduate levels in college, and I always default back to the same principles when it comes to leadership. That principle is modeled after Jesus Christ, Himself and is called, *Servant-Leadership*.

So often, the world tells us to follow a corporate leadership model in which the founder or CEO is at the top of a pyramid and everyone else is positioned below him or her ending at the foundation of the entire structure, which are the members of the company who are positioned at the very bottom. What if the pyramid were reversed? What if the founder of the corporation invested his or her time primarily in the lives of the foundational members of the corporation, and likewise, every level did the same until you reached the bottom, in which the founder was served the least and the foundation was served the most? An upside-down pyramid, if you will.

This is exactly how Jesus lead His followers. The Apostle John recalls when Jesus washed His disciples' feet:

> He came to Simon Peter, who said to him, "Lord, are you going to wash my feet?" Jesus replied, "You do not realize now what I am doing, but later you will understand." "No," said Peter, "you shall never wash my feet." Jesus answered, "Unless I wash you, you have no part with me." "Then, Lord," Simon Peter replied, "not just my feet but my hands and my head as well!" Jesus answered, "Those who have had a bath need only to wash their feet; their whole body is clean. And you are clean, though not every one of you."[10]

To be part of Jesus Christ, means that we must be willing to serve others, regardless of our position on the corporate ladder. And, it's not always comfortable, but we must go beyond our comfort zones to live the gospel message. Always remember, that even the Son of Man came not to be served, but to serve.[11]

---

10. John 13:6-10 (NIV).
11. Mark 10:45 (Emphasis, mine).

On the Seventh Day

My wife and I have been married for almost twelve years now. We got married in a small chapel in Reno, Nevada on March 2, 2008. Not long after, our son, Brett was born followed by our beautiful daughters, Michelle, and Makayla.

The biblical definition of marriage is different than the world's definition of marriage. I once posted on social media that I support traditional marriage and was un-friended by several of my more liberal friends. The irony is, I never said I didn't support someone's right to love someone else, nor did I unfriend *them* for supporting same-sex marriage. I simply stated that according to the Bible, marriage is defined in a certain way. Actually, marriage is defined by God in the Old Testament (Gen. 2:24), Jesus in the Gospels (Matt. 19:4-6), and Paul in the New Testament (1 Cor. 7:3), and they all refer to marriage as being a covenant made between a man and a woman; never referring to two men or two women marrying each other.

I have some friends in ministry who try and justify the practice of same-sex marriage by stating that nowhere does the Bible prohibit same-sex practices between two adult partners, but the fallacy to that argument is that the Bible prohibits all sexual practices before marriage, and the very definition of marriage is between a man and a woman. Technically, if members of the same sex cohabitate with each other, never marry each other, and never act upon their sexual urges, then they are not living in sin. In that case, they are no more sinful than the rest of us. But how realistic is that? Purposefully sinning is far worse than making a mistake and asking for forgiveness. I personally know of same-sex couples who have repented and accepted Jesus Christ. They now have wonderful traditional marriages. Earthly marriage is representative of our eternal marriage to Jesus Christ. Both are holy covenants made to honor God and our spouse. I pray that you have a strong and long-lasting marriage, and honor God in the process.

On the Eighth Day

The dark skies above are filled with menacing clouds as the smell of rain permeates the air. The calming sound of the rain outside helps me to relax when I begin to feel overwhelmed by life's many demands and obligations.

Last February, I purchased a painting by Greg Olsen entitled, "Worlds Without End." In the painting, Jesus is reclining on a rock, gazing up at the heavens that He created. The image is powerful to me in so many ways. It reminds me of how I feel after I've built, deep-cleaned, or organized something. I'll often take a step back and admire my handiwork for a few minutes. It also reveals something that Jesus often enjoyed doing; spending time in solitude with His Father. Lastly, the portrait demonstrates just how small we actually are in God's grand scheme of things; how an all-powerful God makes the time to care for each and every one of us individually.

As Jesus meditates on the celestial heavens that He once created, I'm reminded of what Paul said to the Philippians many years ago: "Finally, brothers and sisters, whatever is true, whatever is noble, whatever is right, whatever is pure, whatever is lovely, whatever is admirable—if anything is excellent or praiseworthy—think about such things."[12]

We should always be thinking and meditating, not only God's Word, but on His creation and everything that exists within His creation. Sometimes, in the quiet of the evening, when I'm making the hour-long drive back to Reno from Lake Tahoe by myself, God speaks to me; answering questions, guiding my motives, encouraging me, and reminding me of my purpose in this life. It's at those times that I realize, God loves me regardless of my faults. And, that in return, I love Him because He first loved me.

On the Ninth Day

The bright lights of the city can be seen from the top of Mt. Rose as the fresh mountain air brings a calm and elated feeling to the frantic traveler. The relaxing, peaceful atmosphere is one of the things that I love most about Lake Tahoe. Whenever my life feels stressful and filled with anxiety, I head towards the mountains where all of my worries seem to fade away.

God is very merciful. Jesus once said, "Blessed are the merciful, for they will be shown mercy."[13] When someone wrongs us, we need to think about all of the times in which we had wronged someone else. How did they react to us? Were they vengeful towards us, or did they show us mercy for making a mistake? God prefers the latter, for that is how He reacts to us once we have sinned and ask for forgiveness.

You might recall reading when the Israelites disobeyed God in the wilderness, and Moses interceded for them so that they would not to be destroyed by YHWH for worshiping false idols. In this way, when we ask for God's mercy, He grants it to us: God's mercy triumphs over His judgment.[14]

No one is perfect. When I was around fourteen years old, I was really into magic tricks. I decided to perform one in front of my family one evening

---

12. Phil. 4:8 (NIV).
13. Matt. 5:7 (NIV).
14. Jas. 2:13 (Emphasis, mine).

and to my dismay, my little sister figured out how I did it and told everyone at the performance! I was so mad that I went upstairs and kicked my wall, which wasn't such a good idea, because I missed the stud and kicked a whole right through the drywall. I thought for sure I would get some type of capital punishment once my stepdad discovered it. Instead, he grounded me for only one day and my grandfather and I repaired the wall. Surely, you have done things in your life in which you thought that you would be severely punished, yet did your parents not show mercy towards you?

On the Tenth Day

Whenever I see a post from a friend on social media who's on a mission trip, for some reason it seems like they are always in desirable places like Romania, or Belize, or Ecuador. Yet, many people need to hear the gospel message right in our own backyards.

A recent study on religiosity by state discovered that less than fifty percent of the states in the United States are considered highly religious. And, out of those fifty percent, only half of the citizens in those states attend church on a regular basis. [15] So, more work must be done, right here in the United States to spread the gospel of hope and peace to those around us who have yet to hear it.

Even before the great commission was given by Jesus Christ to His disciples, The Psalms instruct us to spread the glory of the Lord to all the nations: "Declare his glory among the nations, his marvelous deeds among all peoples."[16]

The Apostle Paul tells us:

> For, "Everyone who calls on the name of the Lord will be saved." How, then, can they call on the one they have not believed in? And how can they believe in the one of whom they have not heard? And how can they hear without someone preaching to them? And how can anyone preach unless they are sent? As it is written: "How beautiful are the feet of those who bring good news."[17]

Therefore, God uses *us* as instruments to speak truth and life into the hearts of others. I was just sharing the gospel message with a co-worker recently and was delighted to hear that he wanted to hear more about the

---

15. Lipka, "How Religious is Your State?"
16. Psalm 96:3 (NIV).
17. Rom. 10:13-15 (NIV).

man called, *Jesus Christ*. If none of us shared the good news with others, then no one would hear it, no one would allow it to change their hearts, and no one would accept Jesus Christ into their lives. It's up to us to share the good news at all times.

On the Eleventh Day

The sunrise casts colors of blue and gold along the horizon as the sun radiates between the scattered clouds. The temperatures have dropped a bit as fall really begins to set in. Some of the leaves have already changed colors, and the evenings have that familiar fall chill in the air.

Money is said to be the root of all evil, right? Technically, no. The *love* of money is the root of all kinds of evils.[18] You see, it's not the money itself that is evil, for we all must utilize it to sustain our lives. Rather, like everything else of God, it goes back to the heart. Does your heart love money more than God? Do you spend hours obsessing with the thought of earning millions of dollars and living happily ever after?

Let me tell you a story, a true story, at that. Many years ago, I was the personal chauffeur for a very wealthy and successful business owner in the Reno area. In fact, he had inherited millions of dollars from his father, who was also financially successful. Believing that money could buy him happiness, he ended up marrying a woman half his age, who, five-years later after he suffered a stroke, divorced him. His so called, "friends" disappeared because no longer could they take advantage of his kindness, and he's now very much alone and without anyone he can truly trust.

My point is this, money cannot buy you happiness. I don't care how much you have or how many people make you believe that they genuinely care about you. Wealth and prosperity can only take us so far in this life. To take us to a place of peace requires a faith and trust in God alone. God wants us to be prosperous, but not on our terms, on His terms. People in the ministry who are wealthy are no exception. I've seen God bring them down just as fast. Put God first in your life and you will have spiritual riches beyond measure.

On the Twelfth Day

God always judges us by our hearts. This is why a young, short, and unknown shepherd was elevated to the status of King of Israel, and a powerful,

---

18. 1 Tim. 6:10 (ESV).

handsome, intelligent Pharaoh was plagued by locusts and death. Both of them sinned, yet both of them had very different hearts. One had a heart after God's own, and the other had a heart for only himself and his possessions.

My wife is studying to be an MRI technician. Her Associate Degree is in Radiologic Technologies and she's in her first semester of MRI school now. I'm definitely not science minded; but both she, and my youngest son, have the gift of the left brain. God decided to gift me and my two daughters with artistic minds instead.

Most people have MRI's done because a doctor needs to see what is happening inside their bodies that he cannot see from the outside. Once the abnormality is revealed, the patient and physician can discuss the best course of action to remedy or treat the issue.

Love, peace, joy, gentleness, kindness, self-control, and the like are not discovered from the outside, for many people do not genuinely possess these attributes, rather, all of these fruits are discovered from within. Conversely, the lack of these fruits is also discovered from within, for there is no hiding our inner selves from the Lord. In a sense, God puts us through a spiritual MRI. He shows us things that we don't want to see and uncovers things that we wish we could see.

When analyzing someone else's character, look to their hearts. Do their actions speak louder than their words, or do their words speak louder than their actions? We should never judge someone's salvation, that is up to God alone; however, we can help correct a brother or sister of faith when they are in error.[19]

On the Thirteenth Day

The beauty of the Sierra Mountains is that they rise majestically over the valley with a beautiful lake at the top. Like the volcanoes of Hawaii, the Lake Tahoe area erupts with life as the winter season draws closer.

God has many names. Once, when Sarai's servant, Hagar fled from her for being mistreated, The Angel of the Lord found her and comforted her. Because of what the Lord saw in her, she named the well, Beer Lahai Roi, for God is a God that really *sees* what we are going through inside.[20]

Moses once asked the Lord what he should call Him if the Israelites inquired. God said, "Tell them that I am who I am."[21] The verb, *YHWH* has this idea of timelessness about it. I AM is in the present tense; therefore,

19. Matt. 18:15-17 (Emphasis, mine).
20. Gen. 16:7-15 (Emphasis, mine).
21. Ex. 3:13-15 (Emphasis, mine).

there isn't a time in which He was not, and there won't be a time in which He won't exist. He is always with us at all times and in all situations.

Adam was given the task of naming everything in creation. Which, sort of symbolically demonstrates that he had dominion over all of the things he named. Kind of like we are in charge of our children and we name them. But Adam could not name the other members of the Trinity, because no one has dominion over Jesus. Jesus' name is above everything else named in creation. "The name above all names."[22]

Often times, when the Lord renames someone in the Bible, it has significance. Abram was changed to "Abraham," Jacob was changed to "Israel," and Simon was changed to "Peter." In the new heavens and new earth, we too will have a new name. One that is written on stone; one that honors the Lord for all time.

On the Fourteenth Day

Yesterday, we learned about the names that God has, and gives to those who He uses to advance His kingdom. So, today I'd like to focus on Jesus' names and how they connect to the beginning of time.

The prophet Isaiah calls the future Messiah, "Wonderful Counselor, Mighty God, Everlasting Father, Prince of Peace."[23] Amazingly, these titles also connect to the one that Abraham tithed ten percent. In the Old Testament, Melchizedek, the king and high priest is also called, "The King of Peace;" "The King of Salem."[24] Jerusalem is known as "The City of Peace." King David established Jerusalem as the capital of Israel; therefore, Jesus is the high priest, not through the tribe of Levi, but through Melchizedek, who existed before Levi. Jesus is also the King of kings because He descended from the tribe of Judah, of which the Davidic covenant was established.

I've heard the argument from non-Christians that nowhere in the Bible does it say directly that Jesus is God, yet I found a place in which Jesus refers to Himself as God: "Very truly I tell you," Jesus answered, "before Abraham was born, I Am!"[25] So, here we see that Jesus connects Himself to YHWH from the beginning of time, which is why the Pharisees picked up stones to throw at Him.

The name of Jesus holds power. This is why we can cast out demons with it, heal people with it, and offend people with it. Jesus even predicted

22. Phil. 2:9 (Emphasis, mine).
23. Isa. 9:6 (NIV).
24. Heb. 7:1-3 (Emphasis, mine).
25. John 8:58 (NIV).

that we will be hated because of His name.[26] We must have strength, courage, and faith when we proclaim the Gospel of Jesus Christ. Use His name, not in vain, but in power.

On the Fifteenth Day

During these colder months, we like to take the kids to indoor activities, such as watching movies, or going to the museum; although, my son Brett still enjoys riding his bike around the neighborhood while I follow slowly behind. It feels like the seasons go by faster each year.

Parenting is both rewarding and challenging. I remember when our kids were all little, they were always scared so we used to let them sleep with us. That was a mistake. Never do that! Well, it's too late now, but ten years later, my back is still feeling the effects of a previous child's foot in it.

The Bible has a few things to say about parenting. God tells us in the fifth commandment to, "Honor your father and your mother, so that you may live long in the land the Lord your God is giving you."[27] Giving honor to our parents involves more than just respecting them.

King Solomon once said, "Listen to your father, who gave you life, and do not despise your mother when she is old."[28] In my wife's home country of Mongolia, once the parents reach an age in which they are too old to care for themselves, it's common for one of the children to care for them in their home. This is unlike us, here in the West, who prefer to send our aging parents to retirement homes so that someone else has to care for them for the last ten years of their lives, even though they took care of us for eighteen years of ours.

Parenting isn't always easy. Sometimes, we're tired and just want to rest, when one of our kids needs something that just can't wait. Sometimes, we end up spending more money than we wanted for that item on Amazon.com that our youngest just couldn't live without. But sometimes, our kids realize that we've had a hard day, and they come over and comfort us in some way, and it makes all of the struggles worth it.

---

26. Matt. 10:22 (Emphasis, mine).
27. Ex. 20:12 (NIV).
28. Prov. 23:22 (NIV).

On the Sixteenth Day

We've discussed God's providence a few times already, but I did have a question arise from one of my church members, about knowing God's plan for us. I've often thought of this myself, and so I thought I'd share some of my insights with you pertaining to God's providence and sovereign plan for our lives.

Seven years ago, I felt a call on my life to become a pastor. I remember that I felt really strongly about the call, but wondered if it was just me calling myself, or if God was actually on the phone. To sort of "test the waters," I decided to meet with my dear friend and spiritual mentor, David and ask his advice. He told me that when he was called by God to start a teaching, healing, and deliverance ministry, God orchestrated the entire event, from his wife confirming through a neighbor that this was in God's plan, to David hearing the Lord's voice. As a result, David has been a true blessing to anyone he teaches about Jesus, and an instrumental figure in the local Christian community for more than fifty years now.

Similarly, when I accepted the call to ministry, I found that my work was willing to give me the time off to attend the courses, my wife was more than supportive, my ability to learn to write papers and study again came back, and I found a small church where I could serve as the senior pastor. God orchestrated everything for me, just as He had done for David.

In contrast, when I look for something that God hasn't intended for me to have, all sorts of obstacles seem to come in my way. Instead of God happily opening the door, I find that I'm trying to kick the door in! In life, we all want success and happiness, but sometimes how we try and achieve it is not in God's plan. God wants the very best for us and He has already established a plan for our lives, we simply have to listen to Him and follow it.

On the Seventeenth Day

September is usually the last month that I mow the lawn; although, last year I think I ended up mowing it into October because it stayed warm longer than usual. Soon the grass will turn color and the leaves will fall.

There are a few things that I'm truly passionate about. I'm passionate about Christianity, my family, music, and loving others. The Apostle Paul once said, "Whatever you do, work at it with all your heart, as working for the Lord, not for human masters."[29] When we choose to take on a task, no

---

29. Col. 3:23 (NIV).

matter how small it is, we should do it with all of our heart and all of our passion. In this way, we reflect the passion that Jesus Christ has for us.

There's nothing more disappointing than someone who promises things, then breaks their promises. If you don't believe you will have the time to take on a task or commitment, it's better to let the person know up front, rather than say yes to everything, only to let them down later when they depended on you. Emergencies come up but making a habit of falling through on your commitments, doesn't benefit anyone, and is certainly dishonoring to God.

The Apostle Paul once told his church members in Rome, "Love one another with brotherly affection. Outdo one another in showing honor. Do not be slothful in zeal, be fervent in spirit, serve the Lord."[30] If we all showed honor to one another, then we would all reflect the passion of the Lord. Being fervent in spirit means to display passionate intensity. How much better will it be if people remember that you were passionate in everything you did? What legacy do you want to leave behind?

On the Eighteenth Day

Rain falls from the melancholy skies above as the winds blow in aggressively from the west. Nautical sailors harbor their boats at the old wooden docks of Lake Tahoe. As the crisp air fills my lungs, I remember so many wonderful trips to the lake in the past. Memories can be a wonderful thing sometimes.

As part of my transportation job, we drive back and forth from Reno to Lake Tahoe multiple times a day. We mostly transport business people, but we have a handful of recreational clients as well. Often times, people will drive slowly up the mountain due to several hairpin turns along the way. I tend to drive slower simply because taking the turns quickly will lead to nauseous clients and a lower gratuity. Yet, along the drive there is always someone right behind me who lacks all patience.

Some believers expect justice to be served immediately to those who have wronged them. Indeed, The Lord is a just God and requires every sin to be accounted for, but the Bible says, "Be patient, then, brothers and sisters, until the Lord's coming. See how the farmer waits for the land to yield its valuable crop, patiently waiting for the autumn and spring rains."[31]

We must practice patience, for the Lord is certainly patient with us. Abraham and Sarah waited almost ninety years before becoming parents to their first, and only son Isaac. How much more patient must we be when

30. Rom. 12:10-11 (ESV).
31. Jas. 5:7 (NIV).

waiting on God's plan for our lives? The Apostle Paul once said, "Do not be anxious about anything, but in every situation, by prayer and petition, with thanksgiving, present your requests to God."[32] Therefore, we must pray that God's will be carried out, but also realize that our blessings are in God's timing, not ours.

On the Nineteenth Day

When Jesus walked the earth, He not only proclaimed the kingdom of heaven, but also, He promoted a kingdom of peace. The prophet Isaiah once foretold:

> Behold, a king will reign in righteousness, and princes will rule in justice . . . Then justice will dwell in the wilderness, and righteousness abide in the fruitful field. And the effect of righteousness will be peace, and the result of righteousness, quietness and trust forever.[33]

Jesus lived His entire earthly life promoting peace and kindness towards one another. Certainly, times of peace are far less stressful than times of war; therefore, we must always work to achieve a peaceful resolution to our differences. The Apostle Paul concludes his second letter to the Thessalonians with, "Now may the Lord of peace himself give you peace at all times and in every way. The Lord be with all of you."[34]

When I take on a large responsibility, I always pray that the Lord will give me peace throughout the experience. This helps to ensure that I make wiser decisions, for when the anxiety is removed, the enemy cannot cloud our minds.

In life, we can choose to make waves, or to calm the waters. So often, I witness people in disagreements over minor things of little importance. This tends to be the case in some marriages. If we can step back from the situation at hand, respond in a calm manner, and use godly wisdom in everything we do, our rewards will be plentiful in heaven. During the Sermon on the Mount, Jesus once taught, "Blessed are the peacemakers, for they will be called children of God."[35]

---

32. Phil. 4:6 (NIV).
33. Isa. 32:1, 16-17 (ESV).
34. 2 Thess. 3:16 (NIV).
35. Matt. 5:9 (NIV).

Remember to think about those who would benefit the most from your peaceful actions. I'll be praying for you in this area of your life. God bless, and peace be with you.

On the Twentieth Day

When I first became a Christian, many years ago, I feared praying out loud in public. I would always remain silent when we were in prayer groups as the other members of the group prayed around me. It wasn't until much later in my walk with Christ, that I began to open up more and pray from my Spirit and heart, regardless of how it sounded.

As a senior pastor, I now pray every week for my congregation as well as every day that I have classes at my seminary school. I pray when someone sends me a prayer request, and I pray at night before bed, thanking the Lord for all He has done to bless me. When my youngest son was seven or eight years old, he would remind me to pray with him before bed, if I had somehow forgotten or was too tired.

Jesus prayed regularly. He prayed in corporate settings, and private settings. He would pray in a garden or on a mountaintop. He would pray with others or alone with God. One of my favorite prayers comes from John chapter seventeen. This prayer is known as, "The High Priestly Prayer, and in it, Jesus prayed:

> My prayer is not for them alone. I pray also for those who will believe in me through their message, that all of them may be one, Father, just as you are in me and I am in you . . . I in them and you in me—so that they may be brought to complete unity. Then the world will know that you sent me and have loved them even as you have loved me.[36]

Jesus prayed for unity. He prayed for unity between Himself and the Father, and for unity between us and Him. Jesus also prayed for love. Therefore, when you pray, remember firstly, to thank God for all He has done, pray that love abounds in Christ, and pray that we will be united in Christ.

On the Twenty-First Day

The clouds overhead are quietly thinning out today as the sunshine peers out between them. The comfort of home is a place where the fireplace glows as the brilliance of the Spirit fills my house with His presence.

36. John 17:20-23 (NIV).

God does promise us the gift of the Holy Spirit once we have accepted Jesus Christ into our lives, but He doesn't promise us that every *earthly* need that we have will be taken care of. Often times, prosperity gospel supporters will quote from John 10:10 or Philippians 4:19 to argue their position. However, this would be a grave mishandling of the text. In John chapter ten, Jesus is proclaiming that He is the gate that gives life as opposed to thieves and robbers who will not enter the gate. In context, Jesus is referring to the riches we will have in heaven from our salvation given freely through Him, not earthly riches that we will gain for having accepted Jesus Christ as our personal Savior.

Similarly, Philippians chapter four says, "And my God will meet all your needs according to the *riches of his glory* in Christ Jesus."[37] Here, Paul is not referring to financial needs, but rather, to spiritual needs and strength during persecution. The "riches of his glory" means that God will be glorified in Jesus Christ through our faith, not from our material possessions.

Be on guard at all times, for the enemy will surely try and distort the Scriptures to his advantage in leading you astray from the kingdom. Did Satan not use Old Testament Scripture out of context while tempting Jesus?[38] Therefore, God does promise us riches, but they are heavenly, not earthly, if you receive both, consider yourself blessed, but be on guard, for it's easier for a camel to enter the eye of a needle than for a rich man to enter heaven.

On the Twenty-Second Day

God is so magnificent! He blesses us continuously, regardless if we deserve it or not. I have been blessed in so many ways, despite my faults and weaknesses. Thank you, Jesus, for loving me enough to show mercy upon me when I have sinned.

Righteousness is important to God. God cannot sin, and at one time, neither did we. Yet, that was long ago and so much has transpired on this earth since then. I once had the pleasure of being a youth leader in the middle and high school ministries at a large non-denominational church in Sparks, Nevada, about fifteen years ago. I enjoyed the company of many of the students there as we talked about Jesus and well-known Bible passages together.

There was a young girl there who was always excited to see me, though she had several emotional issues. She had many questionable boyfriends who didn't treat her so well. As far as I could tell, she loved the Lord and

---

37. Phil. 4:19 (NIV).
38. Matt. 4:5-7 (Emphasis, mine).

loved being at church, but I often worried about what would happen to her when she was old enough to leave her aunt and uncle's house. Would she survive out in the world by herself?

Well, as fate would have it, she found me on Facebook some ten years later. We met for coffee and caught up on the past ten years. Unfortunately, she was still involved with a boyfriend who engaged in criminal activity, drugs, and promiscuity. She recently messaged me that she had contracted a sexually transmitted infection and wasn't sure if it was curable. I've sent her several resources for employment, counseling, and churches in her area, but I don't think she's followed up on any of them.

Sometimes, we can only help people so much before we have to let God work on them in His own way. I continue to pray for this young lady, and if you happen to be reading this, know that it's never too late to turn your life around.

On the Twenty-Third Day

The morning and late evenings display frigid temperatures, yet the afternoons are still quite warm. It's always a challenge figuring out how to dress my kids because it's cold when they go to school and hot when they get out. My wife always errs with the side of caution and dresses them extra warm, just in case.

One of my favorite things about Scripture is that you can read it over and over again and get something new out of it every time! Just the other day, I was reading the passage in John's Gospel about the Samaritan woman at the well. I've probably read that story over one hundred times, yet I didn't realize until the other day when I heard it read on Pilgrim Radio, that Jesus was telling her that after His death, there will no longer be a separate place to worship God, for He will be available to anyone who accepts His Son as their personal Lord and Savior. Thanks to the Holy Spirit, He is now being worshiped in Spirit and in truth.[39] No longer are Samaritans separated from Jews, or Gentiles separated from Jews, or men separated from women, we are all equal in Christ Jesus.

I can't tell you how many times I've prayed before reading a passage and after reading it, God illumines the Scripture for me. The more I mediate on His Word, the more connections I can make to other passages, the church today, and my life. The Holy Spirit will reveal the truths about God's word if you simply ask Him to. The Apostle Paul once told Timothy, "All Scripture is breathed out by God and profitable for teaching, for reproof, for

---

39. John 4:19-24 (Emphasis, mine).

correction, and for training in righteousness."[40] Therefore, continue reading your Bible and allow God to train you in righteousness.

On the Twenty-Fourth Day

I've always enjoyed the sunshine more than the clouds. I do like a cloudy day every once and a while that bursts forth in warm summer rain, but in general, I prefer a bright day over a gloomy one.

The Apostle John once wrote:

> This is the message we have heard from him and proclaim to you, that God is light, and in him is no darkness at all. If we say we have fellowship with him while we walk in darkness, we lie and do not practice the truth. But if we walk in the light, as he is in the light, we have fellowship with one another, and the blood of Jesus his Son cleanses us from all sin. If we say we have no sin, we deceive ourselves, and the truth is not in us. If we confess our sins, he is faithful and just to forgive us our sins and to cleanse us from all unrighteousness.[41]

In life, we will encounter the darkness. There's no escaping it and no hiding from it, but the darkness does not have to define who we are, for we have the light of Christ inside of us. God purifies us from our sins with the light and with the blood of Jesus Christ.

Not long after King David's sinful encounter with Bathsheba, David wrote this, "Create in me a clean heart, O God, and renew a right spirit within me."[42] When we sin, it's important that we ask for forgiveness, repent, and ask that God renew our Spirit. Many believers think that repentance is a once and for all event, yet if that were the case, we would never have to fear sinning after we are saved. Even though our past, present, and future sins have already been paid for by Jesus Christ, active repentance is an ongoing activity.

We cannot simply sin and say that God has already forgiven us for it, therefore we do not need to ask for His forgiveness. To do so greatly breaks the relationship between God and us, as well as disrupts the harmony between faith and good works.

---

40. 2 Tim. 3:16 (ESV).
41. 1 John 1:5-9 (ESV).
42. Ps. 51:10 (ESV).

On the Twenty-Fifth Day

Once in a while I'll read a Christian or a secular article about purpose. I actually just finished a Biblical Leadership course for my master's degree and one of the profound statements made in an article we read dealt with the metric by which God will assess our lives. We often worry about the prominence we receive, but God worries about how we loved Him and others. Did we spend our time criticizing others, or did we spend our time relating to others? Did we focus on making people better, or making ourselves look better? Did we love our neighbor with all of our heart, soul, mind, and strength, or did we only love what our neighbor could do for us?

Hard questions, indeed, but ones that surely God will ask when we see Him face to face. God once told the prophet Jeremiah:

> For I know the plans I have for you," declares the LORD, "plans to prosper you and not to harm you, plans to give you hope and a future. Then you will call on me and come and pray to me, and I will listen to you. You will seek me and find me when you seek me with all your heart.[43]

My wise and kind Spiritual Direction professor, Kristopher Dahir, rightly pointed out to us that we often only quote from the first part of the Jeremiah twenty-nine passage. Yet, we must read the next verse; always read the next verse, because it will contain biblical truths that we did not read when we simply pulled a popular verse out of its context.

Yes, God has plans to prosper us like He did with Jeremiah, but like Jeremiah, we must pray to Him and seek Him with all our hearts. Our purpose in this life is to honor, worship, and glorify our Father in heaven and His Son, Jesus Christ. Sharing the Gospel of Jesus Christ to the ends of the earth will certainly help to accomplish this purpose. This is how we build a powerful relationship with Him. God already knows us, now we must work to get to know Him.

On the Twenty-Sixth Day

The alabaster clouds seek shelter from the thunder as another storm rolls into the Sierra Nevadas. The water pours down now like the great monsoon rains of Southern Nevada, and the Truckee River is full as it rushes east towards Pyramid Lake.

In the Parable of the Lost Coin, Jesus says:

---

43. Jer. 29:11-13 (NIV).

> Suppose a woman has ten silver coins and loses one. Doesn't she light a lamp, sweep the house and search carefully until she finds it? And when she finds it, she calls her friends and neighbors together and says, 'Rejoice with me; I have found my lost coin.' In the same way, I tell you, there is rejoicing in the presence of the angels of God over one sinner who repents.[44]

This is such a powerful image of how happy God is when someone repents from their sins and turns to Him. When my parents and I first moved to Sparks, Nevada, from Lakeport, California, we rented a small home in an older part of the city. One day, we couldn't find my younger sister in the house. Searching all over, and ultimately, walking around the neighborhood with volunteers looking for her, my mother found her asleep in one of the kitchen cabinets. That was scary, especially looking back at that event now through an adult lens with small children of my own. You can imagine how happy my parents were to discover my sister safe and sound in her own home.

That is exactly how happy the Lord is when we are lost and then found. The Apostle John once had a vision in which the church in Ephesus was warned to repent and do the things that they did at first, or risk losing their church.[45] In the same way, we must repent of our sins and turn towards God. He who is loving and just will surely welcome us back into His arms. How great it will be on that day when the Lord says, "Well done, good and faithful servant."[46]

On the Twenty-Seventh Day

The Lord is a mighty God of restoration. We've seen this restoration take place several times in Scripture. God restored the people of Israel, as well as the Holy Temple as prophesied by Jeremiah:

> This whole country will become a desolate wasteland, and these nations will serve the king of Babylon seventy years. 'But when the seventy years are fulfilled, I will punish the king of Babylon and his nation, the land of the Babylonians, for their guilt,' declares the Lord, 'and will make it desolate forever.' I will bring on that land all the things I have spoken against it, all that are

---

44. Luke 15:8-10 (NIV).
45. Rev. 2:5 (Emphasis, mine).
46. Matt. 25:23 (Emphasis, mine).

written in this book and prophesied by Jeremiah against all the nations.[47]

Once the seventy years were completed, Cyrus, issued a decree for the Jews to return to the land to restore and rebuild their temple, exactly as Jeremiah had predicted.

Furthermore, Jesus, Himself restores sight to the blind, sanity to the insane, and clear skin to the leper. God's purpose is to restore all things back to His original design in Genesis chapter one. We, ourselves are restored in Jesus Christ from our old selves to a new creation.[48] Some that hold an annihilistic view of the end times, foresee God fully destroying the heavens and earth and creating entirely new ones, yet God's pattern throughout Scripture has always been restorative. Indeed, the Apostle John mentions, "A *new* heaven and *new* earth," in Revelation 21:1. Yet, perhaps a better rendering of the Greek word used by John, "καινὸν" is the word "renew." When we put on the *new* man according to Ephesians 4:24, our old bodies are not vaporized, but rather we are putting on a new self in Jesus Christ by the renewing of our minds.

We should pray that God restore us and grant us a willing spirit of sustenance.[49] There are many ways in which the Holy Spirit can restore us. Have you prayed to Him lately?

On the Twenty-Eighth Day

The beautiful power that the Lord possesses is mightily manifested in the love we have as members of Christ's body. With or without earthly recognition, the Lord of hosts comforts and encourages us to be better people; to be better spouses, parents, and friends. There is nothing under the sun that God has not seen or been a part of. Allow His light to shine through the darkest storms of your life and find the peace and tranquility that has been available to you since the foundation of the world.

The evils of slavery did not originate in the deep south of the United States. In fact, slavery goes back to the time of Moses, and perhaps even before that. The Bible tells us that the Israelites were slaves in Egypt, but the Lord had redeemed them.[50] The Egyptians treated the Israelites horribly, forcing them to make bricks without straw, beating them, even killing

---

47. Jer. 25:11-13 (NIV).
48. 2 Cor. 5:17 (Emphasis, mine).
49. Ps. 51:12 (Emphasis, mine).
50. Deut. 15:15 (Emphasis, mine).

them in some cases. Yet, God freed them from their slavery to the Egyptians through the great prophet and servant, Moses. Similarly, God freed us from our bondage to slavery through the death and resurrection of His only Son, Jesus Christ.

The Apostle Paul once wrote to a slave owner in the first century named Philemon, "Perhaps the reason he was separated from you for a little while was that you might have him back forever, no longer as a slave, but better than a slave . . . as a brother in the Lord."[51]

Regardless of how the world treats us, we need to treat each other, and the world as brothers and sisters, made in God's image. People should not be treated poorly because of race, gender, ethnicity, or socio-economic status. We are all equal in Christ Jesus. Every life is important to God; therefore, every life must be important to us as well.

On the Twenty-Ninth Day

Rosh Hashanah

The cold wind blows aggressively past the biggest little city in the world as the storm clouds begin to form in the skies above. The streets are covered in the wax-like gloss of the rain as passersby walk along the sidewalks with lonesome visitors who traverse the town.

Today marks the Jewish New Year known as "Rosh Hashanah." According to Jewish tradition, the world was created on this day. How did they know that the earth was created on this day? Because the first words of the Book of Genesis (Bereishit), "In the beginning," when changed around, read, "Aleph b' Tishrei, or "on the first of Tishrei." Therefore, Rosh Hashanah is known as the birthday of the world.[52]

The Psalms tell us, "How blessed are the people who know the joyful sound (*blast of the Shofar*)! O Lord, they walk in the light of Your countenance."[53] Rosh Hashanah is referred to as the day of the sounding of the Shofar, or the "Day of the Awakening Blast."

Rosh Hashanah is also known as "Yom HaKeseh" or, "The Day of Hiding," because Satan, the accuser, is not to be given notice about the arrival of Rosh Hashanah, the Day of Judgment. Therefore, "Of that day and hour no one knows, only the Father," is actually a Near-East idiom for Rosh Hashanah.[54]

---

51. Phlm. 1:15-16 (NIV).
52. Chumney, *The Seven Festivals of the Messiah*, 105.
53. Ps. 89:15 (Emphasis, mine).
54. Chumney, *The Seven Festivals of the Messiah*, 138-139.

It is interesting to note that all of the Old Testament Jewish feasts and festivals have already been fulfilled by Jesus Christ, except for Rosh Hashanah. Could it be that this is a clue as to when the end will come? Many have predicted the end of the world, and many have been wrong, therefore always be on guard, for Jesus will come when it's least expected, and He will most certainly come like a thief in the night.

On the Thirtieth Day

Glory to God in the highest! Thank you, Lord, for every single blessing you give to us. Thank you for your Son for dying on the cross for our sins, thank you for your Holy Spirit which dwells inside of us, and thank you for giving us a life to enjoy.

Well, we've made it to the end of September. How was your journey this month? Were there triumphs? Setbacks? Challenges? Revelations? Did you find a spiritual calm within the storms you faced? I pray that you did.

When we get discouraged and feel like giving up, we must remember that we are not alone in our struggle. God is still present there with us, throughout our experiences. I can't even count the number of times I felt like throwing in the towel in my Greek studies. Having to memorize paradigm after paradigm, hundreds of vocabulary words, hours spent on translations, yet I stuck with it because I knew that God was helping me get through it.

Perhaps, you have a storm that you're facing right now. How are you dealing with it? Are you internalizing your feelings? Are you reaching out to another brother or sister in faith and asking them for advice? Are you allowing the stress to build up to the point where you lash out at the people you love the most? It can happen, I know, I've been there.

We must think of God as the loving Father that He is. Just like the plans God had for Israel, He has plans not to harm you, but to . . . ? That's right! So, whatever storm you are in, realize that Jesus Christ is walking beside you and will reach down and lift you up should you begin to perish. May God continue to bless you all.

Chapter 10

"Spiritual Battles"

The Month of October

On the First Day

Darkness encompasses the surrounding forest. As I peer out into the eerie void, I'm reminded that the prince of darkness inhabits our surroundings at all times. He is there, watching us, waiting for us to fall prey to his temptations. He is eager to watch us fail and devastated when we succeed. He prowls around like a roaring lion, waiting to devour us.[1]

My kids get excited in October because on Halloween they get to dress up and solicit all of my neighbors for candy. Last year, the city actually blocked off some of the streets near our home because trick-or-treating was so popular in the area. Some Christians are against celebrating Halloween, I personally don't have a problem with it because I am not celebrating Satan; but rather, mocking him in light of the fact that as a believer in Jesus Christ, he is not someone that I need to fear. If anything, I need to fear God for my transgressions. Satan is actually powerless unless we give him power.

We all face spiritual battles. Society likes to label them as mental illness or genetic abnormality. But going beyond the science, there are real battles going on daily in the spiritual realms. The Apostle Paul once wrote, "For though we live in the world, we do not wage war as the world does. The weapons we fight with are not the weapons of the world. On the contrary, they have divine power to demolish strongholds."[2] We must all use our spiritual weapons wisely. Take the Sword of the Spirit everywhere you go, for it is the only offensive weapon that we have.

---

1. 1 Pet. 5:8 (Emphasis, mine).
2. 2 Cor. 10:3-4 (NIV).

On the Second Day

When I think of sacrifice, I think of many things. Personal sacrifice, which may include giving up time for someone or something. Financial sacrifice, which would include cutting back on spending to maintain a better personal budget, giving to the church, or helping someone that is in need.

Though there are many types of sacrifices that we make each day for our spouse, significant other, or children, yet there is none quite like the sacrifice that Jesus made for us on the cross. The author of Hebrews tells us this: "Christ was sacrificed once to take away the sins of many; and he will appear a second time, not to bear sin, but to bring salvation to those who are waiting for him."[3] Jesus Christ, a man who was blameless, took on the sins of the world and became a living sacrifice as a propitiation to God and as an atonement for us. No longer does the enemy have any power over us, because Jesus has paid the ultimate price and has defeated death by overcoming it.

Scripture tells us that "Through Jesus, therefore, let us continually offer to God a sacrifice of praise—the fruit of lips that openly profess his name. And do not forget to do good and to share with others, for with such sacrifices God is pleased."[4] God prefers us to sacrifice our time in worship and in praise of Him. The first churches didn't meet in grand cathedrals, they met in hidden catacombs and the homes of other believers. They would praise the Lord, have a meal together, and help someone else financially, if they were in need.[5] In this way, we are all able to sacrifice something to advance the kingdom of God. What will you sacrifice today?

On the Third Day

The glorious heavens awaken as the birds of the air fly overhead in search of food along the way. The river flows rapidly through the middle of downtown as passersby enjoy walking along the trail that leads to their ultimate destination. Like the waters of Lake Tahoe at the break of dawn, I sit still and enjoy God's beauty as my mind drifts off into delightful ecstasy.

God once prophesied through Isaiah, "I will also make you a light for the Gentiles, that my salvation may reach to the ends of the earth."[6] God has had a plan of salvation for us since the fall. Zacchaeus once climbed up a

---

3. Heb. 9:28 (NIV).
4. Heb. 13:15-16 (NIV).
5. Acts. 2:42-47 (Emphasis, mine).
6. Isa. 49:6b (NIV).

tree to see Jesus Christ. After Jesus saw him, He told him to come down and invite Him into his house. Zacchaeus received Jesus gladly, and even assured Him that he would sell half of his possessions and give them to the poor, and if he had defrauded anyone, he would pay them back four times as much. Jesus told him that salvation has come to his house for the Son of Man had come to seek and save that which was lost.[7]

We are all in need of a Savior. *Jesus Christ* literally means, "Save us, Anointed One." Before I came to accept Jesus Christ into my life, I was just one of many among the lost. I couldn't understand who God was or what He could do for me. After I believed with my heart and mind, I realized that I could not live life without Jesus Christ, for there would be no purpose for my life without the saving grace of the Lord most high.

If you are reading this and have not accepted Jesus Christ as your personal Lord and Savior, don't delay. God has already chosen you before the foundation of the world.[8] Now it's your turn to choose Him. "This is good, and pleases God our Savior, who wants all people to be saved and to come to a knowledge of the truth."[9]

On the Fourth Day

As Christians, we should always be striving for total obedience in our walk with Christ. Surely, this is unattainable, because if we could save ourselves, why did Jesus have to die for us? Nevertheless, our goal should always be to live our lives in a way that honors and brings glory to the Father.

Sanctification is the process of becoming like Jesus Christ in our thoughts, actions, and deeds. The Holy Spirit sets us apart, making us Holy before God through our trust and faith in Christ Jesus. At the beginning of time, God created the heavens and the earth and made them perfectly, calling them "good,"[10] but the imperfect state of creation is a stark reminder that God's fully sanctified purpose for it has been disrupted by sin.

The Apostle Paul had encouraged the Thessalonians to be sanctified in his first letter to them: "May God himself, the God of peace, sanctify you through and through. May your whole spirit, soul and body be kept blameless at the coming of our Lord Jesus Christ."[11] Not that Paul thought they

---

7. Luke 19:1-10 (Emphasis, mine).
8. Eph. 1:4 (Emphasis, mine).
9. 1 Tim. 2:3-4 (NIV).
10. Gen. 1:31 (Emphasis, mine).
11. 1 Thess. 5:23 (NIV).

could be kept from sinning entirely in thought, word, and deed; but that they might be preserved in purity from the unrefined horrors of life.

Similarly, Paul writes: "When you were slaves to sin, you were free from the control of righteousness . . . But now that you have been set free from sin and have become slaves of God, the benefit you reap leads to holiness, and the result is eternal life."[12] In this way, we are all seen as righteous before the Almighty, despite our faults.

Sanctification is not easy. If we're honest with ourselves, we could all use more of it. This is why spending time in God's word, with God, and meditation on God is so vital.

On the Fifth Day

The beautiful mountaintops have the faintest hint of winter as some of the elevations are high enough that the snow stays upon them year-round. Like the details of a Thomas Kinkade painting, the log cabins illuminate with gold and amber colored lights through the sheets of glass that inhabit their window frames.

The old adversary knows the end is near, which is why he has ramped up his evil influences on the impressionable. Though Satan can inflict us with pain and disease, he cannot inflict our Spirit, for it is Holy and belongs to God. In fact, nothing Satan can do to us is without God's permission.[13] The Apostle John tells us, "The one who does what is sinful is of the devil, because the devil has been sinning from the beginning. The reason the Son of God appeared was to destroy the devil's work."

Satan always seems to know our weaknesses. I cannot tell you how many times my wife and I have argued and all of a sudden, some woman that I dated from my distant past would appear in my social media feed asking how I'm doing or wanting to get coffee together. I am certain that Satan uses social media to tempt even the godliest of men.

In our walk with Christ, we must realize that temptation is all around us; however, we can choose to give into the temptation or not. To help us make the right choice, God has blessed us with the Holy Spirit. Jesus, Himself was tempted genuinely in all ways. Certainly, He was tempted directly by the Accuser when He was in the wilderness. If you are constantly backsliding, or giving into sin, trust in the Lord to deliver you from your strongholds and pray that the enemy will be bound and removed from your

---

12. Rom. 6:19-22 (NIV).
13. Job 1:12 (Emphasis, mine).

presence. When Jesus encountered evil within someone, He commanded the demons to come out of the host, and so can you.

On the Sixth Day

Jesus is love, and in love we should emulate His passion for others. If everyone could learn to value everyone else, the world would be so much better. Yet, sadly the results of the fall are still felt, even today.

Jesus overcoming Satan has been foretold from the beginning of time. For, did not God tell Eve that her seed will crush Satan's head?[14] Or, that Jesus will sit at His right hand until His enemies are a footstool under His feet?[15] There are so many prophecies of Jesus' first coming that it's undeniable that the Messiah who was promised to the Jews was indeed, Jesus Christ.

We can overcome Satan as well. And to be sure, we already have because Christ has overcome the world. If we are in Christ, then we no longer need to fear Satan and his adversaries, for we have weapons to protect us. The Helmet of Salvation, the Breastplate of Righteousness, the Shield of faith, and the Belt of Truth are our defensive weapons against the enemy's attacks.[16]

I've spent a good majority of my life looking back and wishing I would have made better choices. Better choices in my relationships, better choices with my older sons, better choices with finances, and better choices with morals. Have you ever noticed how much better you feel when you stand up to temptation and rebuke the enemy once he enters into your mind? I certainly have. In fact, I've never regretted saying no to a temptation. In contrast, the times when I gave into temptations, I most certainly regretted.

Sin does not have to have mastery over us. Don't let Christ's work on the cross be in vain. You now possess the necessary tools to overcome your temptations, so use them, and enjoy your time away from Satan and in the presence of God instead.

On the Seventh Day

The brisk air reminds me of winter as the leaves begin to fall. We have a huge tree in our front yard that must have millions of leaves in it. I usually start

---

14. Gen. 3:15 (Emphasis, mine).
15. Ps. 110:1 (Emphasis, mine).
16. Eph. 6:14-17 (Emphasis, mine).

by raking once a week and then as the leaves pour down even more aggressively, I increase my raking cycle to once a day. Last year, I had twenty-five large trash bags full of leaves! I felt bad for the garbage man, so I tipped him twenty dollars since he had to physically throw all of the bags into the back of the garbage truck. Most of my neighbors have these weeping white birch trees whose leaves seem to disappear in the fall. I wish I could be so lucky. I always dread raking leaves.

The positive side to raking leaves is that I get to spend time with my kids while doing it. When I was young, I used to have to rake the leaves in my backyard by myself as my parents enjoyed talking together over coffee. Fortunately, I'm not as delegatory with my children, so I prefer to lead by example.

Servanthood comes in many forms. Of course, Jesus Christ was the perfect example of a servant-leader and one in which we should all try to emulate. Jesus once told His disciples:

> You know that the rulers of the Gentiles lord it over them, and their high officials exercise authority over them. Not so with you. Instead, whoever wants to become great among you must be your servant, and whoever wants to be first must be your slave, just as the Son of Man did not come to be served, but to serve, and to give his life as a ransom for many.[17]

Everything in Jesus' example is the opposite of the world's servanthood practices. In the world, the employee with least amount of authority or power within the company serves the person above him or her. Likewise, that person serves the one above them, and so on until you reach the top of the corporate pyramid in which the owner/CEO is being served the most. But not so in the kingdom of heaven. The greatest is the one who serves the most.

On the Eighth Day

Yom Kippur

Today is the Jewish remembrance of the time that Moses interceded on behalf of the Israelites in the wilderness after they made an idol to worship instead of God. In the Old Testament, atonement for sins could only take place once a year on Yom Kippur. The high priest would sacrifice one goat on behalf of himself and his family, and the other goat would be sent off

---

17. Matt. 20:25-28 (NIV).

into the wilderness as a "scape goat" representing the sins of the Israelites. Therefore, Yom Kippur marks a time of divine favor known as the Day of Atonement: Jesus Christ atoned for our sins once and for all.[18] Yet, sadly there are still many dark sins that occur in this world.

Around ten years ago, I was attending my regular Wednesday night Bible study when I was introduced to a friend of the study leader. Her name was Melissa Holland. Melissa is a faithful believer as well as an advocate for sex trafficking victims in the Reno area. I remember when she first told our study group that God had been pressing on her heart to quit her regular job and pursue trafficking advocacy full-time. Since then, *Awaken* has helped hundreds of local girls escape the horrors of the sex trade.

Sex was intended to be enjoyed between two people who are in love within a marriage covenant.[19] It was never intended to be used as a way to fulfill the temptations of sin. God designed everything perfectly. It's we who decided to go against that design, and we can see the ramifications of that choice everyday in the world around us.

If you know of someone who is a sex trafficking victim, please reach out to your local law enforcement agency or trafficking advocacy group. There are too many victims who need someone to show them that they are valuable to God and deserve to live normal and healthy lives.

On the Ninth Day

The quietness of the early morning is a time of great reflection. Alone with my innermost thoughts, I am captivated by the glory of my Lord and Savior and can hear Him speak into my heart. As the leaves fall down from the tree branches above, I realize that God has created the world in such a way that it sustains itself. Honorably, we are His greatest creation who are the humble observers of that provision.

The Bible tells us that Jesus went up on a mountainside by Himself to pray. And that later that night, He was there alone.[20] Have you ever spent time in complete silence, praying to God? Try it sometime, I guarantee it will be worth the effort. I can't tell you how many times I've had Scriptures come alive to me when I took the time to pray and read them without distraction. Surely, if Jesus found it important to speak with God in solitude, we should as well.

---

18. Heb. 9:27-28 (Emphasis, mine).
19. Gen. 2:24 (Emphasis, mine).
20. Matt. 14:23 (Emphasis, mine).

Proverbs tells us that "Even a fool who keeps silent is considered wise; when he closes his lips, he is deemed intelligent."[21] How much greater are we than fools who do not know the Lord at all? Sometimes, people simply want to be heard. I just listened to a story about a homeless man who came into a friend's church only to have the youth leader send him away, thinking he was just wanting a hand-out. Yet, my friend, who is also a minister, offered him money and instead of leaving, the man opened up as to why he was in the position of life that he was in. He needed something far more valuable than money; he needed someone's time.

Silence and solitude are honoring to God in so many ways. I always pray before meeting with anyone who wants my advice on marriage, God, employment, or life in general. This way I allow God to control my silence. He knows when someone He loves just needs to be heard.

On the Tenth Day

In the cool breeze of a fall afternoon, or late at night in the confines of my own seclusion, I meditate on the Word both day and night. Such beautiful words of Scripture were written by both, inspired authors, and the Holy Spirit. God's Word is timeless. The world will fade away, but God's Word will never fade away.[22] I must guard my strengths in allowing the Holy Spirit to illumine the word of God for me. I must nurture and work on the areas of pride and intellect so that I stay humble in my knowledge of the Word. Scripture is important in spiritual battle. Like Jesus, we too can resist temptation by utilizing the Scriptures.

The Apostle Paul once advised young Timothy saying, "Have nothing to do with godless myths and old wives' tales; rather, train yourself to be godly. For physical training is of some value, but godliness has value for all things, holding promise for both the present life and the life to come."[23] Spiritual disciplines are important for this very reason.

When I was in middle school, I joined the track team. Realizing that I wasn't a sprinter, I chose long distance running instead. Every day after school, we ran two or three times the distance of the event we were training for. I ran the 1600-meter race and the 4 x 4 relay race. So, to train for such an event, I would run three, four, and five miles sometimes. Eventually, I ran one of the events at a track meet with a 5:37 mile. Now that I'm 43 years old,

---

21. Prov. 17:28 (ESV).
22. Matt. 24:35 (Emphasis, mine).
23. 1 Tim. 4:7-8 (NIV).

I'm quite certain I will never be able to do that again, but the point is that to win, I had to train hard.

If we want to win spiritual battles, we must train hard as well. Disciplining our minds, spirit, and soul in order to overcome the enemy's temptations is much like my track and field experience, it involves a journey, not a sprint. Pray in the Spirit at all times and renew your minds with the washing of the Word. I will be praying for your success.

On the Eleventh Day

The Spirit is with me at all times. Where the wind blows, He is there also. He is guiding me at all times, discerning the Word from evil. Oh, how I long for the presence of the Holy Spirit to continue to step before me as I make important decisions in my life. The Spirit is helping to teach me; helping lead me toward Christ Jesus in my walk-through sanctification. The Spirit is willing and strong, but the flesh is weak. The Spirit was there with me during the hardest times of my life. He prevented me from making rash decisions; He helped rescue me from dire situations. He spoke love and truth into my life when I felt far from God's grasp. I thank the Holy Spirit for continuing to dwell in me; for continuing to guide my steps.

The Apostle Paul wrote to the church at Colossae:

> We continually ask God to fill you with the knowledge of his will through all the wisdom and understanding that the Spirit gives, so that you may live a life worthy of the Lord and please him in every way: bearing fruit in every good work, growing in the knowledge of God, being strengthened with all power according to his glorious might so that you may have great endurance and patience.[24]

Tying in with yesterday's devotional, spiritual growth should be the outcome of spiritual discipline. Paul mentions endurance and patience in his encouraging words to the Colossian church. Indeed, we all must have these two attributes if we are to succeed in our mission. Life will knock us down if we let it. Therefore, we must be patient and endure the challenges of this life in order to emerge victorious on the other side.

"Blessed is the one who does not walk in step with the wicked or stand in the way that sinners take or sit in the company of mockers . . . That person

---

24. Col. 1:9-11 (NIV).

is like a tree planted by streams of water, which yields its fruit in season and whose leaf does not wither; whatever they do prospers."[25]

On the Twelfth Day

As the skies darken, the Lord's light shines through the fiercest storm. I can feel your presence manifest itself when I pray, when I witness someone's baptism, and when I read your words within the Holy Scriptures. I never take for granted the power you have given me to persevere, and to fight the good fight of faith. I will continue to guard my relationship with you by trusting in your guidance, and by living the Spirit-led life that Jesus Christ Himself, modeled. I will do my best to allow you to walk before me through this world that so often rebels against you. In order to nurture the areas in which I am weak, I will pray earnestly and in solitude until I hear you speak through that inner voice that has spoken to me so many times before.

What is the measurement of Christian maturity? Must we be seventy years old? Must we have taken many Theology or Bible courses? Must we have attended church all of our lives? Of course, the answer to all of these questions is, no. Spiritual maturity is not measured in the same way as earthly maturity is measured. Spiritual maturity is measured in the heart.

When I worked for the City of Reno Aquatics Department, I was the youngest full-time manager of any aquatic facility. I had just turned nineteen and was in charge of people much older than I. Learning many lessons the hard way on how to manage people, over time, I eventually earned the respect of many of my employees.

I've known Christians who are young in age, but far advanced in their walk with Christ. I've also met Christians who are old in age, yet just beginning in their walk with Christ. The Apostle Paul gives some advice to his young protégé: "Don't let anyone look down on you because you are young, but set an example for the believers in speech, in conduct, in love, in faith and in purity."[26] Focus on your walk with Christ and remember that age is just a number.

---

25. Ps. 1:1,3 (NIV)
26. 1 Tim. 4:12 (NIV).

On the Thirteenth Day

Feast of Tabernacles

To live the holy life is not easy. I have always envisioned a life free of sin, but alas, if that were possible, why did Jesus have to suffer and die for me? Utilizing God's Word gives me strength to overcome temptations as they arise. As the Apostle Peter once said, "Love covers a multitude of sins."[27] God viewed David's holiness, not through the many sins that he committed, but rather, God looked at David's heart. In this sense, I, too, strive to live a holy life through the actions of my heart.

Today is the Jewish feast of Tabernacles. This day is a reminder of God's provisions for the Israelites during their time in the wilderness.[28] It may surprise some that Jesus observed this feast as well: "On the last and greatest day of the festival, Jesus stood and said in a loud voice, "Let anyone who is thirsty come to me and drink. Whoever believes in me, as Scripture has said, rivers of living water will flow from within them."[29]

As God provides for us, we should also provide for Him, not for Him directly, of course, but for His church. In the Parable of the Bags of Gold, Jesus uses the example of three different servants who were given bags of Gold from their master. Two of the servants had invested their money within the community and saw a double return on their investment, but the third had hidden his gold away so that it was of no use to anyone.[30]

This parable is not about investing our money with the hopes of getting a high return on our investment, this parable is about sharing what we have with others so that God will bless us even more greatly than He already has. The one who hides his money away, serves no one.

On the Fourteenth Day

The cold of winter is quickly approaching. Last year, we had a late winter, but one that set all kinds of records in terms of snowfall. I think we had somewhere around six to eight feet of snow fall in the mountains one weekend. I love watching the snow; driving in it, not so much.

I really love studying the Bible. There are so many benefits to reading Scripture. One, and perhaps the main one, is that we get to know God by

---

27. 1 Pt. 4:8 (Emphasis, mine).
28. Lev. 23:34-37 (Emphasis, mine).
29. John 7:37-38 (NIV).
30. Matt. 25:14-30 (Emphasis, mine).

studying His word. Most people do not audibly hear from the Lord, so by studying the Bible, we can build a stronger relationship with Him.

Another benefit is that we have the ability to teach other people about Jesus Christ and God's redemptive plan. We can also correct those who are interpreting Scripture incorrectly. The Apostle Paul once advised Titus that elders, "must hold firm to the trustworthy word as taught, so that he may be able to give instruction in sound doctrine and also to rebuke those who contradict it."[31]

In Bible college, we get a lot of practice in the area of biblical interpretation. Sometimes, there is not a clear-cut interpretation of a Scripture. For example, when the Apostle Paul writes to Timothy telling him that women must be silent during church services, and are forbidden to teach a man,[32] is Paul addressing a specific issue with women who were false teachers in Ephesus where Timothy was overseeing the church, or was this a mandate for all women in church for all of time? I tend to lean towards the former and arrived at my conclusion by careful examination of the culture and context in which Paul was writing these words. Therefore, we must treat God's word with extreme care as not to jeopardize the gospel message or lead people astray.

On the Fifteenth Day

My good friend had recently lost his father to cancer. Having counseled both him and his wife in the past, I realized that this was just another hardship that he had to endure.

Suffering is something we all experience in one way or another. I guess you could say, it's a part of life. Yet, suffering was never present before the fall of mankind. Suffering is a result of the fall and is something we all go through because we live in a broken world.

The Bible tells us that:

> Not only so, but we also glory in our sufferings, because we know that suffering produces perseverance; perseverance, character; and character, hope. And hope does not put us to shame, because God's love has been poured out into our hearts through the Holy Spirit, who has been given to us.[33]

---

31. Titus 1:9 (ESV).
32. 1 Tim. 2:11-12 (Emphasis, mine).
33. Rom. 5:3-5 (NIV).

Even though we suffer at times, if we allow the Holy Spirit to guide us during our suffering, we will persevere through it and come out stronger than ever before. Our faith and trust must be placed in Jesus Christ. Once we trust in Him, we can handle anything that the enemy throws at us.

When I was going through my divorce with my oldest son's mother, I was experiencing tremendous grief, anxiety, guilt, and shame. I wondered how God could allow such things to happen to me; but, like Job, I persevered through it and came out with double the blessings that I'd had before. I didn't let Satan define who I was, I let God define who I was.

If you are suffering in some area of your life, please realize that we have all been there. I would encourage you to reach out to a spiritual mentor or friend that has your best interests at heart: meet up for coffee or tea and share your feelings. God uses moments like those to speak hope into our hearts.

On the Sixteenth Day

The sky is overcast as the sun tries its best to peek through the clouds. Rain is in the forecast today. I think I'll light a fire and enjoy my time reading a great novel. Sometimes, I relish absorbing myself in the silent lucidity of the day.

The philosopher Aristotle once said, "It is best to rise from life as from a banquet, neither thirsty nor drunken." Indeed, we all face triumphs and challenges in this life. Sadly, many cannot handle the challenges and resort to taking their own lives. King David once said, "When the righteous cry for help, the Lord hears and delivers them out of all their troubles. The Lord is near to the brokenhearted and saves the crushed in spirit."[34] This should give us comfort that, even when no one on earth is there for us, God is always there for us. Speak to Him and allow His Spirit to respond.

I've faced depression a few times in which I thought that I would surely take my own life. The last time was when I was involved in an emotionally toxic relationship with a woman and her children. She thought that moving to Las Vegas would help her deal with her issues of alcoholism and depression, but it only made things worse. Not only that, but sexual temptations around me at all times led me to give in to sin.

I remember praying one night that God would give me the courage and strength to leave Las Vegas and head back to Reno. The Lord answered my prayers and within a few days, I was able to secure a full-time job in Reno over the phone, find an apartment to live in, and start my own

---

34. Ps. 34:17-18 (ESV).

cleaning business. To think, I could have listened to Satan instead of God, and I would never have been able to share this story with you, because I would not have survived to tell it.

God has a plan for us, but we must walk in faith and obedience to see His plan unfold.

On the Seventeenth Day

Being in God's presence is so important. The ability for me to allow His words to speak into my heart must be guarded at all times. I intend to make a better effort in escaping the pandemonium of everyday life and allow the Holy Spirit to speak to me. It is important to me to be quick to listen and slow to speak, for in the stillness of the night, God's voice echoes within my soul.

There is nothing more productive than to have a team of believers working together to advance God's purposes. King Solomon once said, "Two are better than one, because they have a good reward for their toil. For if they fall, one will lift up his fellow. But woe to him who is alone when he falls and has not another to lift him up!"[35]

Throughout time, people have been lifting each other up. It's very hard to go through life alone. My wife and I used to watch those survival shows on television where someone is by himself in the wilderness and has to survive living off of the land. Usually, the one who stays the longest, wins. In most cases, the contestants who left early, didn't leave because they could not survive living off of the land, but they left because they could not survive without the company of someone else.

One of the greatest things about my wife is that she is there to help encourage and motivate me when I feel down. I encourage her as well, and because we have a strong support system within our marriage, we are able to overcome many obstacles that we could not have overcome alone.

Teamwork helps us to sharpen each other in weaker areas of our lives. Healthy relationships always involve a team effort, and God will always be a part of that team.

On the Eighteenth Day

The sun escapes the cloud covering as the wind blows in from the west. The crisp air of the evening fills my lungs as the amber sky darkens and the

---

35. Eccl. 4:9-10 (ESV).

moon rises up to offer its nightly brilliance. The city is quiet tonight with very few people walking about. I can't wait for another evening to enjoy time with my wife and kids.

Temptation is all around us. Jesus, Himself was tempted in the desert by Satan for forty days and forty nights.[36] However, we must guard our minds so that we are able to resist the temptation before it's acted upon. Herein, lies the challenge, how do we stop the temptation in our minds before we act upon it?

When writing to the Corinthian church, the Apostle Paul once said, "I am afraid that just as Eve was deceived by the serpent's cunning, your minds may somehow be led astray from your sincere and pure devotion to Christ."[37] In order to counter Satan's mental attacks, we must put on the armor of Christ. Use the Sword of the Spirit wisely, correcting Satan's deceptions as he speaks them to you. This is not an easy task, but I assure you, once you have mastered it, Satan will flee your presence, for he cannot continue to tempt those who immediately run to Christ. Satan's goal is to separate us from Christ, not draw us closer to Him. Rebuke that old adversary as soon as an impure thought enters into your mind. Stand firm in the faith, and when you are on your way home to your loving spouse who has been nothing but faithful to you, a sense of accomplishment and gratitude will overpower you because you resisted the temptation that so many believers give in to.

Throughout our lives, we will win some battles and we will lose some battles but keep fighting the good fight, because in the end, God knows you'll be the one standing.

On the Nineteenth Day

I took a Church Polity and Leadership course as an undergraduate and we spent many hours focusing on how the church should function from a biblical perspective. Along with Rick Warren's book, *The Purpose Driven Church*, our professor used Acts 2:42-47 as the biblical example of what a church should be:

> And they devoted themselves to the apostles' teaching and the fellowship, to the breaking of bread and the prayers. And awe came upon every soul, and many wonders and signs were being done through the apostles. And all who believed were together

---

36. Mark 1:13 (Emphasis, mine).
37. 2 Cor. 11:3 (NIV).

and had all things in common. And they were selling their possessions and belongings and distributing the proceeds to all, as any had need. And day by day, attending the temple together and breaking bread in their homes, they received their food with glad and generous hearts, praising God and having favor with all the people. And the Lord added to their number day by day those who were being saved.[38]

Indeed, many were being added to the church because Christianity is so unlike the way that the world functions. By selling possessions and giving the proceeds to those in need, trust and faith was being established among these early believers. God's hand was surely in the lives of these early believers; God's hand is in our lives as well.

No church can function properly when Christ is not put at the head of it. This is why non-Christ centered churches have several challenges within their organizations. The Apostle Paul notes, "And he is the head of the body, the church; he is the beginning and the firstborn from among the dead, so that in everything he might have the supremacy."[39]

Once in a while I'll hear someone say, "I believe in God, I just don't go to church." That's like saying you have a college degree, but you don't use it. Church is so valuable. To be amongst other believers who are all of one mind and accord, worshiping the Father together in unity is truly priceless. I've had so much great revelation from God at church, and so can you.

On the Twentieth Day

The wind has blown almost all of the leaves off of the trees that adorn the Reno area. The rumble of the street sweeper is like the engine of a Zamboni carving fresh tracks in the ice. I enjoy watching the activities out of the window of my favorite coffee shop near the river. The colors of red, yellow, and light brown in the fall are beautiful.

Have you ever watched, "The Passion of the Christ?" It was a film that came out in 2004 about Jesus' life and death and was directed by Mel Gibson. In the movie, when Jesus is carrying the cross to the mountain, on which He will be soon crucified, He's physically exhausted and drops the cross many times. Ultimately, Simon of Cyrene helped Jesus carry the cross to Golgotha, but during that scene, the actor does something very powerful. He crawls towards the cross as if He cannot be separated from it! This would probably be the last thing I would think of doing if I was separated from the

38. Acts 2:42-47 (ESV).
39. Col. 1:18 (NIV).

instrument of my own torture and crucifixion. It's as if Jesus accepted His fait to atone for the sins of the world, and nothing was going to stop Him from carrying out that mission.

The cross, while originally an instrument of carrying out capital punishment, has since been vindicated as a symbol of freedom from sin through the atoning sacrifice of Jesus Christ. Jesus once said, "Whoever wants to be my disciple must deny themselves and take up their cross and follow me."[40]

In this way, all of us have our own crosses to bear. Some, in the West will bear them financially or emotionally, while others in the East will bear them physically and mentally. But make no mistake, all of us who follow Christ must deny ourselves and live to advance the gospel message.

On the Twenty-First Day

When I think of how I personally identify with being a Christian, aside from placing my faith and trust in Jesus Christ, I think of having unconditional love for both God, and my fellow human beings.

When Jesus was asked what the greatest commandment was, He didn't answer with one of the ten commandments given to Moses. Instead, He responded with part of a prayer that has been prayed to the Lord since ancient times and is recited morning and night. The prayer is called, *The Shema*. The portion of the prayer that Jesus uses to justify the Great Commandment comes from the book of Deuteronomy:

> Hear, O Israel: The Lord our God, the Lord is one. Love the Lord your God with all your heart and with all your soul and with all your strength. These commandments that I give you today are to be on your hearts. Impress them on your children. Talk about them when you sit at home and when you walk along the road, when you lie down and when you get up.[41]

Jesus Christ didn't come to abolish the Law, but to fulfill it, therefore He adds to this commandment with another law from God:

> You shall not hate your brother in your heart, but you shall reason frankly with your neighbor, lest you incur sin because of him. You shall not take vengeance or bear a grudge against the sons of your own people, but you shall love your neighbor as yourself: I am the Lord.[42]

---

40. Mark 8:34 (NIV).
41. Deut. 6:4-7 (NIV).
42. Lev. 19:17-18 (ESV).

Quite brilliantly, Jesus connects these two regulations from God into one continuous commandment. This makes sense, because we cannot genuinely love our neighbor without loving God, and we cannot genuinely love God without loving our neighbor. Remember, *loving* our neighbor is much different than *liking* our neighbor. If we loved our neighbors as God loves them, then we would have to be willing to lay down our lives for them; Jesus Christ did just that.

On the Twenty-Second Day

A few years ago, I came home to discover a pamphlet from the Jehovah's Witnesses on my door. Usually I discard them, but this time I couldn't help but notice that the front cover had a dramatic picture of Jesus being hung on the cross and the title at the bottom said, "Come celebrate Jesus with us." Intrigued, I opened it up to see if there were any other mentions of Jesus Christ. To my surprise, there was. It said, "This Easter, come and celebrate Jesus' *death* with us."

Sadly, I came to realize what they were actually saying. By celebrating Jesus' death, they are not really celebrating anything, except maybe some poor person dying over two-thousand years ago at the hands of the Roman and Jewish authorities. Anyone can be killed for something that they believe in. The power of Jesus Christ wasn't manifested with His death, but rather the power of Jesus Christ, is revealed through His resurrection.

The resurrection is what separates an incarnate God from an ordinary human being, for even the greatest of the prophets have not returned from the dead and walked among us. Jesus referenced the Old Testament when speaking of His death and resurrection: "For as Jonah was three days and three nights in the belly of a huge fish, so the Son of Man will be three days and three nights in the heart of the earth."[43] Jonah did not perish inside the depths of the ocean and neither did Jesus when He went into the depths of the earth, for He returned in resurrected form.

The Apostle Peter once said, "Praise be to the God and Father of our Lord Jesus Christ! In his great mercy he has given us new birth into a living hope through the resurrection of Jesus Christ from the dead."[44] Because Jesus died and resurrected, we are able to be born again through the gift He left behind; the gift of the Holy Spirit. Thank you, Jesus, for loving us so much.

---

43. Matt. 12:40 (NIV).
44. 1 Pet. 1:3 (NIV).

On the Twenty-Third Day

A moonlit night overshadows the streets below. The mist of the cold air fills the lungs of a lonely traveler who walks along the broken streets of the city. Standing under a lamp post is a man whose sinful nightlife is evident to all who look closely into his eyes. Pray for your city. The people there need it.

The second coming of Christ will be a much-welcomed event by those who have put their faith and trust in Him and will be a time of eternal judgment for those who have not. Jesus will come back the same way He left, in the clouds, for all to see. Many of us look for answers in the book of Revelation when it comes to the end times, yet we can also find some of the clues to the end times from Jesus' own words recorded by the Apostle Matthew:

> Then will appear in heaven the sign of the Son of Man, and then all the tribes of the earth will mourn, and they will see the Son of Man coming on the clouds of heaven with power and great glory. And he will send out his angels with a loud trumpet call, and they will gather his elect from the four winds, from one end of heaven to the other.[45]

The Apostles once asked Jesus if He would return after they received the Holy Spirit. But Jesus said to them, "It is not for you to know the times or dates the Father has set by his own authority."[46] Once the great trump sounds, be ready for the end to occur, but until that time, we have more evangelism to still do.

I'll never forget when the year two-thousand was approaching. Many people had assumed that because of Jesus' birth, two-thousand years later would be the fulfillment of the age of grace. Yet, the age of grace doesn't begin with Jesus' birth for He Himself lived under the Old Covenant. The age of grace began with Jesus' resurrection, some thirty years later. We must be ready at all times for Jesus to return because no one truly knows the day or the hour.

On the Twenty-Fourth Day

I have several friends of various faith traditions. Some of them come from a "high church" tradition such as Catholic or Episcopal churches. Others have backgrounds in non-denominational ministries, but regardless of their faith traditions, they all have a strong love for Jesus Christ.

---

45. Matt. 24:30-31 (ESV).
46. Acts 1:6-7 (NIV).

I've always respected the theological viewpoints of people that I may not agree with, as long as we all can agree on the basic essentials of the Christian faith, such as: the deity of Christ, the virgin birth, and the resurrection of Christ. Other doctrines can be worked out when we see Christ face to face and have Him reveal to us all of the answers that we've gotten wrong.

When it comes to church traditions, the Apostle Paul himself acknowledges them: "I praise you for remembering me in everything and for holding to the traditions just as I passed them on to you."[47] Yet, even Paul acknowledges that Jesus Christ is the head of every man.[48] Therefore, since Christ is the Word of God, we must always place God's Word before tradition. This is in the spirit of what Martin Luther referred to as, *Sola Scriptura*, or "Scripture Alone."

If we suddenly start placing our church traditions above God's Word, then we are inferring that our authority in the church is greater than Christ's. May it never be so, for Christ is, and will always be, the head of all things.

When we participate in traditional ceremonies or events at our churches, it's important to check them against Scripture. The two sacraments that we know for certain were to be continued on were Baptism and Holy Communion.[49] Other traditions that are not mentioned in Scripture are open for debate as to whether or not they benefit the body of Christ as a whole.

On the Twenty-Fifth Day

The best things tend to come in threes. The strongest shape is a triangle because it has three sides. There were three people on display at the Mount of Transfiguration. Jesus was buried three days and three nights before He resurrected, and a chord of three strands is not easily broken.[50] But the greatest power of three in the Bible can be found within the Father, Son, and Holy Spirit.

The Trinity is a mystery that no living person has ever solved. I remember in my Theology I course; we talked about the Trinity and watched a funny YouTube video with St. Patrick and his attempts to explain the Trinity to a leprechaun who refuted his every explanation as a heresy.

The truth is, the word "trinity" never appears in the Bible, but the doctrine can be inferred from the many times the Father, Son, and Holy Spirit

---

47. 1 Cor. 11:2 (NIV).
48. 1 Cor. 11:3 (Emphasis, mine).
49. Matt. 28:19/1 Cor. 11:26 (Emphasis, mine).
50. Eccl. 4:12 (Emphasis, mine).

are all associated with each other. The Apostle Peter uses all three in his first epistle:

> To God's elect, exiles scattered throughout the provinces of Pontus, Galatia, Cappadocia, Asia and Bithynia, who have been chosen according to the foreknowledge of *God the Father*, through the sanctifying work of *the Spirit*, to be obedient to *Jesus Christ* and sprinkled with his blood.[51]

Though we cannot define the Trinity in an objective way, we can admire the fact that God has chosen to reveal Himself in three different forms throughout the Bible. Each of these three revelations of God has significance. The triune Godhead has shaped the course of spiritual history since the creation. YHWH revealed Himself to Moses, Christ revealed Himself to the entire Middle East, and the Holy Spirit reveals Himself to us each and every day. Therefore, there is not one God, One Holy Spirit, and One Jesus Christ, they are indeed, three-in-one.

On the Twenty-Sixth Day

The cold rain falls lightly on the valley as the Truckee River fills with water. The mountains radiate with God's glory as the forest absorbs the nutrients from the ground. The deer run cautiously across the highway, seeking shelter and safety on the other side.

Trust is a virtue that is scarcely found in our society today. I was driving a client from Lake Tahoe to the airport in Reno a few months ago and he told me all about his motel business and how several managers had been caught embezzling from him. Apparently, the last one was actually marking the rooms as vacant but renting them out for cash on the side and pocketing the money. Ultimately, the manager walked away with over $50,000.00 in cash. Luckily, the owner figured it out and was able to recover some of his money, but not after the legal system was involved.

Trusting the Lord involves a different kind of trust. The Bible says, "Trust in the Lord with all your heart and lean not on your own understanding."[52] Through trusting God with all of our hearts, we give Him the glory whether things go good or bad for us. Godly trust is knowing that even when things are not going the way we want them to, God is still with us and has orchestrated a plan for us to get through it, emerging victorious on the other side.

---

51. 1 Pet. 1:1-2 (NIV).
52. Prov. 3:5 (NIV).

One of the successors of King Solomon, King Hezekiah, placed his trust in the Lord, the God of Israel. He held fast to the Lord and did not stop following Him; he kept the commands the Lord had given Moses. And the Lord was always with him; he was extremely successful in whatever he undertook.[53]

You can be successful in whatever challenge lies before you if you simply trust in the Lord to get you through it. Trust and obey, for there's no other way.

On the Twenty-Seventh Day

When I was a kid, a few friends and I went exploring the fields near my house. As evening approached, we found flashlights and ended up going into a large open pipe that was being set up for a new housing development in the area. Naturally, our parents couldn't find us, so we told them we were at a park and lost track of time. That story would have worked except one of my friends had a pipe wrench with him that he took from the construction site. After discovering the pipe wrench in the back of my parents' car, I had no choice to tell them what we were really up to.

The truth is something that we often decide on telling based upon extenuating circumstances. Because of the brokenness of the world, we learn to lie from a very young age to avoid consequences. The first lie ever told was by Satan himself: "You will not certainly die," the serpent said to the woman. "For God knows that when you eat from it your eyes will be opened, and you will be like God, knowing good and evil."[54] Indeed, Adam and Eve's eyes *were* opened, but they also died from old age, just as we do.

Cain told the next lie that we read of in Scripture after he murdered his own brother: "Then the LORD said to Cain, 'Where is your brother Abel?' 'I don't know,' he replied. 'Am I my brother's keeper?'"[55] Clearly, Cain knew where he was, for he murdered him just moments before.

We can know absolute truth, not from mankind, but from God, Himself. The Apostle John tells us, "But when he, the Spirit of truth, comes, he will guide you into all the truth."[56] Therefore, by possessing the Holy Spirit, we have all the truth that we need within us.

---

53. 2 Kgs. 18:5-7 (Emphasis, mine).
54. Gen. 3:4-5 (NIV).
55. Gen. 4:9 (NIV).
56. John 16:13a (NIV).

On the Twenty-Eighth Day

The first signs of snowfall appear as the cold rain transforms into light snowflakes. It's common for us to get a little snow in October or November prior to the winter season; however, it usually only lasts for a few hours. The kids always get excited when it snows. I enjoy looking at the snow, but not so much driving in it.

One of the greatest things about Christianity is the unity we have in Christ Jesus. Unity helps us overcome our challenges, face our fears, stand up to our adversaries, and glorify God. The Apostle Paul once told the Roman church, "together you may with one voice glorify the God and Father of our Lord Jesus Christ."[57]

Being unified in one Spirit and voice has great power. The Father, Son, and the Holy Spirit are all unified within each other. The Holy Spirit is the great unifier for us. He dwells within us and guides us towards Christ and away from evil. He confirms truths about Jesus Christ and prevents us from making poor decisions.

About seven years ago, I was attending a charismatic church in Sparks, Nevada, and as the pastor was preaching on giving, something came to me about giving not being from our finances as much as it is from our hearts. I turned to a fellow worship team member who was sitting next to me and told him my thoughts. Immediately after that, the pastor said the same exact words that I said to my friend! We both looked at each other and smiled, because we knew that the Holy Spirit was confirming what I had said.

Satan's goal is to cause disunity amongst believers. If unity was not a powerful part of the Christian faith, the devil would surely give up on this area of our lives. The fact that he continues to try and separate us demonstrates his desire to send us down a path of destruction.

On the Twenty-Ninth Day

Whenever I attend management seminars or clinics, there's almost always a hands-on segment of the training that involves developing mission and vision statements. Often times, the two are thought to be synonymous, but there are subtle differences between them.

I like to think of a mission statement as something that is relatable and practical and can be applied in the moment. To me, a vision statement is more of a future goal that takes much more planning in order to benefit the person or organization. The prophet Habakkuk once had a vision in which

---

57. Rom. 15:6 (ESV).

the Lord told him to, "Record the vision and inscribe *it* on tablets, That the one who reads it may run. For the vision is yet for the appointed time; It hastens toward the goal and it will not fail. Though it tarries, wait for it; For it will certainly come, it will not delay."[58]

The Lord spoke to His prophets using dreams and visions. Great prophets such as: Daniel, Ezekiel, Isaiah, Joel, and the Apostle John, among others, all had great dreams and visions of future events that the Lord would orchestrate, and the days are near when every vision will come to pass.[59]

I have a friend from college who graduated a few years before me. He's always posting on social media how he wants to teach secular education at the secondary level but keeps scoring low on the praxis exam in mathematics, preventing him from getting a teaching license. I can definitely sympathize, as my wife had to help me with my college math classes, but perhaps the Lord has a different vision for him?

I've found that if the door God wants us to go through is shut, we must try another door. If things work out for us, then that is the place God wants us to be. There's no sense in breaking through a locked door, for God has locked it for a reason.

On the Thirtieth Day

There is joy in the Lord! It never ceases to amaze me how some believers possess such little joy in their lives. Certainly, faith, hope, and love remain, and the greatest is love,[60] but what about joy and happiness?

The Apostle Peter tells us that "though you have not seen him, you love him; and even though you do not see him now, you believe in him and are filled with an inexpressible and glorious joy."[61]

For me, joy comes as a direct result of my faith. I experience happiness in knowing that Jesus Christ is present at all times with me through the Holy Spirit. He brings endless joy and comfort to my heart. If you are unhappy with your life, or don't possess joy as a fruit of the Spirit, remember all that God has done for you, and is now doing for you in order that you prevail victorious in Christ. When Paul and Silas were arrested and beaten for preaching the good news of Jesus Christ, and casting out a fortune-telling demon, they didn't display sadness or anger; rather, they sang joy and praises to the

---

58. Hab. 2:2-3 (NASB)
59. Ezek. 12:23 (Emphasis, mine).
60. 1 Cor. 13:13 (Emphasis, mine).
61. 1 Pet. 1:8 (NIV).

Lord.[62] If the followers of Christ, who lived over two-thousand years ago could possess joy and happiness, even when persecuted, how much more should we be experiencing joy and happiness, while living in the twenty-first century, and not facing a fraction of the persecution that they faced?

There are going to be times of sorrow and sadness in our lives. God gave us emotions for a reason, so embrace them, but if you are experiencing depression or anger regularly, pray that the Lord remove the demon that hides within you. And remember, sorrow is only for a night, but joy comes in the morning.[63]

On the Thirty-First Day

All Hallows Eve

The wind is picking up this evening as our children get ready for Halloween. In medieval times, Halloween was known as "All Hallows Eve" and represented a time of extra spiritual activity in anticipation of All Saints Day. Some Christians frown upon Halloween and taking kids out for trick-or-treating, but for me, it's more of a time to mock evil spirits as opposed to celebrating them.

When I was younger, I used to dress up as my childhood hero, Superman every year for Halloween. I must have been Superman for at least three years, from the age of four years old to seven years old. My grandmother used to sew my costume for me, and I was so excited to try it on. It's fun to pretend we are someone we admire. It's too bad most young adults who dress up like Jesus Christ, do so in somewhat of a mocking way.

We began this month with the theme of spiritual battles. We all face spiritual battles of some type in our lives. The danger occurs when we no longer recognize Satan's involvement in our battle. That is the moment when we tend to give in and give up on overcoming the enemy. We must never give up in our fight to live a holy life. We will always face setbacks, but rest assured that when Christ returns, there will be no more tears and no more suffering, because He will make all things new.[64]

I hope this month was a success for you. What demons did you face this month? Were you able to overcome them with the power of the Holy Spirit? Did you cast them out in Jesus' name? Did you pray for your home this month, or pray for loved ones, or pray for the world? There is power

---

62. Acts 16:22-34 (Emphasis, mine).
63. Ps. 30:5 (Emphasis, mine).
64. Rev. 21:4-5 (Emphasis, mine).

in Jesus Christ; demons shutter at the very sound of His name, so use that power to your benefit and keep the enemy at bay. I'll be praying for your continued spiritual success.

Chapter 11

"The Fellowship of the Saints"
The Month of November

On the First Day

All Saints' Day

Legend has it that because All Saints' Day commemorates the saints and martyrs of the Catholic church, there is extreme spiritual activity on the night before, also known as Halloween, or All Hallows Eve.

To appease the evil spirits, families would put out bowls of candy on Halloween night. If that didn't work, they would try and scare the evil spirits away by carving out pumpkins and placing candles in them. Today, we still practice this century's old tradition, only now, we add the additional element of costumes which mock evil characters and honor good ones.

Quietly, I fold my hands in prayer as I think of all of my brothers and sisters in the faith who have given their lives for the sake of Christianity. There's a certain sense of comradery within the body of Christ that is most apparent during fellowship. My beautiful friends in the faith, Michael, Danny, Eileen, and James all came together one evening as we went to share our testimonies and the gospel message with a high school youth group in Sparks, Nevada.

It was such a powerful evening, because not only did we speak into the lives of the next generation of Christian leaders, we also had the privilege of spending time getting to know them as we ate dinner and fellowshipped. Some of the students said they would always remember that night and thanked us profusely for taking the time out of our day to spend with them. To me, that is what Christianity is all about; sharing God's love with those who need it the most.

On the Second Day

The snow falls along the streets of downtown as frost begins to form on the car windshields. Steam emerges from the manholes in the streets like a boiling tea kettle that whistles on top of a heated stove.

God is truly magnificent! He has been there for me so many times when I've gone astray. He has reeled me back in when I ventured out into the sea of despair. He has loved me, guided me, helped me, and glorified Himself through me. I am so blessed to be chosen by Him from before the foundation of the world. I cannot repay Him for all of the times He's spared me from poor decisions, or shown me grace when I've gone against His will.

Jesus Christ once prayed, "And now, Father, glorify me in your presence with the glory I had with you before the world began."[1] Even the Christ glorified the Father's greatness in this prayer. The wisdom of God was present with the Father before the world began.[2]

The prophet Haggai once spoke on behalf of the Lord saying, "The glory of this present house will be greater than the glory of the former house,' says the Lord Almighty. 'And in this place, I will grant peace,' declares the Lord Almighty."[3] The Lord cleans house spiritually as well. Our old dwelling place of sinful flesh has been replaced by a new dwelling place of light and the Holy Spirit.

I pray that you will see how great the Lord truly is. When you have struggles, hardships, and feel rejected, Jesus is there to comfort you. When you triumph in life, achieving the goals you set out for yourself, Jesus was the One who made it possible. Take the time to thank Him today for the blessings He's already given you, and the future blessings that are still to come.

On the Third Day

When I think of physical strength, I think of my Dad who, at sixty-six years old, still works extremely hard in the logging industry. When I think of emotional strength, I think of my brother Justin, who seems to never be emotionally phased by any of life's difficult situations. When I think of spiritual strength, I think of my good friend David, who does everything in the highest obedience to the Lord. Yet, God's strength combines all of those characteristics and more.

---

1. John 17:5 (NIV).
2. Prov. 8:12-23 (Emphasis, mine).
3. Hag. 2:9 (NIV).

King David once wrote, "The Lord is my light and my salvation; whom shall I fear? The Lord is the stronghold of my life; of whom shall I be afraid?"[4] The Bible tells us that "The steadfast love of the Lord never ceases; his mercies never come to an end they are new every morning; great is your faithfulness."[5] Compassion takes strength, especially when we do not want to give it. How many times did Israel sin against the Lord, and how many times did God show compassion upon them? More to the point, how many times have we sinned against the Lord, and how many times has He shown compassion upon us? Seventy times seven? Not even close.

In the first three chapters of Jonah, there is a dilemma due to disobedience, repentance happens, then God provides a resolution. But, in the last chapter of Jonah, YHWH doesn't provide a resolution to the problem; but rather, He leaves Jonah with a question, "You had compassion on the plant for which you did not work and *which* you did not cause to grow, which came up overnight and perished overnight. Should I not have compassion on Nineveh?"[6] In this way, we too should show compassion upon others, even if they have hurt us.

On the Fourth Day

The stores are filling up with fall decorations. Thanksgiving is around the corner and many people have left out their Jack-o-lanterns. I leave mine out as well but turn them around so no one can see that they were once used for Halloween. One can feel the winter in the air as snow flurries blow in from the mountains of Lake Tahoe. The seasons change so quickly; time keeps moving forward at a rapid pace.

God's sovereignty involves the foreknowledge of all things working together for His good purposes. The Lord forms light and creates darkness, He brings prosperity and creates disaster. He does all these things.[7] Therefore, there is nothing beyond the Lord's control. If we walk in obedience to Him, surely things will go well for us. Even when the evil one of the world manifests his ugly head, we can withstand his arrows, for we have the shield of faith to protect us.

When we disobey the Lord, we have to be prepared for the consequences. The prophet Obadiah once wrote, "The day of the Lord is near for all nations. As you have done, it will be done to you; your deeds will return

4. Ps. 27:1 (NIV).
5. Lam. 3:22-23 (ESV).
6. Jonah 4:10a (NASB).
7. Isa. 45:7 (Emphasis, mine).

upon your own head."[8] I've said this before, but it's important to realize that there are always consequences for our actions. Some are earthly and some are heavenly; some are both.

When we have a healthy fear of the Lord, we should not fear that He will strike us dead; but, rather, we should fear that we will continue to damage the relationship we had with Him by our sins. Personally, I always feel better when I confront my sins head on and rebuke the enemy in the moment, versus when I give in to my temptations and regret the decision in the morning. You have the power within you to stand up to Satan; the Holy Spirit will see you through.

On the Fifth Day

In conjunction with God's sovereignty, there is what is known as our freewill. I remember many years ago, debating with fellow students who leaned in full favor of predestination. I personally believe there is a juxtaposition of both, and the debate will never be solved while we still dwell here on this earth. In that way, it's kind of like the Trinity. If we could know all of God's thoughts, then He would no longer be God. He would be broken just like us, so some things are revealed to us, but other things are meant for only God to know.[9]

Freewill has its place in Scripture. The Apostle Paul once wrote to the Galatian Church, "You, my brothers and sisters, were called to be free. But do not use your freedom to indulge the flesh; rather, serve one another humbly in love."[10] God has complete control over everything in this universe, including you and me; however, from our human perspective, we still have a choice to accept God's will or reject it. If we didn't, then there would be no need for evil to exist.

We see it time and time again with church leaders who choose to continue in their sin as opposed to confronting their sins before it's too late. A verse that should haunt us all is from the book of Numbers: "But if you will not do so, behold, you have sinned against the Lord, and be sure your sin will find you out."[11]

I pray that you will choose to repent and turn back towards the Lord. If you have already chosen Jesus Christ, please work towards sanctifying yourselves in humble obedience to the Father. Jesus will return one day, and

---

8. Obad. 1:15 (NIV).
9. Deut. 29:29 (Emphasis, mine).
10. Gal. 5:13 (NIV).
11. Num. 32:23 (ESV).

wouldn't it be better to say you tried your best to serve God and others in love and obedience than to have Him say to you, "I never knew you?"

On the Sixth Day

The sunshine peeks out through the overcast sky like a child looking through a closet door during a game of hide and seek. The robin and blue bird gather seeds from the ground that fall from the trees since winter is just around the corner.

Abraham was said to be the "father of many nations."[12] Indeed, Abraham began the Hebrew nation through a covenant made by God Himself. One night, God walked with Abraham to show him the stars in the sky. He said, "as many stars fill the skies, thus will be all of your decedents, if you can count them?"[13]

There was a time when we were very close to God, so close that we could audibly hear His voice. In fact, Adam, Cain, Noah, Abraham, Isaac, Jacob, Moses, as well as all of the prophets heard God's voice. Some even walked with God and experienced the glory of His presence. So, why do we not hear Him today? Or do we?

I've only met one person, who is well respected and admired in the local Christian community, who said that he heard from the Lord audibly. With no reason to doubt him, I believe that God gave him a very special gift. I personally, hear from God in the form of the Holy Spirit speaking into my mind. How can I tell that it's He and not me? Or, more importantly, how can I tell that it's He and not Satan? I discern between the three enemies of the world and the Holy Spirit by asking if Jesus Christ came in the flesh, and by confirming what entered into my mind with the Holy Scriptures. Interestingly enough, and for what it's worth, When the Spirit has told me to strike up a conversation with someone whom I've just met, I have yet to find out that they were not a fellow believer. Conversely, the people whom the Spirit doesn't prompt me to speak to, almost always have something derogatory to say about Christianity or religion.

On the Seventh Day

In my early twenties, I ended up dating a woman who really wasn't a good fit for me. Perhaps, because of my recent divorce I was looking for someone

12. Gen. 17:5 (Emphasis, mine).
13. Gen. 15:5 (Emphasis, mine).

to fill the emotional gap that was left behind from my ex-wife and I ignored all of the red flags early on. Yet, regardless of the reason, we ended up dating off and on for about five years before finally parting ways.

During that relationship, I ended up moving back and forth from Reno to Las Vegas at least three different times. She wanted to have a fresh start to our relationship in another city, and I went along with her suggestion, except, Las Vegas ended up being a nightmare for me morally. Eventually, I let go of my own desires and asked God what He wanted. He said to move back to Reno, so I did.

New beginnings are always a good way to refresh our mind, soul, and spirit. After God flooded the earth, cleansing it from its unrighteousness and unrighteous people, Noah and his family got a fresh start; a new beginning to life on the earth that God once created and called "good." Unfortunately, Adam's sin followed Noah and his family. No sooner did they depart the boat and settle in to this newly cleansed earth, did Noah's own son view his nakedness and receive the curse.[14]

The Apostle Paul once told the Corinthians, "Therefore, if anyone is in Christ, the new creation has come: The old has gone, the new is here!"[15] Indeed, as believers, we have the honor of receiving the Holy Spirit which enables *us* to have a new beginning. No longer are we held prisoner to our past sins, for Christ has paid the price for us and now intercedes for us to God the Father. How glorious He is, and how fortunate we are to have someone love us so much.

On the Eighth Day

The day breaks as the dawn of the morning gives way to the brightness of the sun, shining through my windows like radiant beams of light that penetrate through even the darkest clouds. The Lord is always present to hear my thoughts and prayers. He never leaves nor forsakes me, and for that I am forever grateful.

Jesus' death is pivotal to our Christian faith because as Christ died for our sins, we too die to our sins once we accept Him as our Lord and Savior. Therefore, we are no longer chained as slaves to sin, but now have a newness of life in Christ Jesus. The Apostle Paul once wrote, "The death he died, he died to sin once for all; but the life he lives, he lives to God. In the same way, count yourselves dead to sin but alive to God in Christ Jesus."[16]

14. Gen. 9:22-25 (Emphasis, mine).
15. 2 Cor. 5:17 (NIV).
16. Rom. 6:10-11 (NIV).

Before our conversion, we were enemies of God due to our sinful nature; however, once we accepted Jesus Christ into our hearts, we became like Christ, in the sense that God sees us through the lens of His Son, and not as we truly are. This is why we should abstain from sexual immorality, or any kind of impurity, or of greed, because these are improper for God's holy people.[17]

As a community of saints, we are called to live a sanctified life. It's not always easy; believe me, I know. Yet, if we are seen as righteous through God's eyes, how then can we live as though we are unrighteous? The fruit of the Spirit should be evident in everyone who professes Christ as Lord. Surely, we will have set backs. I just spoke to one of my professors the other day, who confessed that he is working on patience because he tends to get frustrated at people driving too slowly in front of him. Perhaps, we can all relate to that. This is why the goal is ahead of us, and not behind us; we must look to Jesus Christ for strength in all areas of our lives.

On the Ninth Day

The wind blows in from the west as the forest yields to its mighty force. Wind storms are not uncommon in the valley, in fact, they will often close part of the freeway because of high winds. Sadly, many truck drivers do not heed the wind warning and end up with severe injuries or dead because they loose control of their vehicles. Seeing the turned over semi-trucks on the side of the road is a chilling reminder that we are all finite and are at the constant mercy of God above who allows us to wake up every morning according to His will.

Wonderful Counselor, Prince of Peace, Mighty God, and Everlasting Father are just some of the many great titles for our Lord, Jesus Christ.[18] How beautiful the Son is, for He gave His life for many, many who took for granted the fact that salvation lies with God alone through faith in His Son.

Every Christmas and Easter, I get gifts from the elders at my church. Usually, they are in the form of outdoor decorations that tie in with the Bible or the Cross. One year, I got a wooden sign that simply says, "Jesus Saves." I decided to hang it next to my front door, inside of my house. This way, every time I walk out of my house or into my house, I'm reminded that Jesus not only saved me, but saves other beautiful people every single day.

Salvation is not earned by our good works, for there is no amount of works that we can do that will satisfy God's requirement of righteousness.

17. Eph. 5:3 (Emphasis, mine).
18. Isa. 9:6 (Emphasis, mine).

In fact, the Bible says that our righteous works are like filthy rags, to the Lord.[19] Therefore, we cannot earn salvation, it must be given to us as a free gift; it was given on Calvary mountain over two-thousand years ago. I encourage you to take the time to thank the Lord for all the blessings you have. Even if you don't have many earthly possessions, you have eternity with Him, and that's more than a lot of people have.

On the Tenth Day

As the day is about to break, I have the honor of spending this morning in solitude with God. Quite often, when I awake before dawn, He has something important He wants to tell me. So, I thought I would share what is on my heart, and hopefully bring God's light into a dark world.

Today, I am forty-three years old. Over the past four decades I have seen and experienced much. I have built dreams, I've had them shattered. I have loved, and I have been rejected. I have been married; I have been divorced. I've had moments of anger and jealousy; I've had moments of happiness and joy. I have experienced watching my children be born; I have experienced watching my loved ones die. I have had so many friends, professors, and mentors pour into my life, and I have poured into theirs. I have lost contact with my son, only to have him walk back into my life several years later. I have served others; I have served myself. I've achieved several goals, and I have been defeated. I've had the pleasure of loving others; I've felt the pain of not feeling loved. I've had much success; and, I have had much loss.

I am nowhere near perfect. I've made plenty of poor choices in the past, but I've also made plenty of good ones. I've learned from my mistakes and not let the enemy defeat me. I've survived through depression so that I could still feel the sunshine upon my face. There are so many things to be thankful for in this life. Sometimes we just have to take the time to recognize them. I look forward to having many more years of blessings.

Blessings and curses are part of life, so surely you will experience both. Don't let the curses be your downfall. Realize that we all experience hardships sometimes. The blessing is that we never face them alone.

---

19. Isa. 64:6 (Emphasis, mine).

On the Eleventh Day

Veteran's Day

The brilliance of the Holy Spirit moves me to reach out and share the gospel message with those I encounter as I make my travels throughout Reno and Lake Tahoe. Some reject the gospel, but many accept it and are happy to hear more about this man called, "Jesus." I never tire of spreading the good news: it is a part of me, just like my hands and feet. Sharing God's word is truly a rewarding experience.

Today is Veteran's Day. A day in which we honor our country's military heroes who have, and still do, continue to keep us safe from foreign oppression. The Bible says, "Greater love has no one than this, that someone lay down his life for his friends."[20] Indeed, young men and women have done just that for so many people in the United States who are unknown to them.

The military has been around for thousands of years. In fact, the book of Genesis tells the story of, The Battle of the Kings and their armies:

> Then the king of Sodom, the king of Gomorrah, the king of Admah, the king of Zeboyim and the king of Bela (that is, Zoar) marched out and drew up their battle lines in the Valley of Siddim against Kedorlaomerking of Elam, Tidal king of Goyim, Amraphel king of Shinar and Arioch king of Ellasar—four kings against five.[21]

The four kings ended up winning the battle and captured Abraham's nephew Lot in the processes. Abraham ambushed the four kings at night and emerged victorious, bringing back Lot, various possessions, and women and children.[22] Ironically, Abraham ends up receiving a blessing from another king; a great king of Jerusalem named, Melchizedek. Similarly, Jesus Christ, our High Priest from the order of Melchizedek still blesses us every single day.

On the Twelfth Day

Many of my friends on social media reach out to me for advice with their lives. What should I do with my life? Where should I travel to? Should I stay

---

20. John 15:13 (ESV).
21. Gen. 14:8-9 (NIV).
22. Gen. 14:14-16 (Emphasis, mine).

with my boyfriend or girlfriend? Should I start a new career? What is God's plan for me?

I usually have to preface my answer with something like, "Just so you understand, I'm not God, so I don't want to speak for Him, but I do have some thoughts on this that I'd like to share with you." I'm always flattered when someone seeks out my advice. I'd much rather they do it from me or another pastor than from a clairvoyant or medium, but I always have to include that caveat, because only God knows His plan for their lives, I can only offer my experience with God in His dealings with my own life.

One morning last spring, I received a message from a young lady who was devastated because she sporadically moved to California with her on and off boyfriend and realized that she had made a mistake. She's been reaching out to me for advice for a while now, and I always see the same pattern. She is not willing to let go of the life she's comfortable with, even though it's hurting her in the long run. She would rather be in an abusive relationship than in no relationship at all.

I've discovered that in life, God will often place two different doors in front of us. One is easy to open because we actually possess the key to unlock it. The other is much harder to open because it's locked and only God, Himself has the key to unlock it. If we force our way through the locked door that we do not have the key to, then we might actually end up in the wrong room; a room that God never intended for us to go in. Yet, if we choose the door that's easy to go through because God has given us the key, then we will always be in the right room because God has indeed intended for us to go through it. So, the question is, which door will you choose?

On the Thirteenth Day

The clouds pass over the cold valley as the rain begins to fall. The animals in the area seek shelter from the storm as they run to the nearby forest of pine trees in the Sierra Nevada mountains. God provided clothing for the first humans,[23] surely, He provides cover for the rest of His creation as well.

When we think of great biblical characters of the Bible, we might think of names like, Moses, Joseph, David, Abraham, or Daniel. Indeed, all of those people were great patriarchs of the Bible, but one that is often overlooked is King Josiah.

Josiah, one of the greatest kings to ever rule Israel, started his reign when he was only eight years old. The Bible tells us that "he did what was

---

23. Gen. 3:21 (Emphasis, mine).

right in the eyes of the Lord."[24] Not long after, the high priest found the Book of the Law which had been neglected and hidden for years. This caused Josiah to tear his clothes and plead with the Lord to not punish Israel for their disobedience to God's word. Josiah read the Book of the Law publicly and made a covenant with the Lord along with his people to obey the Lord with all of his heart and with all of his soul.[25]

This story demonstrates how kingly leadership, with a heart for repentance, can lead to God's mercy upon a nation. Perhaps, something our own country could benefit from. If we have a truly repentant heart, it doesn't matter if we come from royalty or poverty, God will turn from His wrath against us and forgive us for our sins. We are ultimately forgiven in Christ Jesus who paid the price once and for all that we might again be in right standing with the Father.

On the fourteenth Day

I've read a lot of books over the past seven years. When I was an undergraduate in college, I got to my junior year and realized that I took everything required first, so I was left with thirty elective credits to complete before I could graduate. I wasn't interested in taking random courses that I couldn't do much with, so I decided to double minor in both English and Pastoral Ministries. This, of course, led to much more reading and I was fascinated by all of the great literature that I had missed out on reading in my youth.

My English professor used to tell us that the difference between regular writing and literature is that literature stands the test of time. Great literature is timeless in its message and impact to the reader. This is why the Bible is so amazing to me. The Holy Word of God goes even beyond literature into realms of prophesy, revelation, learning, and application. When we read God's word, we are reading the words penned by both the human author and the Holy Spirit. No other book exists that has so much revelation and application to our lives as the Bible does. No other book has over three-hundred specific prophecies of Jesus Christ written by dozens of different authors over a fifteen-hundred-year period. No other book contains the inspired word of God.

The author of Hebrews tells us, that "the word of God is alive and active. Sharper than any double-edged sword, it penetrates even to dividing soul and spirit, joints and marrow; it judges the thoughts and attitudes of

---

24. 2 Kgs. 22:2 (NIV).
25. 2 Kgs. 23:3 (Emphasis, mine).

the heart."[26] God's word not only convicts us, but penetrates into our souls, revealing the true feelings of our hearts. Most Bibles sit on the dust-filled bookcases of neglected home offices, but God's word is meant to be read every single day. Have you read your Bible lately?

On the Fifteenth Day

The mountains and valleys call out to Him. All of creation will one day bow at His feet. The great lakes and rivers reflect the life-giving water that He provides for us. And, the stars, planets, and heavens remind us how great and powerful He truly is. He has the power to heal and destroy; to grant life, and to take it away. I take nothing that I have in this life for granted, and I make sure I set time aside each and every day to thank God for what He has done for me.

When I set out to write this devotional, a few things inspired me. One, was the way in which the medieval and desert fathers, such as Anselm and Antony, wrote their devotions to the Lord. They wrote them in almost a stream of consciousness allowing the Holy Spirit to enter into their thoughts. A second thing that inspired me was spending time in solitude with God as a Spiritual Formation course assignment. I realized that simply looking out at God's creation is enough to verify that He is there amongst it.

People worship God in many different ways. Singing worship songs is probably the most common way in contemporary churches today, but many people worship Him through dance, prayer, meditation, journaling, fasting, or sharing the good news of Jesus Christ with others. King David once wrote, "Ascribe to the Lord the glory due his name; worship the Lord in the splendor of his holiness."[27]

God's name is glorious. When Moses came upon the burning bush, the Lord revealed His name as YHWH, or "I Am."[28] Many years later, Jesus Christ would also refer to this name for Himself when asked how He could have seen Abraham's day at less than fifty years old.[29] We worship the name of the Lord because He is the great I Am; nothing compares to Him.

26. Heb. 4:12 (NIV).
27. Ps. 29:2 (NIV).
28. Ex. 3:1-14 (Emphasis, mine).
29. John 8:57-58 (Emphasis, mine).

On the Sixteenth Day

On this day, five years ago, on a brisk fall morning full of hope and sunshine, I began serving as the senior pastor of 1st Church of God in Reno, Nevada. I've been so blessed to be the pastor of this loving and Christ-centered church for all of these years. We are few in number, but strong in Christ.

Sometimes, it can be discouraging when a person takes over as the pastor of a church and the membership seems to increase only ever so slightly. However, one thing that I learned early on in my ministry is that the goal is not to fill the seats; rather, the goal, is to fill the individuals who occupy the seats, regardless of how many or few they may be. My goal is to grow people in Christ; and, as a result, God will send me more people to help grow. In fact, God sends people to me outside of my church all of the time. If everyone who reached out to me for soul care outside of church actually attended my church, we would be at least three times as big.

I have many friends who are pastors of small churches. When I say small churches, I mean churches of less than fifty members. To you, I commend you, for I know how challenging it can be at times to wear all of the hats. But please know that you are still doing God's work, whether you have ten members or ten thousand members. One thing I enjoy about a smaller congregation is that I can spend time getting to know them as people. I can help in times of struggle with one-on-one spiritual care because I have the time and energy to care for each member of my flock.

Just last week, we had a visitor from Florida attend our church for the first time. He is a Church of God member in Florida and was visiting some friends of his who are members of our church. After the service, he said something that stuck with me. He said, "What you lack in quantity, you make up with quality." Thank you, Lord, for continuing to motivate me.

On the Seventeenth Day

As the last leaves fall from atop the maple tree in our backyard, the cold cement of the ground reveals the frost of the coming winter. The sun rises over the great lake as the cloud formations reflect the majestic glory of God, the Father.

When I look out at the water as the wind blows through the pine trees, I can feel God's presence all around me. The serenity of my surroundings allows for God to speak to me, touching my soul with His love and guidance. Reflecting back on my times alone with God, I appreciate His patience with me, for we all fall short of His glory.

Jesus once said, "Ask and it will be given to you; seek and you will find; knock and the door will be opened to you. For everyone who asks receives; the one who seeks finds; and to the one who knocks, the door will be opened."[30]

When I was in seminary, we studied contemporary church models of various traditions. Many of the more popular, non-denominational churches have what's called a "seeker-friendly" church service, which involves making the experience so comfortable, inviting, and friendly that the person attending will feel compelled to give their lives to Jesus Christ.

Ironically, we don't have to seek God out, for He seeks out us.[31] You see, salvation is completely the act of God; He draws and empowers the dead sinner with what is necessary to believe.[32] At some point, someone in your life planted a seed that there even was a God and that He created all things. In my own experience, it was through a dear friend of mine who invited me to church, and it was there, that God made me grow. Therefore, after God first seeks us, we in turn, seek to get to know Him and the result is that the door of salvation is opened to us.

On the Eighteenth Day

We've all seen them, I'm quite certain of it. We've all heard how successful they are, how much good fortune has come their way, how many fancy homes, cars, and even private jets they own. We've watched in shock as they continue to ask for even more from naive and vulnerable people who support them. I'm not referring to a famous celebrity or business owner, I'm referring to televangelists.

A funny thing happens to those who abuse what God blesses them with. God humbles them in the most public ways. You may recall the popular televangelist, Jim Baker and his wife Tammy Faye? Jim ended up being investigated by the FCC for using money to build his mansion that was originally donated for missions. He also faced a sexual misconduct allegation, and a fraud conviction, of which he spent five years in prison. Oh, and he also ended up divorced.

False prophets are everywhere. There is a reason that the love of money is the root of all evil. It's because it can corrupt even the most humble and God-fearing men. In that sense, money is a curse. Jesus reveals the intentions

---

30. Luke 11:9-10 (NIV).
31. John 6:44/Rom. 3:11 (Emphasis, mine).
32. John 6:37 (Emphasis, mine).

of the lovers of money by stating, "The thief comes only to steal and kill and destroy; I have come that they may have life and have it to the full."[33]

Living the abundant life is not the health and wealth gospel message. In fact, it's quite the contrary. Living a life of abundance means living a life rich in the love of Jesus Christ. True prosperity is revealed in how strong our relationship is with Christ Jesus.

The Apostle Paul once exhorted the Ephesians by saying, "Now to him who is able to do immeasurably more than all we ask or imagine . . . to him be glory in the church and in Christ Jesus throughout all generations, for ever and ever! Amen."[34] I pray that same immeasurable ability is given to you, once you realize where your true wealth can be found.

On the Nineteenth Day

The omniscience of the Father is a wonder to behold. His knowledge is beyond all understanding. If we *could* understand everything about Him, then we would be bringing Him down to our human level, a place He can never go. We serve a God that is absolute truth; we serve a God who possesses ultimate wisdom.

My first name, Craig, is actually a derivation of the Celtic word, "creag," meaning rock. The great psalmist, David once wrote, "The Lord is my rock, my fortress and my deliverer; my God is my rock, in whom I take refuge, my shield and the horn of my salvation, my stronghold."[35] Indeed, a rock is a symbol of unbreakable strength.

I remember a few years ago, a huge bolder fell from atop of a South Lake Tahoe mountain and onto Highway 50 below it. It took nearly two years just to break apart the boulder with several jackhammers and other construction equipment and secure the rest of the remaining boulders on the mountain. That situation proved to everyone who witnessed it that rocks are not easily broken.

Jesus once told Peter, "I tell you, you are Peter, and on this rock, I will build my church, and the gates of hell shall not prevail against it."[36] This was said in the context of Caesarea Philippi, as there was a stone cliff face surrounding the cave entrance with votive niches for pagan offerings. The name of the cave opening was, "The Gates of Hades." The name of the wall was, "The Rock." So, what Jesus was doing is drawing attention to the last

33. John 10:10 (NIV).
34. Eph. 3:20-21 (NIV).
35. Ps. 18:2 (NIV).
36. Matt. 16:18 (ESV).

place the disciples wanted to be, with a play on words from Peter's name. "Simon, your Greek name means rock (*Petros*), and speaking of rocks, it is upon *this* here rock (and places like this) that I will build my church." Too often, we seek to build churches where it is easy, convenient, safe and predictable.

On the Twentieth Day

Seven years ago, I received a call upon my heart to pursue the ministry full-time. While I still work a second (and sometimes) third job to help support my family, I have always pursued that goal. The small church I serve as senior pastor for is a round-the-clock position, and I wouldn't want it any other way. My passion is to serve God and serve His creation, and I truly enjoy teaching people about Him.

The Apostle Paul once wrote:

> As a prisoner for the Lord, then, I urge you to live a life worthy of the calling you have received. Be completely humble and gentle; be patient, bearing with one another in love. Make every effort to keep the unity of the Spirit through the bond of peace. There is one body and one Spirit, just as you were called to one hope when you were called; one Lord, one faith, one baptism; one God and Father of all, who is over all and through all and in all.[37]

Notice, that Paul is not writing to a specific pastor, rather, he is addressing the entire church of Ephesus. This is because if we profess Jesus Christ as our Lord and Savior, then we are all called in some way to serve Him. In light of this, we are all to be unified in one faith and baptism, even though our callings may all be quite different.

I am friends with several Christians who all serve the Lord in various ways. Some are teachers, some are healers, some are evangelists, some are carpenters, some are mechanics, some are cable television installers, and some are housewives, but *all* are called to share the good news with those around them.

If you are currently attending a church and wondering how you can serve, don't be afraid to reach out to one of the pastors or leadership team members and ask how you can volunteer using your God-given talents. We can all help advance the Kingdom of God in some way.

---

37. Eph. 4:1-6 (NIV).

On the Twenty-First Day

The wind begins to blow as the clouds clear to make way for the sunshine. The bright sun reminds me of the radiance of the Holy Spirit who shined down upon each of the disciples at Pentecost like tongues of fire.[38]

It's amazing how much power our words have. If we say something encouraging or inspiring, it can help to uplift even the most down-trodden individual. Yet, if we use our words to hurt and embarrass someone else, it may help to end the life of even the most positive person. Children are especially susceptible to hurtful comments now that social media has taken over our lives. I've read too many tragic stories of young people taking their own lives because of being bullied online.

The book of Proverbs tells us, "The tongue has the power of life and death, and those who love it will eat its fruit."[39] Those who love life are the first fruits of God's beautiful harvest. Jesus once said, "A good man brings good things out of the good stored up in his heart, and an evil man brings evil things out of the evil stored up in his heart. For the mouth speaks what the heart is full of."[40]

The way we speak of others reflects our own hearts. If we speak well of others, then we speak well of ourselves, yet if we speak poorly of others, then we speak poorly of ourselves. As with everything, God judges us by our hearts. If you struggle with gossip or intentionally speaking ill of others that you know, please ask God to deliver you from the demon that torments you. We should always use our words to encourage and edify. I pray that you will continue to use your words to build others up.

On the Twenty-Second Day

Genuine belief in something is hard when there is a lack scientific proof. Most unbelievers use science against religion, but they actually are compatible with each other. Science reinforces biblical truths once they are discovered. In fact, I have yet to read or hear of an archeological find that has disproven a historical event in the Bible; they only reinforce them. The ones that have not been scientifically proven, simply haven't been discovered yet.

The Lord's brother *James the Just* once wrote, "But when you ask, you must believe and not doubt, because the one who doubts is like a wave of

---

38. Acts 2:2-3 (Emphasis, mine).
39. Prov. 18:21 (NIV).
40. Luke 6:45 (NIV).

the sea, blown and tossed by the wind."[41] We must be confident in our faith. The enemy is quick to bring doubt into our minds, but if we have the strength to rebuke him, our faith will be restored and our relationship with Jesus Christ will grow even stronger.

Once, a man came to Jesus with his son who was having multiple seizures. After rebuking the crowd for their lack of faith, Jesus rebuked the demon and the boy was healed immediately. When questioned by the disciples why they could not cast the demon out, Jesus said, "Because you have so little faith. Truly I tell you, if you have faith as small as a mustard seed, you can say to this mountain, 'Move from here to there,' and it will move. Nothing will be impossible for you."[42]

If we have just a small amount of faith, we can do many great things. Imagine if we have great faith, we can do even greater things. Mustard seeds are not that big, but when planted, they often grow into large nine-foot plants that sprout forth many seeds. Even if we start out with just a little faith, through prayer, reading God's word, and life experience, our faith can grow as well.

On the Twenty-Third Day

The love of the Father is quite evident. I mean, you're still alive, aren't you? Sometimes, we take for granted that God controls our very heartbeats. God gave us life and continues to sustain our lives as we travel throughout this broken world. We should wake up every morning and thank the Lord for another chance at life.

Godly wisdom is very different from earthly wisdom. We can be wise in intellect, yet foolish in the wisdom involving our fear of the Lord. The Bible tells us that, "the wisdom that comes from heaven is first of all pure; then peace-loving, considerate, submissive, full of mercy and good fruit, impartial and sincere."[43] Godly wisdom will never lead you astray, never give you false information, and never let you down. I can't tell you how many times I've made poor choices in life, because I've relied on my own wisdom instead of God's wisdom. Some of my choices, I still suffer from today.

The great prophet Daniel once awoke from a vision and said, "Praise be to the name of God for ever and ever; wisdom and power are his. He

---

41. Jas. 1:6 (NIV).
42. Matt. 17:14-20 (Emphasis, mine).
43. Jas. 3:17 (NIV).

changes times and seasons; he deposes kings and raises up others. He gives wisdom to the wise and knowledge to the discerning."[44]

The Lord, Himself actually gives us the wisdom we need to obey Him. This is the beauty of Christianity. Once you've accepted Christ into your heart, you possess all of the tools to succeed in the kingdom of heaven. Nothing will be impossible for you, if you simply trust in the Lord and listen to His Spirit who is constantly speaking to you.

On the Twenty-Fourth Day

The rain pours down as the dim clouds slowly crawl across the menacing sky. The mix of rain and snow fall on the valley floor as lonely travelers find themselves susceptible to the dangerous road conditions. I always dread driving clients on the snow-filled, icy roads of Lake Tahoe during the extreme winter season. Too often, my heartbeat has nearly beat out of my chest from hydroplaning or sliding while driving in those conditions. Fortunately, God has always kept me safe; He has always answered my prayers.

Lake Tahoe has many pine trees. I once learned that there were several species of pine trees that naturally grow there. The Alpine, Ponderosa Pine, and Sugar Pine are just a few of the species that adorn the Sierra Nevada mountains. Trees are beautiful to look at and seek shade under. They provide homes for several forest creatures and food for many other animals and insects.

Like the many branches that extend from a tree, we are all a part of Jesus Christ's kingdom. Do you ever stop to think that you are an extension of Jesus Christ? I had never really thought about it in that way before, but after re-reading *The Gospel according to John*, I meditated on this verse: "I am the vine; you are the branches. Whoever abides in me and I in him, he it is that bears much fruit, for apart from me you can do nothing."[45]

The Bible tells us that if we abide in Christ, then we should walk in the same way that He walked.[46] When we walk in Christ's footsteps, we are reflecting the very best that God has to offer. When we love as Christ loved, we are loving in the way that God loves us. Therefore, put your best foot forward as you abide in Christ, for your reward is already paid in full.

---

44. Dan. 2:20-21 (NIV).
45. John 15:5 (ESV).
46. 1 John 2:6 (Emphasis, mine).

On the Twenty-Fifth Day

When we think of "the church," images of large buildings with stained glass or a full stage often come to our minds. Yet, the church is not really about the physical structure at all; the church is about the people inside of the building. In fact, the early church met secretly in homes much smaller than any church we see today on a busy street corner.

The fellowship of the saints involves sharing the gospel message, supporting one another, reaching the unreachable, praying for the lost, and helping those who cannot help themselves. The Apostle John once wrote, "If we walk in the light, as he is in the light, we have fellowship with one another, and the blood of Jesus his Son cleanses us from all sin."[47]

In addition to simply going to church, we should also work on *being* the church in a community of those who are lost and seeking the truth of why they are here and what their purpose in life actually is.

Buildings are great, but only temporary. Jesus once said that the great temple of marble and gold will be destroyed and rebuilt in three days.[48] Of course, Jesus was talking about His body, which can never be destroyed. Since we are all members of the body of Christ, our souls can never be destroyed either; therefore, have confidence that He who began a good work in you will continue that good work until the return of Jesus Christ.[49] Part of our sanctification is helping to grow the church by growing the people that make up the church.

If you belong to a large church, please know that God has blessed you and that you should be thankful that He has sent so many people to you; however, you must realize that there are a high percentage of people that attend church regularly and assume they are saved.

On the Twenty Sixth Day

The snow falls lightly upon the dry ground as the river flows forcefully towards downtown. The neighbor continues on his morning jog as the sidewalks begin to fill with white powder. My kids love the snow, but it's so much work getting them dressed, then undressed from their wet clothes, then they want a bath. After all of that, I just really want to take a nap.

It's important to take the time to care for your brothers and sisters of faith. They may not always be around, as God decides if we will live or if we

---

47. 1 John 1:7 (ESV).
48. John 2:19 (Emphasis, mine).
49. Phil. 1:6 (Emphasis, mine).

will die. Does not the Bible tell us to break bread, give of our abundance, praise God, and greet each other with open arms, each time we gather?[50] Therefore, embrace one another on all occasions, for we know not when the Lord will take us home.

There once was a man who was attacked by robbers and was left to die on the road. Many people, including a Levite and Priest, passed by not giving him a second look. But, an unlikely fellow from Samaria saw him, had pity on him, bandaged his wounds, and even paid for him to stay at a hotel and recover.[51] Those who show mercy to others are like this good Samaritan. We should always be willing to help those in need, regardless of where they are from, what race they are, or what possessions they have. Does not the Scriptures tell us that others will know we are disciples of Jesus Christ if we have love for one another?[52]

Pray for each other, build each other up, and show mercy towards those who have wronged you. We must be kind to others at all times, for no one but the Father knows what they are really going through.

On the Twenty Seventh Day

Glory to God in the highest! I thank the Lord for the ability to wake up and enjoy another day to serve Him and His creation. I love Jesus Christ with all of my heart, mind, soul, and strength, and I can't wait until the day I can dwell with Him in eternity, face to face and Spirit to Spirit.

My children have a lot of questions about God and our life after this earth. I wish I could tell you that I have all of the answers, but some things, none of us will know until we go to be with Him someday. I do know that His love is never ending and whatever form of love we experience here on earth is nothing compared to the unconditional love that the Father has for us.

In my youngest daughter's bedroom, there is a depiction of Jesus holding a small child as she has just entered into heaven. I decided to hang it up in my daughter's room because I wanted to let her know that if anything ever happens to any of us, Jesus will always be there to hold us. I cannot imagine what it would be like to lose a child, and I pray that I will never have to find out, but I do know that they are never alone. Christ is there to take over where we left off.

50. Acts 2:43-47 (Emphasis, mine).
51. Luke 10:25-35 (Emphasis, mine).
52. John 13:35 (Emphasis, mine).

Once, the disciples were gathered around Jesus as children ran towards Him, longing for His attention. The disciples selfishly rebuked them for bothering the Messiah, but Jesus said to them, "Let the little children come to me and do not hinder them, for to such belongs the kingdom of heaven."[53]

I pray that you have a strong relationship with your children. If you have lost a child, I pray that you can find peace in the fact that your child is in the loving arms of Christ and you will be reunited with them again.

On the Twenty-Eighth Day

Thanksgiving Day

One of my favorite prayers for Thanksgiving Day is from the book of Thessalonians, which says to "give thanks in all circumstances; for this is the will of God in Christ Jesus for you."[54] Every time that I pray, I begin my prayer with thanksgiving to God. I thank Him for saving me, watching over me and my family, watching over my church members, and for dying a death that I deserved to die for my rebellion against the Father.

When I walk down the lively streets of downtown Reno, I notice that there's always a strong homeless population present. Some are there by choice, many are there due to alcohol or drug dependencies, and still some are there wanting to get out of homelessness but simply can't. I mentioned in a previous devotional that my dear friend and brother in Christ, Bill Muck has a strong heart for the homeless and takes time out of his busy schedule to minister and serve them every single week through the Reno-Sparks Gospel Mission.

One of my friends from high school asked how she could help her children to appreciate what they have instead of complaining all the time (something my own children could do better), so I suggested she have them serve food down at the homeless shelter. It's very humbling to serve and give to others. Moses once said, "There will never cease to be poor in the land. Therefore, I command you, 'You shall open wide your hand to your brother, to the needy and to the poor, in your land.'"[55]

I pray that this thanksgiving, you will be truly appreciative of all that the Lord has blessed you with. When you feel like you're not doing that well, remember that someone is always worse off than you are. For that reason alone, we should all be thankful to God Almighty.

53. Matt. 19:14 (ESV).
54. 1 Thess. 5:18 (ESV).
55. Deut. 15:11 (ESV).

On the Twenty-Ninth Day

The sunset adorns the sky as God's tapestry is in full effect. I'm at awe at such a beautiful painting that I have the honor of admiring every single day. God controls the earth, the universe, and everything in it. Nothing is here by chance. We all have a purpose in this life; we all have something to thank God for.

At the church where I serve, we have had many different people from all walks of life come through our doors. They say that the church is not a museum of saints, but a hospital for sinners. Perhaps, there's some truth to that statement, but I feel that some of the loneliest people walk into a church hoping to be noticed.

I had a class not long ago with a good friend of mine who said that he invited some of his friends to his church, which is a popular church with the young adult demographic in town. To his shock, no one even said hello to his friends, so they decided not to return.

Sadly, this is not all that uncommon. A person may walk into a church alone on a Sunday morning and leave the church alone. Although, they appreciate the free coffee and doughnuts in the foyer, what they really want is someone to notice them and get to know them.

I've had the honor of ministering to people within my church, outside of my church, and people who attend other churches. Jesus Christ spent most of His time ministering to people outside of the temple walls. Only once in a while do we have a record of Him actually inside of a temple. I can't say that I blame Him, for when He did visit a temple once, He found moneychangers there instead of worshipers.[56]

If you attend a church, please take the time to get to know the people visiting. For, Christ has taken the time to get to know you.

On the Thirtieth Day

Jesus Christ has died for our sins. He paid the ultimate price so that we can enjoy time with Him in eternity. The love of the Father is like no other love we can experience here on earth. Heaven is such a wonderful place; yet, we only get a foretaste of the feast to come. How much greater will our lives be when God restores everything back to the way He intended it to be. How glorious is His name that because of it, every knee will bow, and every tongue confess?[57]

---

56. John 2:14 (Emphasis, mine).
57. Rom. 14:11 (Emphasis, mine).

"THE FELLOWSHIP OF THE SAINTS"

Well, you've made it through another month. How do you feel? Have you worked on fellowshipping with other believers? Have you worked on spending time with those outside of the church? I pray that this month was successful for you in those areas of your Christian walk. Have you taken the time to speak to God lately? He truly longs to hear from you, and He is always listening.

It's important to ask ourselves the question, why do we go to church? Is it merely to visit with friends or family members that we don't normally interact with during the week? Are we there to enjoy the free coffee, the worship team, or the message? Are we trying to earn points in heaven by attending each week? We must realize that God does not need us. I know, that sounds harsh, but the reality is that God functions just fine without us. In fact, if God could get stressed out, it most certainly would be because of us. Imagine how stressed out you get when your kids are fighting with each other for hours, now multiply that by seven billion. That's how many people God keeps track of every single day.

We should be attending church to worship and glorify God with other like-minded believers. It's not about us, it's about Him. It's always been about Him. To God be the glory.

Chapter 12

"The Promise"
The Month of December

On the First Day

First Sunday of Advent

Icicles form on the edges of the roof as winter sets in. The frigid temperatures are all too familiar as the steam rises off of the wet ground on this first day of December. Looking out of my frosted window I can see the barren, lifeless trees in the distance.

The Advent season is upon us as we reflect back on when our Lord Jesus Christ broke into our fallen world giving us hope; we look forward to His return as well. To some, hope can be a discouraging word. My biological father and I have always had a loving relationship, but when I was little, he used to tell me that he was planning a trip to Disneyland and wanted to take me along with him and my half-brother and sisters. He would call and say that we would go the following summer. Excitedly, I waited for summer to arrive. When it did, my dad would say that he was sorry, but something had come up and he would try and reschedule for the fall. Fall came along, and again something would come up and the trip was canceled. After a while, I stopped believing him whenever he would promise that we would go to Disneyland. You could say that my *hope* in him regarding Disneyland was lost.

Consider God's servant Job. How many times do we experience only a fraction of what Job went through and yet we blame God for the smallest deficiencies in our lives? Rather than curse God and die, Job responded: "Though He slay me, yet will I hope in Him."[1] Like Job, I have never lost hope in my heavenly Father, for He has never let me down. Oh, and my earthly father finally did take us to Disneyland a few years ago, all expenses paid.

---

1. Job 13:15a (NIV).

On the Second Day

The coldness of winter reflects the emptiness inside for those who have yet to know the Savior. A numbness takes over when we have no one to turn to as we struggle; no one to turn to when we are alone. Our feelings are rigid, like the hardened ice that rests beneath the fallen snow. Life passes by as the seconds of time tick away.

I enjoy reading. In fact, I probably have over seven hundred books in my home library. Most of them are theology or spiritual formation books, but many of them are novels, classics, and poetic works from well-known authors of the past. My wife often complains that I buy too many books, to which I jokingly reply, "Would you rather I spend my money at the bar?"

No matter how much head knowledge we have, if we are not connecting with God on an intimate level, we have not achieved true knowledge. The Apostle Paul longed that the people in Ephesus receive this type of knowledge through the Holy Spirit: "I keep asking that the God of our Lord Jesus Christ, the glorious Father, may give you the Spirit of wisdom and revelation, so that you may know him better."[2]

The amount of literature and historical books that deal with doctrine and theology are endless. I once posted on social media that I've read over six hundred books, taken forty college level classes in Theology, Philosophy, Biblical Studies, and Church History, been a Christian for over thirty years, pray regularly, and make a genuine effort to love God with all my heart, and my neighbors as well. Yet, despite all of that, I'm barely scratching the surface in building a relationship with Jesus Christ.

We can spend our entire lives learning about God and still not know everything there is to know about Him. Have you taken the time to get to know Him lately?

On the Third Day

I enjoy traveling. I prefer to travel by car, but sometimes airplane travel makes the most sense. This Christmas we are going to my parents' house in Denver, Colorado. The scenery along the way is truly something to marvel at. I've always admired the variety of landscapes that God created. Flat lands, to mountainous regions, valleys to lakes, deserts to oceans. Like with us, God used a diverse range of aesthetics in nature, which are all pleasing to the eye.

---

2. Eph. 1:17 (NIV).

Sometimes during long travels, we can annoy each other more than originally anticipated. Young children will fight with each other over who gets which seat, or who can watch which electronic device. Yet, through it all God enables us to persevere through it. This is where patience comes in. The Bible says that, "The end of a matter is better than its beginning, and patience is better than pride."[3]

A wise man once said, "You can be right, or you can be happy."[4] Indeed, I'm not always right, but I am pretty happy. Having humility may involve us swallowing our pride and letting the other person that we care about gain a sense of it. If we remain stubborn at all times, we will surely engage in an endless banter that allows the enemy to enter into our minds with thoughts of giving up or resentment. Do not let this happen. Have an honest and open dialogue in your relationship. Surely, there will be times of trials and temptations, I know, I've been there, but don't let the enemy win. The divorce rate is way too high because people fail to communicate, fail to have faith in both God and their partners, and fail to work at their relationships when times are hard.

On the Fourth Day

God will often send me people that He wants me to interact with. I can't explain it fully, but it's like the less I try to seek out people to share God's Word with, the more often He finds those in need who reach out to me. For this, I am truly grateful.

A friend of mine recently reached out to me through social media and asked me to pray for him. He's been struggling with toxic family members for years and is trying to find balance in his relationship with them. I told him that the enemy is a great deceiver. He has always been a deceiver, and until he is bound, will always be able to deceive. Therefore, this should come as no surprise to us. When we feel that we cannot persevere in our lives or in our faith in the Lord, it is not us failing to have the strength to get through it. It is the great deceiver who is putting thoughts of doubt and bitterness into our minds.

Family can often be the hardest ones to reach with the gospel message. This is why Jesus rightly proclaimed:

> For I have come to set a man against his father, and a daughter against her mother, and a daughter-in-law against her

---

3. Eccl. 7:8 (NIV).
4. Source unknown.

mother-in-law. And a person's enemies will be those of his own household. Whoever loves father or mother more than me is not worthy of me, and whoever loves son or daughter more than me is not worthy of me.[5]

These are not harsh words, for it is not Jesus' intent to separate us from our families; but, rather, it is a natural result of the fall. Satan has always tried to separate us. This is why Adam hid from God after the fall; this is why Cain killed Abel; this is why division still takes place. Through the promise of the Savior, the curse of Adam has been reversed. We can now dwell in unity once again with both each other and with the Father. The Holy Spirit makes it possible to remain unified. If not physically, at least in a spiritual sense.

On the Fifth Day

The snow lightly falls down as the windows of my house begin to frost over. My wife and kids are asleep in their beds as the heater warms up our home. A few of the logs crackle in the fire as I begin to pray on my thoughts for the day.

Having good virtues will lead to a life filled with happiness and triumph. Even during our setbacks, our virtuous attributes will allow us to overcome any obstacles that we might face. The Apostle Peter knew the importance of godly virtue all too well, for he once denied knowing the Christ, then later made up for the denial with the three "I love you's," and ultimately, as legend has it, was hung upside down on a cross, giving his very life for the Messiah that he once denied following.

Like Peter, we sometimes let the enemy get in front of us. We allow our virtues to be tainted by Satan's lies and deceptions. Yet, we must work harder at allowing our true godly nature to shine through. The Bible tells us, "Make every effort to supplement your faith with virtue, and virtue with knowledge."[6] Faith and virtue must work together. If we have no faith, do we really have honor or integrity? What is our moral compass? And, to what ethical standard do we hold ourselves? Surely, not mankind's standards, for God must be the ultimate moral standard.

Virtues were very important to the ancient Greeks. Philosophers, such as Socrates and Plato, held human virtues in very high regard. If you are not living a virtuous life, ask God to increase your faith in Him. Through prayer,

---

5. Matt. 10:35-37 (ESV).
6. 2 Pet. 1:5 (ESV).

time spent with the Lord, and love for one another, the godly attributes that you desire will surely increase over time.

On the Sixth Day

Christmas is fast approaching as the stores and shopping malls are filled with consumers. My wife usually buys our gifts online which saves us the hassle of physically shopping at the store. Most of the time, we can't think of things to get for people, so we usually send them a gift card or money instead of a wrapped present.

The holidays can be hard for those who have lost a friend, relationship, or loved one. Every Christmas I send a card and money to my oldest son, Collin; every year I fail to get a response from him. Sometimes, I wish I could go back in time and make better choices in life.

When Collin was a teenager, I didn't always make enough time to be with him. I should have made more of an effort to build a relationship with him, but I was too busy being depressed, preoccupied with work, and taking care of my girlfriend and her children at the time.

A few years ago, the principal of the high school that I taught at asked the faculty if we could come up with a piece of advice for the graduating seniors that year. Many teachers had words of inspiration such as, "Don't take life for granted," or "Always do your best." Based on my own experiences right out of high school, I chose to say, "Make wise choices."

Trust me when I say that if you are in a new relationship, never allow yourself to be so overcome by it that you neglect making time for your children from your previous relationship. The poor choices that you make now will surely haunt you for the rest of your life.

We can't go back in time and fix the mistakes of our past, but we can move forward and make better choices in the future. It's never too late to change course and become a better parent, spouse, or friend. God will help you in your quest to be a better Christian, but you must do your part as well. Life is too short to take things for granted.

On the Seventh Day

God works in mysterious ways. Just yesterday, I wrote that I hadn't heard anything back from my oldest son, Collin in quite some time. A few years, as a matter of fact. Well, today he wrote me back! He's doing well, moving into an apartment of his own, and working full time at a hardware store. What a blessing, and right before Christmas. Thanks be to God!

I've mentioned this before, but we tend to always be in a hurry. God is not in a hurry, I promise you. I would have loved to hear back from my son a few years ago, but instead I heard back from him today. Perhaps, the Lord had other plans for him during that time and interacting with me would have altered those plans. The Lord *is* sovereign, after all.

Is there someone in your life that you haven't spoken to in a while? Perhaps, they had wronged you in the past, or you had wronged them? It's never too late to forgive someone and build your relationship back with them. The Apostle Paul tells us to: "Bear with each other and forgive one another if any of you has a grievance against someone. Forgive as the Lord forgave you. And over all these virtues put on love, which binds them all together in perfect unity."[7]

You will find that true peace of mind comes when you have little worries about yourself or someone else in your life. If we always act in an upstanding and godly way, the enemy has little to convict us of. You can build a strong relationship with Jesus Christ, as well as with others around you, simply by honoring God in all that you do.

I pray that this Christmas season will be one of joy, hope, and remembrance of the one who was born into this world to become a living sacrifice for each and every one of us. "Through Jesus, therefore, let us continually offer to God a sacrifice of praise; the fruit of lips that openly profess his name."[8]

On the Eighth Day

Second Sunday of Advent

With all that is going on in the world today, peace seems like a far cry from reality. Yet, peace is something we should never stop striving for. This Advent Sunday, I encourage you to find peace within yourselves, and with others you interact with. Peace on earth and goodwill toward men will only help to bless the relationships with those closest to you.

The Apostle Paul tells us to let the peace of Christ rule in our hearts.[9] In this way, we are to remember Christ's actions while He was here among us. Christ even forgave those who persecuted him, in the midst of the persecution. Likewise, we too should conduct ourselves in a peaceful manor.

Have you ever had an argument with someone and by yelling back at them, they only got more frustrated and increased the intensity of the

---

7. Col. 3:13-14 (NIV).
8. Heb. 13:15 (NIV).
9. Col. 3:15 (Emphasis, mine).

argument? That was how I used to try and settle disputes with people. Yet, this method never settled anything and would only lead to more frustration on both of our parts. Have you ever considered speaking in a calm tone when someone is upset with you and agreeing with them on areas of mutual agreement? I'm quite sure it will work much better to resolve whatever disagreement you might have with someone else.

The Bible tells us, "Make sure that nobody pays back wrong for wrong, but always strive to do what is good for each other and for everyone else."[10] Revenge can only lead to more heartache and despair. I encourage you to take the higher road. When someone has wronged you, make sure they know that they have hurt you, but that you have forgiven them. This will lead to a relationship similar to the one Christ had with both His friends, and enemies. I'm confident that you can do it. I'll be praying for your success, and peace be with you.

On the Ninth Day

The brisk walk along the river leads me to one of my favorite coffee shops as I greet the baristas and order my usual mocha latte. The coffee shop has a panoramic view of the river and streets below. I just love to sip coffee and ponder life's questions as I stare out into God's creation and marvel at how this beautiful landscape was once spoken into existence.

One of my favorite theology professors, Dr. Tim Allen, is very kind and compassionate. He's always the first to welcome his students with a big hug, infectious laugh, and words of encouragement. If he ever does get angry, I haven't seen it in the six years that I've known him.

Like Dr. Allen, we should be friendly to one another, especially if we profess Jesus Christ as our personal Lord and Savior. Jesus commands us to love our enemies, so how much more would He prefer that we love our friends? This seems like it should be common sense, but you'd be surprised at how many "Christians" I've met who either pretend to love one another when it's convenient for them, or do not show love for their friends at all, let alone their enemies.

Sanctification is truly a lifelong process. The Apostle Paul tells us that salvation is not only past and future but happens in the present as well.[11] In this way, salvation can be viewed in a similar way to sanctification, since it is an ongoing process. This means that we cannot expect to be fully sanctified in Christ's likeness at salvation. Which is why we must work out our salva-

---

10. 1 Thess. 5:15 (NIV).
11. 2 Cor. 2:15 (Emphasis, mine).

tion through fear and trembling.[12] Paul knew all too well the consequences of sin. Yet, Paul focused on love as the greatest of the gifts.

If you are struggling to love someone unconditionally, pray and ask the Lord to soften your heart for that person. We never know what someone else has been through or is now going through.

On the Tenth Day

Most scholars would argue that Paul, himself believed that the end of time would occur during his own lifetime. And, I think that Paul did believe that. Jesus tells us that no one knows the day or the hour except the Father.[13] Therefore, every generation must be ready for Christ's return.

I just got back from a nice vacation with my family in California a few days ago and naturally, I was thrust back into full work mode at all of my jobs. Yet, I did get to spend some time with one of our drivers the other day on a multiple driving trip. She has somewhat of a rough past, but she's a Christian and tries to attend church services when she can. She was telling me (before I left for California) that she needed a counselor for some of her past issues and struggles. So, I reached out to a few of my counseling friends that are also involved in ministry and found some referrals for her. When I followed up with her during our conversation a few days ago, she said she didn't have enough time to get in touch with any of them. And then I thought, we never know when Christ will come back or when we will go to see Him. So, when it comes to bettering your life and turning from sin, don't delay. The time is now! Think of how bad it will sound when you stand before the Almighty and explain to Him that you were too busy to work on your obedience. That conversation may not go so well.

No one is perfect, and certainly we all sin, whether in our minds or physically, or both. Yet, it's important to take the time to work on our relationship with Jesus Christ because you don't want Him to return and say, "I never knew you."[14]

On the Eleventh Day

The naked branches of the trees are rigid this morning as the frost from the evening air settles in. The cold of winter can be a time of great reflection as

---

12. Phil. 2:12 (Emphasis, mine).
13. Mark 13:32 (Emphasis, mine).
14. Matt. 7:23 (Emphasis, mine).

I peer out at the endless valley below. From the top of the mountain, I can see God's beautiful design, laid out in vibrant colors of taupe, forest green, turquoise, yellow, and crimson. The fresh air fills my lungs as I inhale the breath of life and exhale the bitterness of sorrow.

Sadly, one year ago today, my beloved stepmother, Joni Prather passed away from a long and strenuous battle with cancer. Being ever so humble, Joni never expressed that she was in such a bad physical place. I only found out much later from my aunt that she only had a few weeks to live. After she passed, it got me to thinking. Does God allow for these diseases to take our lives so that we can spend time with Him in eternity, sooner than we expected to? Or, is cancer and other deadly diseases the result of the fall, in which God doesn't control whom it affects or when it affects them? Is there a difference in reasoning as to why an evil person can get cancer just the same as a righteous person? Why did both Michael Landon and Steve Jobs die of cancer, when one could be considered close to God and the other could be considered very distant from God?

I pondered these thoughts for quite some time. Perhaps, like Jesus calming the storm, we have to look at who is delivering the storm? Jesus could not rebuke Himself; therefore, the storm on the Sea of Galilee was clearly sent by Satan. Yet, in other natural disasters, God delivers the calamity Himself, such as when Sodom and Gomorrah was destroyed through fire and volcanic activity.[15] Some things, we cannot know in this lifetime. We must simply trust in God's plan and know that He loves us.

On the Twelfth Day

Lust is a nasty four-letter word that can destroy men and their families. Suffering through two tragic break-ups in my own life, I can attest that Satan uses this sinful tactic quite often and quite powerfully against God's children. From King David, to popular 70's evangelists and televangelists, to modern day theologians, sexual immorality truly plagues us all.

Solomon tells us that, "The eye never gets enough of seeing or the ear enough of hearing, for there is nothing new under the sun."[16] In this way, we have all experienced lustful thoughts as a result of the fall. Jesus once said, "And if your eye causes you to fall into sin, pluck it out. It is better for you to enter the kingdom of God with one eye than to have two eyes and be thrown into hell."[17] This hyperbolic statement isn't far from the truth. We

---

15. Gen. 19:23-25 (Emphasis, mine).
16. Eccl. 1:8-9 (Emphasis, mine).
17. Mark 9:47 (NIV).

must proactively work towards a healthy relationship with the Lord. Short of plucking out your eyes, what else can you think of to help prevent you from falling into sin?

A Christian friend of mine once told me that he struggled with adultery during his marriage. Instead of dissolving the marriage, his wife stayed with him, but only on the condition that she could check any of his electronic devices at any time, to help build back trust in the relationship. He not only agreed to those terms, but also made her his accountability partner. Meaning, that he gave her the passwords to all of his email and social media accounts.

Sometimes, to save what is important to us, we must be willing to sacrifice what is important to Satan. Satan doesn't care about your marriage succeeding, or about you succeeding. He only cares about separating you from God by tempting you to sin. So, resist him and enjoy a wonderful marriage. It's never too late to stop sinning.

On the Thirteenth Day

When I was much younger, we used to have a family golden retriever as a pet. My mother loves golden retrievers and would often have at least one, if not two of them at a time. In fact, she still has one now, though he is growing older. I enjoyed the company of our dog, but personally, didn't have a strong connection to him, other than he was cute and fun to be around.

Many people have strong connections to their pets. When I started college, a friend and colleague of mine mentioned that he had baptized his dog in order to ensure that he would see him again in heaven. After most of us stopped laughing, we began to question whether or not animals need salvation. Instinctively, animals attack and kill other animals, but is that the same as murdering them? It's interesting to note that unlike animals, God actually breathed His Spirit into Adam to create him; thereby, instilling in Adam an immortal soul. Since Eve was part of Adam, she would have had an immortal soul as well, as do the rest of us. Animals can be obedient only through training and rewards; whereas, human beings have the ability to make moral choices apart from a survival instinct.

I hope we see our favorite pets in heaven. Perhaps, they will be there, not because they have been forgiven of their sins, but because God wants us to be happy and knows that reuniting us with our longlost cat or dog, may just be the thing that keeps a smile on our face:

> Surely the fate of human beings is like that of the animals; the same fate awaits them both: As one dies, so dies the other. All

have the same breath; humans have no advantage over animals. Everything is meaningless. All go to the same place; all come from dust, and to dust all return. Who knows if the human spirit rises upward and if the spirit of the animal goes down into the earth?[18]

On the Fourteenth Day

The dry desert is overshadowed by the Sierra Nevada mountain range which is snow-capped this winter and breathtaking to look at. I never grow tired of driving to the Lake Tahoe area for work since I can relive the pleasure of seeing God's creation every time I go. The beauty of the lake never gets old.

Jesus Christ came into the world, not to judge it, but to save it.[19] God set His plan of redemption in motion long ago so that a Messiah would be sent to us to save us from our sins. Though He was among us, we did not recognize Him.[20] Yet, He still dwells with us, even today, in the form of the Holy Spirit. You are never alone, for Christ is with you. Many of the prophets predicted His coming. The prophet Jeremiah once said, "The days are coming," declares the LORD, "when I will raise up for David a righteous Branch, a King who will reign wisely and do what is just and right in the land."[21]

Jesus is the light and without Him, only darkness would inhabit our souls. This is why light is always better than darkness.[22] When we love one another, spend time with one another, pray for each other, and encourage one another in godly love, we are shining Christ's light into those around us. We are not the source of the light, but we inhabit the light that we might be reflections of Jesus Christ who can shine brightly into someone else.

Therefore, we should never fear the light, for the light has already overcome the darkness. The Greek philosopher Plato once said, "We can easily forgive a child who is afraid of the dark; the real tragedy of life is when men are afraid of the light."

---

18. Eccl. 3:18-21 (NIV).
19. John 3:17 (Emphasis, mine).
20. John 1:10 (Emphasis, mine).
21. Jer. 23:5 (NIV).
22. Eccl. 2:13 (Emphasis, mine).

On the Fifteenth Day

Third Sunday of Advent

The third Sunday of Advent is traditionally celebrated by lighting a pink candle within the Advent wreath. Pink represents the joy of Mary, the beloved mother of Jesus Christ. For many years, the early church fathers debated whether God could indeed have a mother. *Theotokos,* or "mother of God" is better translated as "bearer of God," and will surely appease those who take opposition to God having a mother.

Certainly, Mary was chosen to give birth to the Savior. The angel Gabriel was sent to Mary and said:

> Do not be afraid, Mary; you have found favor with God. You will conceive and give birth to a son, and you are to call him Jesus. He will be great and will be called the Son of the Most High. The Lord God will give him the throne of his father David, and he will reign over Jacob's descendants forever; his kingdom will never end.[23]

What a glorious event this was! God had orchestrated the birth of Christ from the beginning of time. From Joseph leaving for Bethlehem for the census, to the angel visiting him in a dream warning him of Herod's plan to kill Jesus,[24] every event had to take place exactly how God had arranged it for our Savior to be born into this world unharmed.

And, so it is with you and me. The Lord has already arranged everything in our lives to take place exactly as He planned it. This is why we must not fear when trials and tribulations come our way, for the Lord surely has a plan for us to persevere through it, but only if we have the faith of a mustard seed.

When we accept Jesus Christ into our hearts, we make a covenant with Him. Jesus never breaks His covenants, so take heart that He will be forever committed to you.

On the Sixteenth Day

The chilly morning fast approaches as the sun begins to rise in the east. Sitting next to a warm fire, I take the time this morning to communicate with God through my thoughts. Sometimes, I wish whatever I thought could be

---

23. Luke 1:30-33 (NIV).
24. Matt. 2:12-13 (Emphasis, mine).

directly recorded without the hassle of writing it down. Yet, many other times, I do not wish whatever I thought could be directly recorded. I suppose whatever God inspires us to write down, we will.

I feel as though the Lord wants me to speak to you about suicide. Not a topic that I would have chosen to write to you about, but God wants me to address it, so I will. Some believers interpret suicidal thoughts in the wrong way. They may think that God, Himself is leading them to take their own lives to be in His presence sooner. Yet, this could not be farther from the truth. The Apostle Paul once said, "Do you not know that you are God's temple and that God's Spirit dwells in you? If anyone *destroys* God's temple, God will destroy him. For God's temple is holy, and you are that temple."[25] The *anyone* who destroys God's temple includes us. You see, the commandment to not murder applies to murdering ourselves, and since you will have already committed the act by the time you ask forgiveness for it, you'll already have to face God and tell Him why you ended the life that He gave you.

Think of the Apostle Paul. How many times was he beaten, shipwrecked, left to die, stoned by his adversaries, scourged, yelled at, made fun of? Yet, he did not once, choose to take his own life. Listen to what the Spirit has to say. You are valuable to God. Even if the world doesn't see your value, God does. He has more work for you to do on this earth. You might not see it now, but you will when you look back on your life and say, "I fought the good fight, I finished the course, and I kept the faith."[26] I love you and I'll be praying for you.

On the Seventeenth Day

When I was a young teenager, I used to always doubt my abilities. I had some support from friends and some family members; but, in general, my self-esteem was not where it should have been. If an exam or assignment was due at school, I would get very nervous; often times, giving up studying when I could have persevered. Other times, I would give into sexual temptations, feeling as though they made up for a stressful homelife.

The Apostle Peter surely experienced some of these setbacks as well. In his second epistle, he reminds us that:

> His divine power has given us everything we need for a godly life through our knowledge of him who called us by his own glory and goodness. Through these he has given us his very great and

---

25. 1 Cor. 3:16-17 (ESV).
26. 2 Tim. 4:7 (Emphasis, mine).

precious promises, so that through them you may participate in the divine nature, having escaped the corruption in the world caused by evil desires.[27]

I believe that God has a plan for us, but I also believe that we can choose to go along with that plan or resist it. Each day, we are faced with temptations, for the enemy is not quick to give up on us. Through the divine power of Jesus Christ, we have everything we need to resist temptation and remain uncorrupted by this world. Evil desires are nothing new. They have been part of our flesh since the fall, yet we are not forced to give into them. If it were easy to resist the devil, he would no longer be motivated to continue tempting us. Since sin is usually pleasurable, we need strong faith and courage to overcome it.

If you are struggling with sin and temptation, seek someone in the faith that you can trust to help you overcome it. Pray fervently that the Holy Spirit will empower you to resist the temptations that Satan burdens you with. If you continue to seek Christ during times of temptation, Satan will flee, and you will live a virtuous life.

On the Eighteenth Day

The landscape is blanketed with snow this morning as the sun peers out between the thick white clouds. Footprints in the ground begin to fill with powder as the wind blows the snow off the branches of the trees.

I had a great conversation yesterday with a Muslim woman that I went to high school with. Her daughter was getting serious with a Christian man and she wanted to know more about our beliefs. I was very happy that she reached out to me. She had some questions about how Christians view the Trinity and what we consider Jesus to be. I shared with her my faith and how many people throughout my life had spent time with me revealing the love of Jesus Christ. I mentioned how the Holy Spirit helps guide me in my decision-making process, and how I felt a connection to Him the instant I underwent baptism. She, in turn, shared with me her experience with the Muslim faith and how the Qur'an teaches many similar principles. She even believes that Jesus will return and judge the world.

Though we had many areas of agreement during our conversation, the area that we disagree was on the divinity of Jesus Christ. The Muslim view is that there is only one God; therefore, Jesus was a great prophet like many of the prophets of the Old Testament. My view is also that there is only one

---

27. 2 Pet. 1:3-4 (NIV).

God, but that He manifests Himself in three different ways. I can see how this would seem hard for an unbeliever to accept, because it's even hard for believers to explain. Yet, I told her that her daughter and her boyfriend are better off finding common ground in areas of agreement, instead of fighting over areas of disagreement.

Being made in the image of God means that, like God, we should love one another regardless of their beliefs. We can love someone, but still hold firm to our own convictions.

On the Nineteenth Day

Have you ever felt pressured into doing something you thought you'd regret later? I'm sure that most of us have. When my wife and I were first married, we were visited by a popular vacuum company sales representative. After telling us, "Let me just show you how this vacuum can clean your grout really quick; it will only take five minutes," I thought to myself, sure, why not?

Well, you can probably guess what transpired after the five-minute demonstration. Soon, he was showing us how the vacuum had extra suction powers, how the cord was super durable and could never break, how it could not only vacuum our house, but shampoo our carpets and paint our siding as well! It even came with a lifetime warrantee. And, all for the low, low price of $3,000.00! "I'm in, where do I sign?" Guess how many times we spray painted our house or cleaned the grout between our floor tiles? Zero. My wife says the vacuum is just too heavy and clunky, so it now sits in our garage collecting dust.

The wise king Solomon once said, "Where there is no guidance, a people falls, but in an abundance of counselors there is safety."[28] Sometimes, we make impulse decisions without taking the time to consult those who have been there and learned from similar mistakes. Of course, God is a great resource to seek advice from, this is why it's important to pray over major life decisions as well as seek the guidance of others.

I've made many poor choices in the past; but, through God's grace, I've learned from my mistakes. I live my life in a much wiser way through obedience to Him, and you can too. If you struggle with impulsive decisions that you might later regret, seek the help of a brother or sister in faith and God will surely provide you with the right answer.

---

28. Prov. 11:14 (ESV).

On the Twentieth Day

When I first applied for the senior pastor position with 1st Church of God in Reno, I was quite nervous. I was only in my second year of Bible College and had only taken one preaching course by the time of the interview; although, I felt that God had directed me to apply there and I knew that His hand was surely in it.

I spent quite a few days preparing my message. I decided to preach on the theme of hope and used Paul's letter to the Ephesians to illustrate how the Gentile believers (us) were once separated from Christ, having no hope, and without God in the world.[29] Thanks to God, the sermon went over really well. My old friend and Sunday school teacher, Rev. Mike Patterson even showed up to support and encourage me.

I've counseled people who have very little hope in this life. After hearing what they've been through, I probably would lose hope in this world as well; however, I have never lost hope in my Savior. He has been through far worse pain and suffering than I could ever go through, yet He still emerged victorious at the end, and so will we. For, anyone who is among the living has hope.[30]

I know sometimes life can make it appear that hope is all but present. And that sometimes, hope can be a dangerous word, but fear not, for the hope we have is in Jesus Christ. He came down from Heaven once in the flesh but will return in the full Glory of His resurrected body to Judge the living and the dead. Those of us who are in Christ have the security of knowing that we already possess the kingdom of heaven. The kingdom of heaven is at hand because the kingdom exists inside each and every one of us who believe in Christ Jesus.

On the Twenty-First Day

The bright snow is almost too radiant to look at as the city experiences a severe storm that has caused many delays for motorists traveling back and forth across the Sierra Nevada mountains. Several weather-related car accidents have taken place over the last few days as ambulances and fire trucks rush to the scene.

Most car accidents are preventable. Often, we are in too much of a hurry to get somewhere because we waited until the last minute or didn't plan ahead for weather or road conditions. I'm just as guilty as anyone else, but truly,

---

29. Eph. 2:8-12 (Emphasis, mine).
30. Eccl. 9:4 (Emphasis, mine).

truly I tell you, being late for work or an event is far better than being in the hospital, or worse. Just because you may have a four-wheel or all-wheel drive vehicle, doesn't make you invincible to slippery conditions.

In college, I would tend to do assignments and research papers far in advance so that I wouldn't be stressed out at the last minute, knowing that they had to be turned in within a few days. A few times, I got ahold of the syllabus before the class even started and was able to work on and finish the final paper by the first day of class (disclaimer: this method can backfire, if the instructor has specific guidelines for the assignment that are not spelled out in the syllabus).

In general, planning ahead is always a smart decision. Does not the ant prepare her bread in the summer and gather her food during the harvest?[31] How much greater are we to God than an ant? Therefore, do not wait until the last minute, but plan ahead for things that could prevent you from accomplishing something on time. In doing so, you will have peace of mind when challenges occur, and will enjoy a life of less stress.

On the Twenty-Second Day

Fourth Sunday of Advent/ Hanukkah Begins

The pine trees sway in the breeze on top of the snow-capped mountains. The hawk floats aimlessly in the sky as snow begins to melt from the afternoon sun. Candescent lights flicker from inside the homes of those whose brazen logs add heat to the fire. The compressed smoke rises from the chimney as children play in the winter wonderland outside.

This last Sunday of Advent includes remembering the love that God has for us. From a human perspective, we tend to love others with conditions. If they treat us well, if they buy us things, if they go above and beyond for us, if they take care of us when we're sick, then we might be able to show love for them. Yet, imagine if someone demeaned you, accused you of things you didn't do, abused you, didn't believe in you, and tried to murder you. Would you still love them? Probably not. Yet, these are the kinds of people that Christ died for. Similar to Jesus, the first deacon of the church age, Stephen once said, "Lord, do not hold this sin against them."[32] Immediately after that, Stephen died from being stoned to death by the very people for whom he asked the Lord's forgiveness.

---

31. Prov. 6:6-8 (Emphasis, mine).
32. Acts 7:60 (ESV).

Godly love is far different from earthly love. Picture a loving parent. If they discipline their child for doing something that might endanger them, is that not still showing love towards them? If they get upset or jealous because their child has neglected them for something that might bring bodily harm or death to them, is that not still showing love towards them? We spend so much time loving others with the expectation that they will love us back in the exact same way. Yet, if we love as Christ loves His Church, we would be showing true love to others without expecting anything in return.

On the Twenty-Third Day

God incarnated Himself, not only to die for us, but to experience life with us. When non-believers question why God does not just come down to the earth and reveal Himself, I always say, "He did! Yet, still many didn't believe in Him." The Messiah was promised to the Jewish people long before He arrived on this earth. Through Abraham's offspring, all the people on earth would be blessed.[33] Indeed, we are blessed through Jesus Christ who has the power to turn each of us away from our wicked ways.

Jesus' existence was foretold by God in Genesis, Moses in Deuteronomy, and several of the prophets throughout the Old Testament. Jesus, Himself fulfilled all of the Old Testament feasts and festivals except one, the Feast of Tabernacles. Ironically, this Jewish festival takes place in the fall, which is when many scholars believe that Jesus was actually born; and some even predict is when He will return.

I get messages sometimes from my non-Christian friends reminding me that Christmas is a pagan holiday and that Jesus wasn't born on December 25th. In response to them I say, "It is of little importance *when* we celebrate a Christian holiday, yet it is of extreme importance *why* we celebrate a Christian holiday." The etymology of the word "Holiday" originates from, "Holy-day," but because of the brokenness of the world, we've moved away from our sacred beliefs towards more scientific and relative truths.

As believers, it is important that we take time out of our busy schedules and remember the sacrifice that Jesus made for us on the cross. The King of the earth was born into this broken and dirty world, placed in a feeding trough, and raised in poverty. He washed the feet of sinful people. He gave His very life so that people like us could keep ours into eternity.

---

33. Gen. 12:3 (Emphasis, mine).

On the Twenty-Fourth Day

My grandparents on my stepfather's side are German and have always celebrated Christmas on Christmas Eve, so growing up, we always got to open our presents early and then excitedly wait for Santa Clause to leave something special in our stockings the next morning. One tradition that we had as a family was driving around the neighborhood and looking at Christmas lights. A tradition that I've carried through to my own wife and children each year around Christmas time.

Yet, the true celebration of Christmas isn't about fancy gifts, video games, or shiny new bicycles, but rather, involves remembering the birth of our Lord and Savior, Jesus Christ, who came into a broken world, only to later die for our sins. The great prophet Isaiah once said, "I will allot Him a portion with the great, and He will divide the spoils with the strong, because He has poured out His life unto death, and He was numbered among the transgressors. Yet He bore the sin of many and made intercession for the transgressors."[34]

When someone asks me if I'm religious, I answer no. I prefer to respond that I'm a Christian. By following Christ, I am not any of the things that religion would expect me to live up to, but rather, I am a broken human being who puts my faith in Jesus Christ, who accomplished in His lifetime what I could not, and who defeated death on the cross.

Thank you, Lord, for dying for my sins. I thank you for caring enough about me to give your very life so that I could enjoy eternity with you. Thank you for sending the gift of the Holy Spirit who dwells inside of me; guiding and helping me to build a closer relationship with you. Amen.

On the Twenty-Fifth Day

Christmas Day

The smell of fresh-cooked turkey, mashed potatoes and gravy, and deep-red cranberry sauce fills the air. The golden biscuits with butter that glistens from the afternoon sunshine peering through the half-draped windows adorn the dining room table. The majestic Christmas tree topped with a plastic angel whose fiberoptic gown changes from purple, to yellow, to pink, to blue, is a central feature in our modest-sized living room. Yes, Christmas Day has arrived.

---

34. Isa. 53:12 (NIV).

It's important to remember that while we celebrate Christmas from the comfort of our warm living rooms, Jesus' mother and adoptive father were making their way to Bethlehem to be registered when Mary went into labor. Having no guesthouse to stay at, she gave birth to Jesus in an animal stall and placed Him in a manger.[35]

The creator of the entire universe humbled Himself to the point of being born into a broken world and laid in a feeding trough. The King of kings and Lord of lords chose to dwell among us and experience first-hand what we experience. We are so very blessed to have a God that loves us so much. Other gods require their followers to try and obey all of their commands to have a chance at entering into eternity with them. Yet, only the one true God of our fathers, Abraham, Isaac, and Jacob, requires nothing more from us other than placing our faith and trust in His Son, Jesus Christ in order that we can live in eternity with Him. St. Luke tells us, "Today in the town of David a Savior has been born to you; he is the Messiah, the Lord. This will be a sign to you: You will find a baby wrapped in cloths and lying in a manger."[36]

I wish all of you a very Merry Christmas. Please take the time to say a prayer of thanks to our Lord and Savior, Jesus Christ for coming into this world to save us from our sins.

On the Twenty-Sixth Day

As the sun glistens off the melting snow, the birds begin to sing as the new day has begun. The very fact that we have another opportunity to wake up, enjoy God's wonderful creation, and worship the Lord, is truly a blessing.

I had the pleasure once of giving a lecture at my seminary school on the Apostle Paul, as well as the book of Acts. When meeting with the head professor, I asked him about his personal preaching style, and he said that it was basically the same as how he taught because that seems to go over best with his church congregation. As I thought about it, I realized that I preach and teach in the same fashion. I would much rather preach in an expository way (deducting principles and doctrine out of the Scriptures in their proper context) than the more popular, thematic or topical preaching style. There's nothing wrong with preaching topically as long as it's done responsibly. The dangers occur when we try and take modern events happening in culture and superimpose them onto Scripture. The reason we can be confident in our message is because we've spent countless hours in study and research

---

35. Luke 2:6-7 (Emphasis, mine).
36. Luke 2:11-12 (NIV).

in order to assure our audience that they are receiving the most sound and accurate teaching of the Bible that is possible.

When we prepare to teach someone else about the Bible, we should do so with humility and scholarship; using passion, words, and ethical principles to enhance our message. Listen first and foremost to the Holy Spirit, for He, Himself will teach you.[37] Then, be sure and research the historical context of the passage you are teaching. Lastly, read or consult with well-respected theologians on the topic that you are teaching on, try and use an illustration or application to speak into the hearts of your audience, and always remember that: "All Scripture is God-breathed and is useful for teaching, rebuking, correcting and training in righteousness."[38]

On the Twenty-Seventh Day

There are so many places in the Old Testament that refer to a Savior being born who will save God's people from their sins. One passage that I enjoy reading can be found in the book of Isaiah:

> For to us a child is born, to us a son is given, and the government will be on his shoulders. And he will be called Wonderful Counselor, Mighty God, Everlasting Father, Prince of Peace. Of the greatness of his government and peace there will be no end. He will reign on David's throne and over his kingdom, establishing and upholding it with justice and righteousness from that time on and forever. The zeal of the Lord Almighty will accomplish this.[39]

Great is the Lord's faithfulness. God has promised us a redeemer for our transgressions from the beginning of time and He has delivered on His promise. We can always trust that the Lord will follow through with His promises. Unlike broken human beings, we can place our full trust in the Holy One and He will never let us down.

Because of our disobedience, the Lord had every right to condemn us all to an eternity with the prince of the earth; however, in His loving heart, God has graciously redeemed us through His only begotten son, Jesus Christ. God had to be made fully human in every way in order to become a merciful and faithful high priest, and also that He might make atonement for our sins. [40]

---

37. 1 John 2:27 (Emphasis, mine).
38. 2 Tim. 3:16 (NIV).
39. Isa. 9:6-7 (NIV).
40. Heb. 2:17 (Emphasis, mine).

God Almighty has the power to speak life into existence. He can bless or curse, He controls the rain and winds, He gives life and takes life away. He is the Lord God, who has existed before all time and who will never cease to dwell in the heavens. How mighty is His power and how loving is He who is, who was, and who will always be.

On the Twenty-Eighth Day

The loving and beautiful Father loves us in many ways. Yet, like Gomer, we do not always love Him back. This saddens me because we too easily allow the enemy to come between us and our creator. After the fall, Adam hid from God, and sometimes so do we. The Lord truly has our best interests at heart. Trust in Him and live a blessed life.

I've done some things in my past that I'm certainly not proud of. Whether it was drinking, sexual fornication, or prideful behavior, I've always received forgiveness from the Lord once I've asked for it. I promise, if you struggle with something that is preventing you from living a righteous life, repent from your sins and ask the Lord for forgiveness. He will surely accept you back into His loving arms. The prophet Isaiah once said, "Let the wicked forsake their ways and the unrighteous their thoughts. Let them turn to the LORD, and he will have mercy on them, and to our God, for he will freely pardon."[41]

God's mercy always triumphs over His judgment.[42] If it didn't, would He not send His only son to die for us? Listen to what the Spirit has to say. Therefore, don't give up on yourself. You can still build a healthy relationship with the Lord. As long as you're still breathing, it's not too late.

Sadly, as the Apostle Paul rightly predicted, the time has come in which people will not listen to sound biblical doctrine. Instead, they turn to their own desires, allowing teachers to tell them what they want to hear.[43] Don't be like the people of the world. They do not have your eternal interests in mind when they lead you astray. Instead, be like those who are in the world, but not of the world. They will help lead you to a better relationship with the Holy One.

---

41. Isa. 55:7 (NIV).
42. Jas. 2:13 (Emphasis, mine).
43. 2 Tim. 4:3 (Emphasis, mine).

On the Twenty-Ninth Day

The dawn is upon me as the warmth of the morning sun begins to light up the world. I glance over at my wife who is sleeping comfortably in bed as I awake to celebrate another day of life. My children are all sound asleep, and it's quiet now. The stillness of the morning is like being in front of the great lake, with only the sound of the wind echoing like white noise in my ears.

We have all experienced hardships in this life. I'd be lying to you if I said that I hadn't. Yet, how we face life's challenges says a lot about our character and our passion to persevere. An old friend of mine, Faith Martinez, used to work as a cocktail waitress at the hotel where I drove limousines. Tragically, she lost her ability to walk several years ago. She had recently moved to Tijuana to be with her children's father who lived down there. One night, he came home drunk and shot her in the back. By the grace of God, she survived, yet was left paralyzed from the waist down.

Faith is a great example of optimism in the midst of challenge. She struggled through countless hours of physical therapy and training and was eventually able to get around by herself using her wheelchair. She often posts on social media how great God is and how happy she is to be alive.

When we think of how hard our life is, think of what Faith had to endure and her amazing perseverance; think of what Jesus Christ had to endure at Gethsemane and His faithfulness. If you think Jesus didn't suffer, both mentally and physically, think again.[44] Life is hard enough to get through, so don't go through it alone. God is there with you, helping you every step of the way.

On the Thirtieth Day

Hanukkah Ends

One thing that I love about being charismatic is that the gifts of the Spirit that God has blessed me with are always present in my life. Whether that gift is a prayer language, discernment, sound teaching, or illumination of Scripture, I can always count on the Holy Spirit to energize my soul in a way that best glorifies God.

Along with the corporate gifts of the Spirit, come corporate revivals. Revivals are quite popular among charismatic circles. Often times, Pentecostals will reference well-known revivals such as: The First Great Awakening, or The Second Great Awakening, or the Azusa Street Revival of the

---

44. Matt. 26:36-38 (Emphasis, mine).

early 1900's. These are all good examples of more modern or contemporary revivals taking place in the church, but what does Scripture tell us about revivals?

King David once wrote, "Will you not *revive* us again, that your people may rejoice in you? Show us your unfailing love, Lord, and grant us your salvation."[45] It's important to note what must take place in God's eyes before He can revive His church. According to Scripture, true revival must begin with ourselves. We as the church, both individually and corporately, must repent of our sins because without repentance there can be no revival. The book of Acts tells us, "Repent therefore, and turn back, that your sins may be blotted out, that times of refreshing may come from the presence of the Lord, and that he may send the Christ appointed for you, Jesus."[46]

By actively pursuing repentance, forgiveness, fervent prayer, and communion with the Holy Spirit, we set ourselves apart to be in the perfect position for revival to take place within our churches.

On the Thirty-First Day

Well, loved ones, we have made it to the final day of the year in the, *Moved by the Spirit Daily Devotional*. How did your year go? Were there challenges that you faced that you overcame? Were there setbacks during the year that you prayed to God to resolve? Did you make any progress in your relationship with friends or family members? Did you make any progress in your relationship with Jesus Christ? How is church going? Have you pursued a ministry in which God has called you to serve in, or are you still seeking a church to belong to?

I hope that this devotional has been edifying to your soul. I spent many, many hours writing it. Yet, I never wrote it alone, for every second of every key-stroke was inspired by the Holy Spirit. I pray that you will continue in your Christian journey long after these words have left your sight. I wish you well in your future, and please know that God is always with you, always guiding and counseling you, always correcting and refining you, and always leading you by the hand to a place of beautiful sanctification in Christ Jesus. Through Him, in Him, and with Him, we all will be *Moved by the Spirit*.

The End

---

45. Ps. 85:6-7 (NIV).
46. Acts 3:19-20 (ESV).

Afterword

My journey with the Lord has been nothing short of magnificent. I cannot express how much love I have for Him, and He in return for me. I've always thought it was important to reveal myself through my writing in such a way that relates to people of every: race, gender, background, and socio-economic status. Regardless of where we are currently in our lives (or what the world deems as successful), we are all sustained by the same God, in the same way, and through the same love that He has for each and every one of us.

At first, I questioned if I could even write enough about all of the great things my Lord and Savior has done for me over the years. Could I possibly fill up 300 plus pages worth of praise, worship, and awe for the creator of all life? Then the Lord reminded me of what the Apostle John once said in his Gospel account, *"Jesus did many other things as well. If every one of them were written down, I suppose that even the whole world would not have room for the books that would be written."*[1]

My very first class at Multnomah University was College Writing with Professor Kathe Berning. I'll never forget the first thing she told us college freshmen. She said: "Developing your writing is so important. You might not realize this now, but someday, someone is going to want to read what you have to say." I hope that this book has made a valiant attempt to honor her passion for teaching and helping to develop future literary artists.

My small contribution fails in comparison to all the great works of the Saints and Martyrs, who have given their very lives to record their experiences with Jesus Christ. I can only humbly offer my gratitude to God the Father, for loving me enough to care for my every need.

—Craig M. Prather

---

1. John 21:25 (New International Version).

Appendix 1

Jewish Festivals and Fasts, by Date and Month

Festival or Feast:	**Length:**	**Hebrew Date:**	**Gregorian Month:**
Rosh Hashana	2 days	1-2 Tishrei	September–October
Yom Kippur	1 day	10 Tishrei	September–October
Sukkot	8 days	15-22 Tishrei	September–October
Simchat Torah	1 day	23 Tishrei	September–October
Chanukah	8 days	25 Kislev	December
Tu Bishvat	1 day	15 Shvat	January–February
Purim	1 day	15 Adar	March
Pesach (Passover)	8 days	15-22 Nisan	March–April
Holocaust Remembrance Day	1 day	27 Nisan	March–April
	1 day	4 Iyar	May
Israel Independence Day	1 day	5 Iyar	May
Jerusalem Day	1 day	28 Iyar	May
Shavuot (Pentecost)	2 days	5-6 Sivan	May–June
Fast of Tammuz	1 day	17 Tammuz	June–July
Fast of Av	1 day	9 Av	August

Appendix 2

"The Traveler"

By

Craig M. Prather[1]

I couldn't sleep at all last night, guess I woke up around four.
Kissed my kids and wife goodbye, as I headed out the door.
And after all this time I realize that I'm lonely where I've been.
I am a traveler, and I'll see your face again.

Many times, I walk alone, and many days I've cried.
Tell my kids that I love them all, it's so hard to say goodbye.
And as the sun goes down, I'm headin' North to a land I've never been.
I am a traveler, and I'll be with you again.

And if all my time on earth expired and I looked back at my life.
I could say I gave my best to you; I could find a reason why.
And even after darkness fades away, and the pain in me subsides.
I am a traveler, and I've seen the other side.

Lookin' up at God Himself, I can see Him in the sky.
Prayin' that He'd give me help and He'd keep the love alive.
And if I ever forsake livin' here, and I feel I can't go on.
I am a traveler, in the heavens I belong.

---

1. *https://craigprather.bandcamp.com/track/the-traveler-2.*

Appendix 3

"Crazy Life"
By
Craig M. Prather[1]

If I could get away, is there something you would say?
Would you follow me again; would you take away my sin?
If I ever walk alone, can you make your presence known?

When I feel this way inside, I can't help but feel alive.
So, I'll make this vow to you; I'll make every dream come true.
If you let me try again, you'll be sure and let me in.

---

1. *https://www.amazon.com/Crazy-Life-feat-Doovy-Tushayde/dp/B00949SL40.*

Appendix 4

"On and On"

By

Craig M. Prather[1]

Today, I woke up in the rain.
Sunflowers kill the pain.
I tried to live again.

So, say, why don't you come on down.
Turn this empty world around.
We're living for today.

And it goes on and on we need it.
And it goes on and on we need it.
And it goes on and on we need it.
And it goes on and on we need it.

Well, I could not imagine why.
The fireflies shine so bright.
When they never had your light.

So please, help some of your children out.
Then no one could ever doubt.
What your love is all about.

---

1. *https://soundcloud.com/craigmprather/on-and-on.*

Bibliography

Chumney, Edward. *The Seven Festivals of the Messiah.* Shippensburg: Destiny Image, 1994.

Lipka, Michael & Benjamin Wormald. "How Religious is Your State?" Pew Research Center. Washington, D.C. February 29, 2016. http://www.pewresearch.org/fact-tank/2016/02/29/how-religious-is-your-state/?state=alabama.

Young, Katherine. "Precision Medicine While Saving Health Care Costs." PRNewswire, Barrons.com, January 7, 2019. http://www.prnewswire.com/news-releases/genomic-health-marks-more-than-1-million-patients-worldwide-who-have-benefited-from-oncotype-dx-testing-in-personalizing-cancer-treatment-decisions-to-improve-outcomes-300773224.html.

www.ingramcontent.com/pod-product-compliance
Lightning Source LLC
Chambersburg PA
CBHW050337230426
43663CB00010B/1887